The MAILBOX®

The Idea Magazine For Teachers®

PRIMARY

1997–1998

YEARBOOK

Diane Badden, Senior Editor
Sharon Murphy, Associate Editor

The Education Center, Inc.
Greensboro, North Carolina

The Mailbox® 1997–1998 Primary Yearbook

Editor In Chief: Margaret Michel
Magazine Director: Karen P. Shelton
Editorial Administrative Director: Stephen Levy
Senior Editor: Diane Badden
Associate Editor: Sharon Murphy
Contributing Editors: Darcy Brown, Susan Hohbach Walker
Copy Editors: Lynn Bemer Coble, Karen L. Huffman, Jennifer Rudisill, Debbie Shoffner, Gina Sutphin
Staff Artists: Jennifer Tipton Bennett, Cathy Spangler Bruce, Pam Crane, Teresa Davidson, Nick Greenwood, Clevell Harris, Susan Hodnett, Sheila Krill, Mary Lester, Rob Mayworth, Kimberly Richard, Rebecca Saunders, Barry Slate, Donna K. Teal
Editorial Assistants: Mickey Hjelt, Laura Slaughter, Wendy Svartz
Librarian: Elizabeth A. Findley

ISBN 1-56234-212-6
ISSN 1088-5544

The Education Center, Inc.
P.O. Box 9753
Greensboro, NC 27429-0753

Contents

Bulletin Boards 5

Learning Centers 23

Arts & Crafts 39

Teacher Resource Ideas 59
    Birthday Tips That Take The Cake! 60
    Hitting The Road…With Class!: Field-Trip Tips 62

Author Units 67
    Audrey And Don Wood 68
    Eric Kimmel 74
    Bill Martin Jr. 79
    Angela Shelf Medearis 84
    Ruth Heller 89

Literature Units 95
    Tornado 96
    The Ghost In Tent 19 100
    Hey, New Kid! 105
    Books For The Funny Bone! 109
    Make Four Million Dollar$ By Next Thur$day! 114
    The Mouse And The Motorcycle 118

Language Arts Units 123
    Getting Started On The "Write" Foot! 124
    Getting The Scoop On Writing Reports 130
    A Harvest Of Reading Motivation 137
    Special Deliveries From First-Class Pen Pals 142
    Another Special Delivery!: More Pen-Pal Ideas 147

Math Units 149
    This Must Be The Place!: Place-Value Activities 150
    Time Races On!: Time-Telling Activities 156
    The Numeral Cafe: Math Games 162
    Math + Poetry = Shel Silverstein 164
    Calculator Roundup! 168

Science Units 169

    The Bone Zone! 170

    Finding Out About Force 176

    Animals In Winter 179

    A Look At Light 186

    The Sensational Six: Activities For The Food Guide Pyramid 188

    A Circle Of Change: Investigating Life Cycles 196

    Discovering Coral Reefs 204

Social Studies Units 211

    On-The-Spot Community Coverage: Literature And Communities 212

    The Island Of Enchantment: Puerto Rico 216

    The Land Of The Midnight Sun: Sweden 222

    Jambo, Kenya! 230

    Native Americans Of The Southwest 236

    Building Character 242

Seasonal Units 257

    Hurrah For Grandparents! 258

    The Wonderful World Of Watermelon! 263

    Spotlight On Fire Safety 271

    Light Up The Season With Holiday Literature! 275

Write On!: Ideas And Tips For Teaching Students To Write 281

Compute This!: Computer Technology Tips And Ideas 287

Lifesavers Management Tips For Teachers… 293

Our Readers Write: Timesaving, Teacher-Tested Tips 299

Patterns 312

Answer Keys 313

Index 314

BULLETIN BOARDS

Bulletin Boards..

Get to the point with this easy-to-make helper display! Label a pencil cutout with each desired job description and label one "Off Duty." Mount the cutouts and title on a newspaper-covered bulletin board. Attach a press-on pocket containing individual student snapshots beside the "Off Duty" pencil; then pin one snapshot from the pocket beside each pencil. Assign weekly jobs using an established method of rotation.

Joan Frickleton—Grs. 2–4, Glen Oak Continuous Progress School, Peoria, IL

Watch your students sink their teeth into this toothy display! Design a blank grid that features the school months; then mount the grid, a tooth "beary" cutout, and the title. Duplicate a supply of white construction-paper tooth shapes using the pattern on page 20. When a student loses a tooth, he labels, cuts out, and attaches a tooth shape to the grid. Periodically discuss the results of your "beary" toothy graph.

Suzanne M. Hudson—Gr. 1, Indian Valley Elementary, Overland Park, KS

If you're looking for a "tree-mendous" back-to-school display, try this one! Mount one or more tree cutouts and a suitable title. On a provided apple cutout, each child writes his name and a short paragraph about himself. Then each child glues his cutout on slightly larger red paper, trims the paper to create a border, and attaches a green paper stem. Have students read their paragraphs aloud before mounting the projects on the display.

Annamaria Vitucci Walters—Gr. 3, St. Joseph School–Fullerton, Baltimore, MD

This year-round display is great for reinforcing geography skills. Ask students to bring to school postcards showing different places in the United States. Have each student who brings a postcard tell something about the site on his card. Then display his card and use a yarn length to show its location on the map. Invite students to continue bringing postcards to school throughout the year. Geography has never been more fun!

Alesia M. Richards—Grs. 1–2, Apple Pie Ridge Elementary School, Winchester, PA

Any way you slice it, this scrumptious display makes a big impression! On a provided seed cutout (white), have each student illustrate her favorite summer memory. Then have each child glue her cutout on slightly larger black paper and trim the paper to create a border. Invite each child to tell her classmates about her summer memory; then mount the projects on a giant slice of watermelon.

Kristin McLaughlin—Gr. 1, Daniel Boone Area School District, Boyertown, PA

If you're planning to invite your students' grandparents and/or older adult friends into the classroom, this display is a must! On a 3 1/2-inch white circle, have each child illustrate one or more grandparents or older adult friends. Then have each child glue her project on a blue construction-paper ribbon (pattern on page 19). Mount the completed projects on a display like the one shown.

Beth Vander Kolk—Gr. 1, The Potter's House, Grand Rapids, MI

Scare up some great student work and a whole lot of fun at this seasonal display. Mount the title, a character, the caption "Bump Board," and samples of exceptional student work. When the display is full, the bumping begins. Each student whose work is chosen for the display gets to bump another paper off the board. You can count on plenty of "boooo-tiful" work during October!

Judy Knight—Gr. 3, Day Elementary, San Angelo, TX

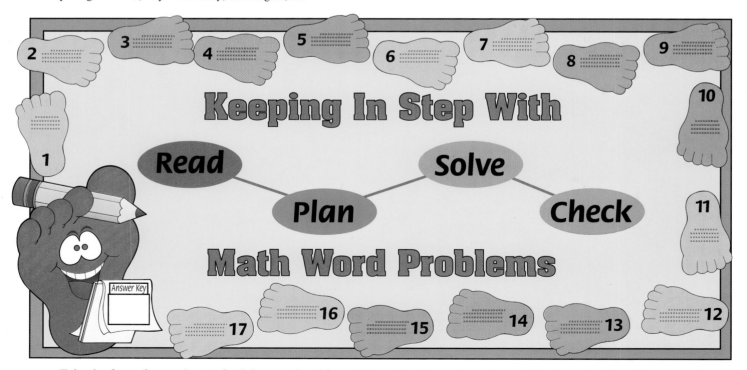

Take the fancy footwork out of solving word problems! Mount the title, a character, and the four steps to solving a word problem. To create the border, have each child write a math word problem on a numbered footprint cutout; then mount the cutouts as shown. Challenge students to use the four-step method to solve the word problems their classmates created. Provide an answer key at the display if desired.

Gina Parisi—Basic Skills Grs. 1–6, Brookdale School, Bloomfield, NJ

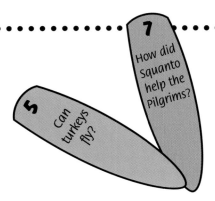

This grinning gobbler has a tail full of questions for students to answer! Number and program feather cutouts with seasonal questions like "What is a female turkey called?" and "What ocean did the Pilgrims cross?" Mount the feathers, a featherless turkey cutout, and the title as shown. Near the display provide books that contain the answers to the posted questions. Great gobbler! Research has never been more fun!

Julie Plowman—Gr. 3, Adair-Casey Elementary, Adair, IA

Harvest a bumper crop of parts-of-speech practice this fall. Each child writes two descriptive sentences; then he copies his edited work on an ear-of-corn cutout. Next he color-codes his sentences by drawing a red box around each noun, an orange circle around each verb, and a green line under each adjective. Mount the title, green paper husks, the colorful ear-of-corn cutouts, and real cornstalks for a one-of-a-kind harvest display!

Cami Shapiro—Gr. 2, Taylor Mills School, Manalapan, NJ

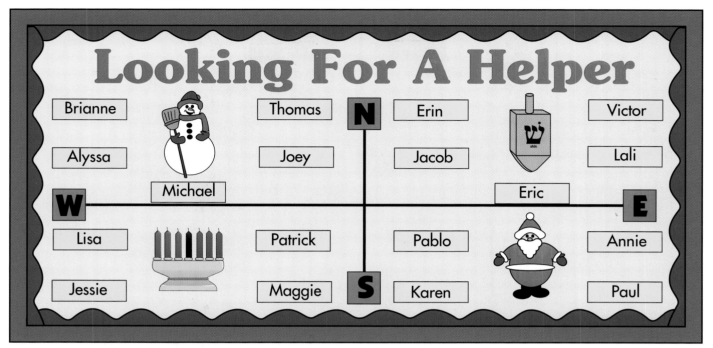

Reinforce cardinal directions with this clever helper display. Visually divide a bulletin board into fourths, label the cardinal directions, and mount a seasonal picture in each quadrant. For each student post a name card that is above, below, or beside a picture or another card. Each day identify a helper by citing a clue like "The name of today's helper is east of the dreidel." Each season or month, replace the pictures and rearrange the cards. To up the challenge, add intermediate directions too!

Vicki Neilon—Gr. 2, Antietam Elementary School, Lake Ridge, VA

Let Rudolph lead the way to super student work! Mount a large Rudolph cutout (pattern on page 20), a sign that describes a class goal, and the title. If desired, tape an inflated balloon to Rudolph's nose. Duplicate and cut out a supply of the award (page 20); then attach an individually wrapped, red candy nose to each one. When the posted goal is met, return each paper with an award stapled to it. Then challenge the class to meet the goal again. Now that's a display that will go down in history!

Julie Plowman—Gr. 3, Adair-Casey Elementary, Adair, IA

Warm students up to wintry writing and create this toasty display! Post a student-generated list of adjectives that describe mittens or wintry weather. Give each student two large mitten cutouts—one lined and one blank. A student decorates the blank cutout; then she writes a descriptive poem or paragraph about her decorated mitten on the lined cutout. Mount the mitten projects and the title as shown. Invite students to take the chill off winter by reading their classmates' mitten-related writing!

Jennifer Balogh-Joiner—Gr. 2, Franklin Elementary, Franklin, NJ

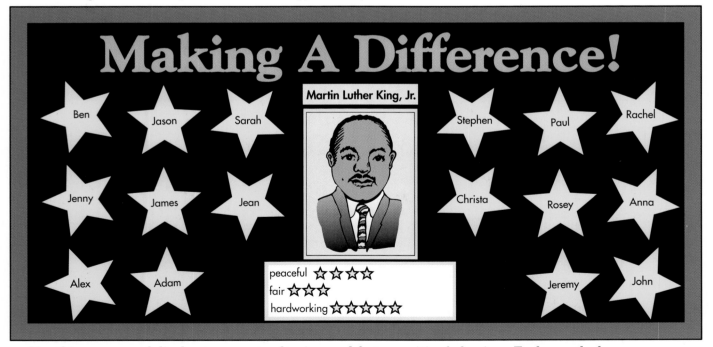

Use this year-round display to promote altruism and foster positive behaviors. Each month showcase a poster or cutout of a person who has contributed to the betterment of others. Add the person's name and a sign that lists his or her most outstanding traits. Then have every student create a personalized cutout for the display. Each time you observe a student or the class exhibiting one of the listed traits, attach a foil star beside that trait. Wow! Look who's making a difference now!

Hope Bertrand—Grs. 2–3, Fremont Elementary School, Bakersfield, CA

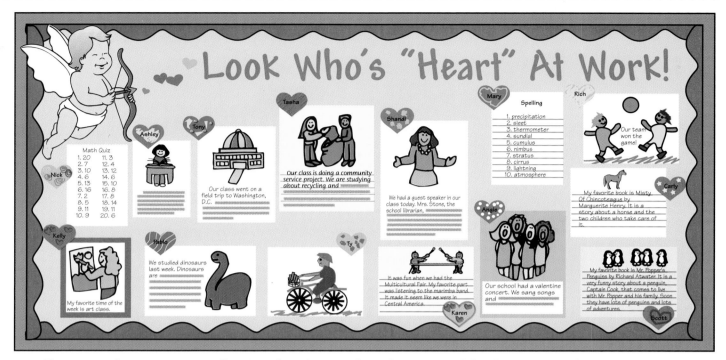

Showcase a heartwarming collection of student work at this seasonal display. Have each student personalize and decorate a heart-shaped paper topper. After each student has chosen a sample of her best work, mount the work samples, paper toppers, and title as shown. Periodically ask students to replace their displayed work with more current samples. Now that's a true work of "heart"!

Colleen Cori Connally—Gr. 3, Rolling Valley Elementary, Springfield, VA

Your youngsters will warm right up to this quilt-making project! Remind students that a quilt displayed outside a home signaled to slaves traveling along the Underground Railroad that the home was safe to approach. Then ask each child to design a precut quilt patch for a class freedom quilt. Explain that this quilt will signal to others that your classroom is a safe place for *all* people. Mount the quilt patches and a title patch on a bulletin board covered with colorful paper. Then use a marker to draw stitch lines between the projects.

Keeping track of March weather is a breeze at this display. Have each child make a lion or a lamb as described in "Lions And Lambs" on page 49. Also duplicate and cut out 33 cards from page 21. Program one lion and one lamb card as shown; then mount these two cards, the student projects, and the title. For each day in March, enlist your students' help in categorizing the weather; then date and display the appropriate card.

Peter Tabor—Gr. 1, Weston Elementary, Schofield, WI

Turn independent reading into a golden experience! Mount the title and a pot-of-gold cutout as shown. Near the display provide a supply of the book-report form on page 21 and 7" x 10" construction-paper rectangles in the colors shown. To make a book report, a child completes a form and cuts it out; then he folds a colored rectangle in half and glues his form inside. Display the completed reports in the shape of a rainbow.

Julie Simpson—Gr. 2, Cherry Elementary, Toledo, OH

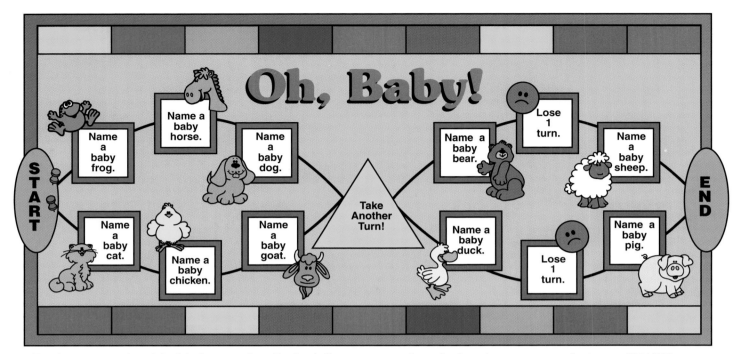

Review any topic with this interactive display! Create a gameboard; then insert two pushpins at START. Make a die that has values of "1" and "2." To play, one of two students (teams) picks a pathway, rolls the die, and moves his pushpin. If he correctly follows the direction, he stays there. An incorrect response at any point along the gameboard returns the player to START. The first player to reach the END wins. Frequently change the programming to keep student interest high.

Terrie Guest Yang—Grs. K–1, Hsin-chu International School, Hsin-chu, Taiwan

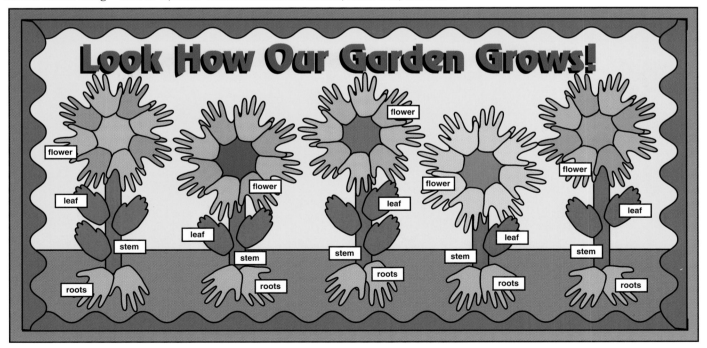

Ask your budding botanists to give you a hand with this eye-catching display! Mount the background paper and title. Give each small group of students glue, scissors, pencils, a paper stem and flower center, and colorful paper. Demonstrate how to trace a hand on paper to create a leaf, a root, and a petal. Mount each group's completed flower in the class garden and label it as shown.

Patti Ghormley—Gr. 1, Liberty Elementary School, Libertytown, MD

Looks who's hard at work! Mount the title and a border of yellow caution tape. Then have each student personalize and cut out a construction-paper copy of the hard-hat pattern on page 19. Laminate the cutouts and slit the dotted lines. Ask each student to choose a sample of her best work; then display the papers with their matching cutouts. Invite students to replace their work samples as frequently as desired.

adapted from an idea by VaReane Gray Heese, Omaha, NE

Sprout a renewed interest in class-made books with this springtime display. Precut several paper leaves and stems, duplicate a supply of the book pattern on page 312, and mount the title and some paper grass. Each day read aloud a different class-written book and ask a volunteer to create a corresponding flower for the garden. Forgotten titles will be remembered and your students' self-esteem will be in full bloom!

Jennifer Farneski—Gr. 1 Instructional Aide, Berkeley Elementary School, Bloomfield, NJ

Our Work Is Nothing But The "Berry" Best!

Showcase your students' "berry" best work at this delicious-looking display! Mount the title and a vinelike border. To make a paper topper, a student uses watercolors to paint a berry pattern (page 22). When the paint is dry, he cuts out the pattern, spreads a thin layer of glue over it, and sprinkles the glue with clear glitter. Exhibit the student's berry project and a sample of his best work at the display. Dazzling!

Sarah Mertz, Owenton, KY

Now that you've featured every child on your "Star Of The Week" display, transform it into an end-of-the-year reading motivator. Change the heading, attach two labeled envelopes as shown, and tuck a supply of paper stars in each envelope. When a student reads a book, she writes her name and the book's title on the desired star and pins it to the display. Each day select a few posted stars and let these readers shine!

Kristin A. McLaughlin—Gr. 1, Daniel Boone Area Elementary, Boyertown, PA

Give your end-of-the-year display a space-age spin! Cover a bulletin board with black paper, accent it with foil stars, and add the title. Have each child describe a highlight from the past school year on a colorful comet pattern (page 22), then cut it out. Next he uses a toilet-tissue roll and assorted other supplies to design a rocket. Mount the projects and you have an out-of-this-world finale to the school year!

Mary Mahaffey—Gr. 3, Harrisburg Academy, Wormleysburg, PA

Students will like lending a hand with this sunny summer send-off. Mount a large sun cutout that sports student-made hand-shaped rays. Ask each child to write a prediction about the upcoming summer on a sheet of white paper, then trim his paper to create a cloud shape. Post the predictions on the display. What a warm welcome to summertime!

Denise Tinucci Farrell—Gr. 3, St. Joseph School, Collingdale, PA

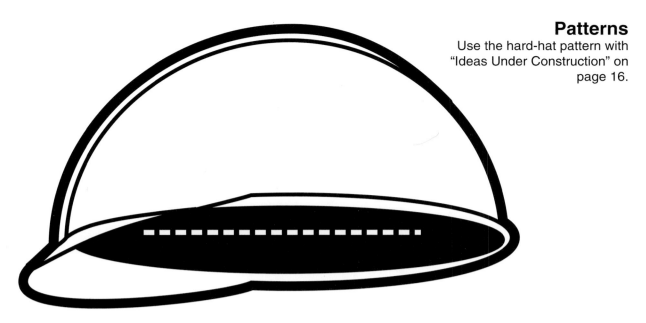

Use the ribbon pattern with "Our
Grand Prizes!" on page 8.

Patterns And Award

Use the reindeer pattern and award with "Rudolph's Challenge" on page 11.

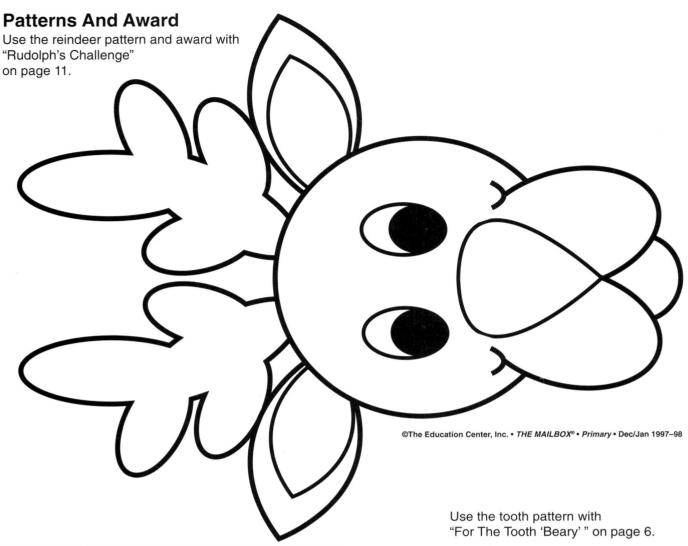

Use the tooth pattern with "For The Tooth 'Beary' " on page 6.

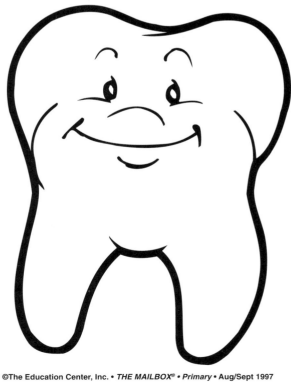

I helped meet Rudolph's challenge!

©1998 The Education Center, Inc.

©1998 The Education Center, Inc.

Use with "A Rainbow Of Reading" on page 14.

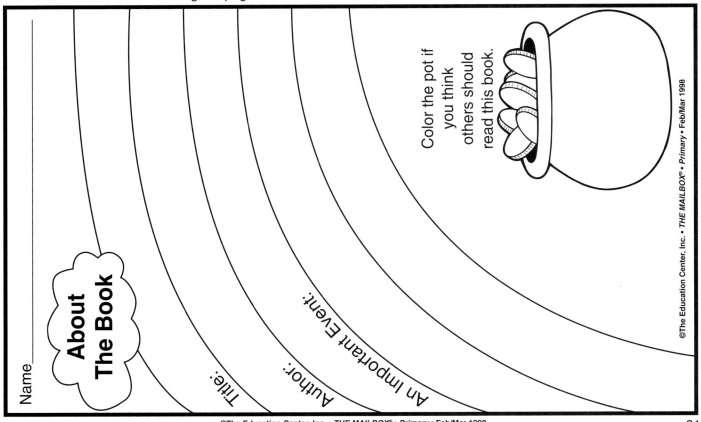

Color the pot if you think others should read this book.

Name

About The Book

Title:

Author:

An Important Event:

©The Education Center, Inc. • *THE MAILBOX®* • *Primary* • Feb/Mar 1998

Patterns

Use the berry patterns with "Our Work Is..." on page 17. Enlarge the patterns if desired; then duplicate them on white construction paper.

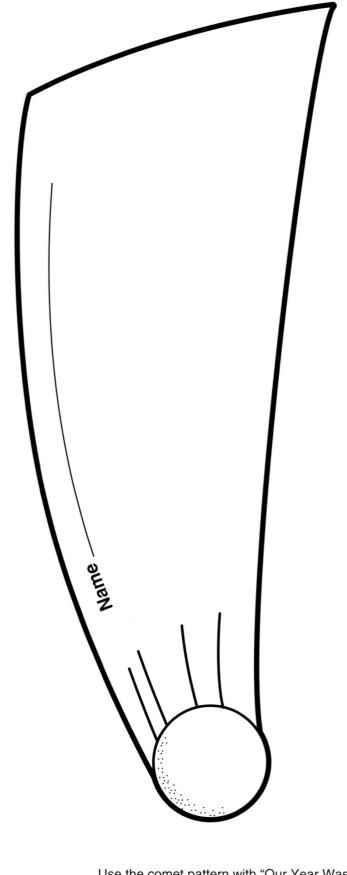

Name

Use the comet pattern with "Our Year Was Out Of This World!" on page 18.

LEARNING CENTERS

Spotlight on Centers

Domino Sums

This partner center adds up to lots of fun! Make several domino mats like the ones shown. Designate a different sum on each mat. Laminate the mats for durability; then store the laminated mats and a set of dominoes at a center. Each partner chooses a domino mat. If individual domino shapes are shown, the student covers each shape with a domino that equals the mat's designated sum. If a trail of domino shapes is shown, the student covers the shapes with dominoes that—when added together—equal the sum shown on the mat. When a student completes his mat, he asks his partner to check his work. Then he chooses a different mat to complete. The partners continue working in this manner until center time is over or they have each completed all the domino mats.

Ruth G. Trinidad—Gr. 1, 28th Street School, Los Angeles, CA

In The Know

You can count on this puzzle center being very popular with your pupils! Take a photograph of each member of the school staff. Mount the snapshots on individual sentence strips. Next to each person's picture, write that person's professional name. Beneath the name, in smaller letters, write the staff position that person holds. Laminate the strips; then use a different jigsaw cut to separate each snapshot and name. Store the resulting puzzle pieces at a center. A student matches each picture to a name by fitting the puzzle pieces together. In no time at all, your students will know the names and faces of the entire school staff!

Jan McManus—Gr. 2
St. Clement School
St. Bernard, OH

What's For Lunch?

Create an appetite for alphabetizing skills with a lunchbox center. Use a permanent marker to program one resealable, plastic sandwich bag to show each of the following categories: "Sandwiches," "Desserts," "Fruits," "Vegetables," "Drinks." On individual cutouts, write the names of five or more different food items in each category. Number the backs of the cutouts in each category in ABC-order for self-checking, and laminate the cutouts. Store each group of cutouts in its corresponding bag. Place the bags of cutouts in a lunchbox and display the lunchbox at a center. A student arranges the cutouts from each bag in alphabetical order, then flips them to check her work.

Diane Benner—Gr. 2
Dover Elementary School
Dover, PA

24

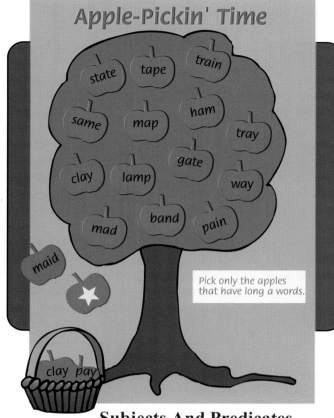

Apple-Pickin' Time

Pick only the apples that have long a words.

Apple-Pickin' Time

Picking apples is the perfect way to reinforce the long and short sounds of *a*. Duplicate 24 apple shapes on red construction paper. Program 12 apples with short *a* words and 12 apples with long *a* words. Next cut tree foliage and a tree trunk from colored paper. Glue the foliage and tree trunk onto a sheet of poster board, and write desired student directions and the title "Apple-Pickin' Time." Laminate the center components for durability, and cut them out. For self-checking, use a permanent marker to program the backs of the long *a* cutouts. Place the apples in a basket; then store the basket and the poster board at a center. A student randomly places all the apples (faceup) on the tree; then she picks only the apples that are programmed with long *a* words. To check her work, she flips over the apples she picked.

Betsy Liebmann—Gr. 1
Gotham Avenue School
Elmont, NY

Subjects And Predicates

Reviewing subjects and predicates is a snap at this easy-to-make center! Program several sentence strips with desired sentences, leaving extra space between the words in each sentence. To program the sentence strips for self-checking, clip a clothespin to each sentence strip to separate the subject and the predicate; then flip the strip over and draw a dot on the back in the corresponding location. Remove and store the clothespins in a decorated container. Laminate the strips for durability; then place the strips and the container of clothespins at a center. A student reads each sentence, clips a clothespin onto the strip to separate the subject and the predicate, and flips the strip to check her work.

Holly L. Cable—Gr. 2
Page Hilltop School
Ayer, MA

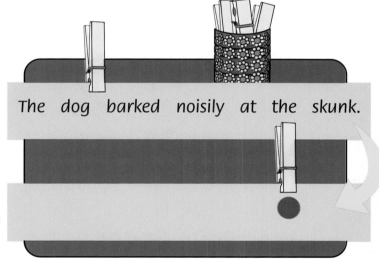

The dog barked noisily at the skunk.

Find five classroom items that are shorter than your shoe cutout.

Find two classroom items that equal the length of your shoe cutout.

Fancy Footwork

Students are sure to get a kick out of this measurement center! At the center place a supply of construction paper and writing paper, scissors, pencils, paper clips, and several measurement task cards like the ones shown. A student traces the outline of his shoe on construction paper and cuts out the resulting shape. Then he uses his custom-made cutout to complete the measurement tasks at hand. He records his answers on a personalized sheet of writing paper. When he has completed all the measurement tasks, he clips his shoe cutout to his answer sheet.

Collect the students' work; then place the completed projects along with the task cards at the center the following week. Ask each student to choose one measurement project (other than his own) and use the provided cutout to check the recorded measurements. Now that's some fancy footwork!

Kelly A. Wong—Gr. 2
Berlyn School
Diamond Bar, CA

Spotlight on Centers

State-Of-The-Art Sentences

Students can show their stuff again and again at this sentence-writing center! Use a colorful marker to label several craft sticks with nouns. Place the color-coded sticks in a container labeled "Nouns." Repeat the procedure to create color-coded sets of verbs and adjectives. Store the containers of craft sticks along with story paper, pencils, and crayons at a center. A student chooses a stick from each container, then uses the words on the sticks to create a state-of-the-art sentence. After he has written the sentence on his paper, he returns the craft sticks to the appropriate containers and illustrates his sentence. Youngsters are sure to enjoy this hands-on approach to sentence writing. For added writing inspiration, post samples of the students' work at the center.

Michelle Wolfe—Gr. 1, Kennewick, WA

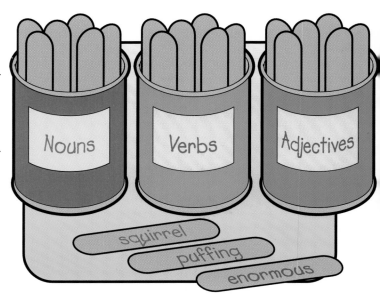

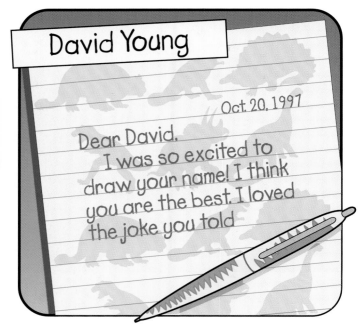

Special Delivery

Deliver year-round letter-writing practice at this versatile center. Write your students' names on individual slips of paper; then deposit the papers in a decorated container. Place the container, a supply of lined paper or stationery, an assortment of writing instruments, and a letter receptacle at a center. Also display a colorful poster that shows the parts of a friendly letter. To complete the center, a student draws the name of a classmate from the container and writes the classmate a letter. Then he places his completed letter in the letter receptacle and discards the paper slip. When each child has visited the center—and the container of student names is empty—ask a student or two to deliver the student-written letters. On his second center visit, a student writes a letter to the classmate who wrote to him. Once these letters have been delivered, restock the decorated container with student names and begin the letter-writing process again. In no time your youngsters' letter-writing skills will be in top form!

Mauri A. Capps—Grs. 1–2, Northlake Elementary, Dallas, TX

An Even Dozen

Reinforce the addends of 12 with this game for two players. Place an egg carton containing 12 small manipulatives, a penny, pencils, and a supply of paper at a center. To begin, one student in the pair flips the penny to determine which student goes first. Then, using the lid of the carton as a shield (so that her opponent cannot see inside the carton), Player One removes from the carton and places in front of Player Two one or more of the manipulatives. Player Two responds by stating how many manipulatives are left inside the carton. A correct answer earns Player Two one point. The manipulatives are returned to the egg carton and the carton is passed to Player Two. The game continues in this manner until one player earns 12 points. Now there's a math center that's all it's cracked up to be!

Cheryl Pilgrim, San Antonio, TX

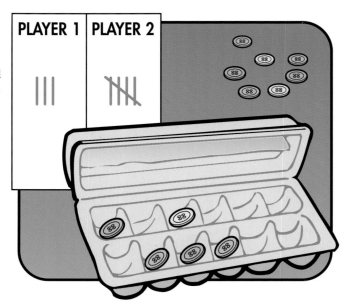

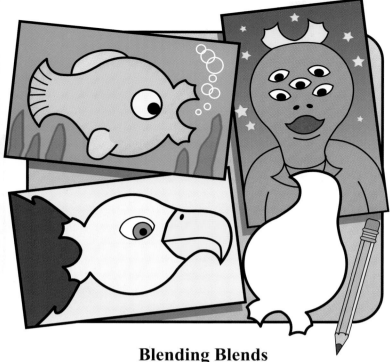

Turkey Transformations

Foster students' creative thinking and artistic talents with this one-of-a-kind center! Use the patterns on page 36 (turkey shapes minus the feathers) to create several tagboard tracers. Place the tagboard tracers; a supply of drawing paper; and crayons, markers, or colored pencils at a center. A student holds a tracer in his hand and studies its shape by turning it around and around. When the student is ready, he traces the shape onto a sheet of drawing paper and transforms it into a totally unrelated object; then he illustrates a coordinating scene. Gobble! Gobble!

Wanda F. Bobo—Grs. K–6 Art
L. P. Cowart Elementary
Dallas, TX

Blending Blends

Whip up a batch of blend practice in a matter of minutes! Program each of ten yellow construction-paper cards with a desired blend. Then, for each yellow card, program two white cards with different word endings. Each word ending must create a word when joined with the blend on the yellow card. Place the programmed cards in a large, nonbreakable bowl. Store the bowl, a wooden spoon, a baking sheet, a chef's hat, pencils, and a supply of paper at a center. A student dons the chef's hat and uses the wooden spoon to gently stir the paper cards. Then he removes a yellow and a white card from the bowl. If the programming on the cards makes a word, he places the cards on the baking sheet and writes the word on his paper. If a word cannot be formed, he returns the cards to the bowl. The student continues in this manner until he has recorded ten different words on his paper.

adapted from an idea by Melissa Springer—Grs. 3–4 Learning Disabled
Greenbrier Intermediate
Chesapeake, VA

Place-Value Practice

This daily math center is the place to reinforce beginning place-value skills! For each child staple a supply of blank 9" x 12" paper between two 9" x 12" construction-paper covers. Have each child personalize his journal and store it in his desk or another desired location. At the center place several rubber stamps and colorful stamp pads. Each day post a different two-digit number at the center. A student takes his journal to the center and copies the posted number at the top of a blank page. Then he uses a rubber stamp and a stamp pad to program the page with a corresponding set of tens and ones as shown. You can count on this center making a lasting impression on your students!

Michele Lasky Anszelowicz—Gr. 1
Mandalay Elementary School, Wantagh, NY

Spotlight on Centers

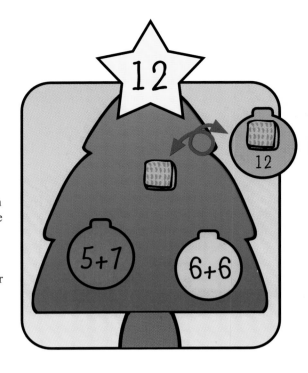

Seasonal Calculations

Reinforce basic math facts at this seasonal center. To create an addition Christmas tree like the one shown, cut a tree shape from green poster board. Cut three ornament shapes from colorful construction paper and one star shape from yellow paper. Program the star with a sum and glue it to the top of the tree. Label each ornament with a corresponding addition sentence and program the back for self-checking. Laminate the cutouts for durability; then use Velcro® to attach each ornament to the tree. Create a desired number of decorated trees. Next remove the ornaments from the trees and store the ornaments in a resealable plastic bag. Place the bag of ornaments and the trees at a center. A student solves an addition sentence, flips the ornament to verify his answer, and fastens the ornament to the corresponding tree. The center is completed when each tree is fully decorated. For variations, make other seasonal shapes to provide practice with skills such as subtraction, initial consonants, or rhyming words.

Cindy Corey—Gr. 1, Lealman Avenue Elementary, St. Petersburg, FL

Easy As ABC!

This nifty sorting activity provides plenty of practice with beginning sounds. For each letter of the alphabet, cut a picture from a discarded workbook or magazine. Glue each picture to a colorful index card. At the bottom of each card, label the picture—omitting the initial letter; then program the backs of the cards for self-checking. If desired laminate the cards for durability. Store the cards in a resealable plastic bag. Place alphabetical dividers in a file box; then place the file box and the bag of cards at a center. A student removes the cards from the bag. For each card, he identifies the missing letter and files the card behind the corresponding divider. The student may check his answer on the back before he files each card. Or he may file the entire card set, then check his answers as he removes the cards from the file box. It's as easy as ABC!

Phyllis Nielsen—Gr. 1, Miller's Point Elementary
Converse, TX

Missing Vowels

This partner game is easy to make, and it provides great vocabulary practice! Write the weekly spelling words on a sheet of paper, replacing each vowel with a blank. Duplicate a class supply of this list. Next create a vowel code that corresponds to the numbers on a die (see the illustration). Place the vowel code, the spelling-word lists, a die, and a carpet square at a center. Each partner takes a spelling list and then, in turn, rolls the die on the carpet square. Using the vowel code as his guide, he writes the vowel he rolled in a spelling word. If a player cannot use the vowel he rolls, his turn is over. The first player to complete each word on his spelling list wins!

Carol K. Budsock—Gr. 1, First Grade Intervale School
Parsippany, NJ

Soup-Bowl Facts

Warm students up to math-fact practice with bowls and beans! Use a permanent marker to program several disposable soup bowls with addition and subtraction facts; then program the bottom of each bowl with its corresponding answer. Partially fill a pot with dried beans. Place the pot, the programmed soup bowls, and a spoon at a center. A student selects a bowl, reads the fact, and uses the bean manipulatives to solve the fact in the bowl. Then she carefully lifts the bowl to check her work. If her answer is correct, she pours the beans back into the pot. If her answer is incorrect, she adjusts her bean calculation before she returns the beans. The student continues in this manner until each math fact has been completed. Soup's on!

Kristin McLaughlin—Gr. 1, Daniel Boone Area School District
Boyertown, PA

Write On!

Hang on to this activity! It's perfect for promoting prizewinning writing! Place writing paper, pencils, a student dictionary, glue, and construction paper at a center. A student writes the first half of an adventure story, stopping his story just as the action begins. Then he mounts his writing on a sheet of construction paper. After each student has completed the writing activity, collect the story starters. Suspend a length of clothesline at the center and use skirt hangers to display several story starters along it. Each time a student returns to the center, he chooses a different adventure story to complete. If desired, have the student clip his story ending behind the appropriate story starter as shown. Keep writing interest high by routinely replacing the story starters. In no time at all, your youngsters will be hung up on writing!

Tammie Boone, Sheldon Middle School
Sheldon, IA

> One day I was walking my dog, Sophie, when it started to snow. Soon it was snowing so hard that I couldn't see. I fell down. When I looked up, all I saw was two big green eyes. Sophie was nowhere in sight!

Weekly Mystery Word

Your supersleuths will have a ball searching for words at this center! Each week select a mystery word that relates to a current topic of study. In each of several resealable plastic bags, place construction-paper squares labeled with the letters needed to spell the mystery word. Place the bags of letters, pencils, stickers, and writing paper at the center. Also post a laminated sign, like the one shown, that can be reprogrammed each week with an appropriate word goal. A student removes the letters from a plastic bag and manipulates them to make words. He writes each word he makes on his paper. He also tries to discover the mystery word by arranging all the letters in his bag to make one word. If he meets the posted goal, he attaches a sticker to his paper!

Lisa Kelly—Gr. 1
Wood Creek Elementary School
Farmington, MI

Stamps For Sale!

Students will give this money-counting activity their stamp of approval! Gather a supply of canceled stamps in various denominations. Glue each stamp to an index card. Then, for each resulting stamp card, use coin stickers or a stamp pad and coin stamps to program an index card with coins that equal the price of the featured stamp. Program the back of each coin card for self-checking; then laminate the cards. Store the cards in a resealable plastic bag at a center. A student matches each stamp card to a coin card; then he flips the coin card to check his work.

Karen Smith—Grs. K–1
Pine Lane Elementary Homeschool
Pace, FL

Party Placemats

Set your students' hearts aflutter at this seasonal art center. Cut a supply of 1" x 12" strips of white and pink construction paper. Place the strips, 12" x 18" sheets of red construction paper, pencils, scissors, rulers, glue, crayons or markers, and construction-paper scraps at a center. To make a placemat, a student folds a sheet of red paper in half. Then he uses a pencil and a ruler to draw parallel lines from the fold. The lines should be eight inches in length and spaced about one inch apart. Next he cuts on the lines, unfolds the paper, and weaves paper strips through the resulting slits. He then glues the ends of each strip to the red paper. To complete the project, he personalizes the placemat to his heart's desire!

adapted from an idea by Sandy Shaw—Gr. 1
Jeannette McKee Elementary
Jeannette, PA

Snack Attack!

Provide tasty skill review with this appetizing activity! At a center, display and label four different snacks. You will also need a supply of the activity sheet on page 37, rulers, pencils, and a small basket containing a class supply of individually wrapped snacks (like small boxes of raisins). For a self-checking center, tuck a completed copy of the activity sheet inside the basket. A student completes a copy of the activity sheet by referring to the snacks on display. When she finishes and checks her work, she helps herself to a snack from the basket. When all students have completed the center, share or raffle off the four displayed snacks. Then restock the center—making sure to display a different variety of snacks—and the center is ready to use again! Basic skill review has never tasted *soooo* good!

Alyce Pearl Smith—Gr. 1
Butzbach Elementary
APO, NY

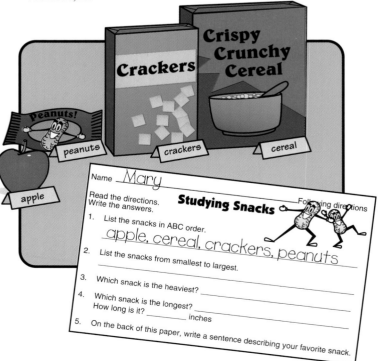

Story Order Cards

Improve students' reading comprehension skills with this nifty sequencing activity. Gather several books that you have recently read to your students. For each book choose five story events that clearly show the sequence of the story line. Write a sentence about each event on an individual index card; then number the backs of the cards for self-checking. Laminate the cards for durability, and store each card set in an envelope labeled with the title and author of the corresponding book. Place the envelopes and the books at a center. A student sequences the sentences from each envelope, referring to the book as needed. Then she flips the cards to check her work.

Karen Smith—Grs. K–1
Pine Lane Elementary Homeschool
Pace, FL

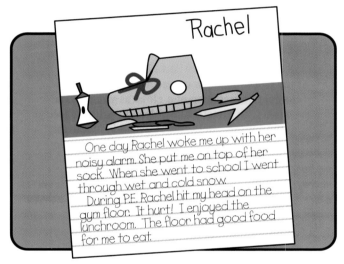

Sneaker Stories

Untieing your students' creativity is a real "shoe-in" at this writing center. Place a supply of story paper and a shoebox containing crayons or markers at a center. A student slips off a shoe and sets it alongside his paper. Then he imagines life as that shoe. Next he writes and illustrates a story from his shoe's point of view. Compile the students' work in a class book titled "Sneaker Stories" for further reading enjoyment. Now that's some fancy footwork!

Marge Schultz
Northside School
Fremont, NE

Pot O' Gold Facts

Check out this gold mine of basic-fact practice! Duplicate, color, and cut out a desired number of the rainbow pattern on page 37. Program each cloud with a math fact. Then program the back of the cutouts for self-checking. Laminate the cutouts for durability before storing them in a resealable plastic bag. Place the bag and a small black pot of wrapped butterscotch candies at a center. A student selects a cutout, reads the fact, and uses the candies to solve the fact. Then she flips the cutout to check her work. If her answer is correct, she places the candies back into the pot. If her answer is incorrect, she adjusts her candy calculation before she returns the candies. The student continues in this manner until each math fact has been completed. When her work is done, she helps herself to a candy nugget!

Brenda Streetman
Briarwood Elementary
Moore, OK

Spotlight on Centers

Fraction Creatures

These fun creatures familiarize students with fractions—and at the same time, challenge students to think creatively. Place a large supply of one-inch construction-paper squares in assorted colors, black fine-tipped markers, a supply of 12" x 18" sheets of drawing paper, and glue at a center. A student folds a sheet of paper in half and in half again; then he unfolds his paper. At the top of each resulting quadrant, he writes a fraction with a denominator of four or less and a color word that describes some of the paper squares at the center. Each quadrant must be labeled differently. Then, in each quadrant, he uses the available supplies to create a creature that represents the quadrant's programming. For example a creature created in a quadrant labeled "2/3 blue" would be made with three paper squares—two of them blue. Fractions have never been more fun!

Belinda Darnall Vose—Gr. 1
Evergreen Elementary
Ocala, FL

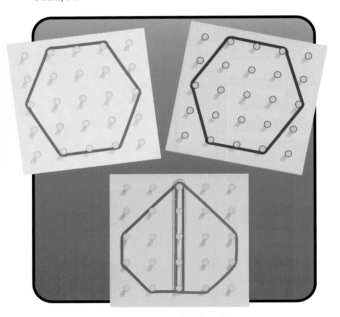

Geoboard Fun

Reinforce congruency and symmetry with these Geoboard partner activities. Place two Geoboards and several rubber bands at a center. To reinforce congruency, each partner needs a Geoboard and a rubber band(s). One partner makes a desired shape on a Geoboard; then the other partner makes a congruent shape on his Geoboard. As soon as the students agree that their shapes are congruent, they switch roles and repeat the activity. Challenge each twosome to create a predetermined number of congruent shapes.

For practice with symmetry, one partner uses a rubber band to create a line of symmetry on one Geoboard. Then, working together on this Geoboard, one partner creates a desired shape on one side of the symmetry line. Next the other partner arranges his rubber band on the board so that a symmetrical shape is created. As soon as the students agree that the shape is symmetrical, they switch roles and repeat the activity. Challenge each twosome to create a predetermined number of symmetrical shapes.

Peggy Seibel—Gr. 2
St. Mary's School
Ellis, KS

Silly Sentences

Reviewing parts of speech can lead to giggles and chuckles at this center! To make a silly-sentence booklet for each student, fold five sheets of blank paper into fourths as shown; then unfold the papers and staple them between two construction-paper covers. Place the booklets, pencils, crayons, and scissors at a center. A student personalizes the cover of a booklet. Then, starting at the top of each blank page, he writes a four-word sentence—one word per section—in the following order: an adjective, a plural noun, a present-tense action verb, an adverb. When all five pages have been programmed, he cuts each page into fourths. To do this he starts at the right margin of every page and cuts along each fold line until he is about one inch from the left margin. To read his booklet, the student randomly flips the strips and reads the resulting four-word sentences from top to bottom.

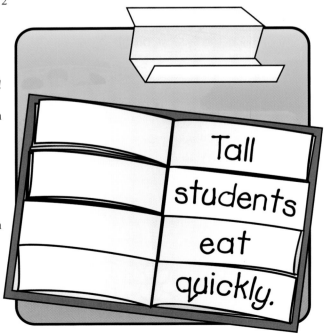

Cindy Marks—Gr. 3
Mark Twain Elementary School
Kirkland, WA

Wanted: Perfect Summer

Put your youngsters' writing skills to the test when you ask them to pen classified ads for the perfect summer! Read aloud several classified ads and discuss with students the kinds of information included in the ads. If desired, also read aloud your local paper's guidelines for writing these ads. Place several samples of classified ads, a supply of writing paper, and pencils at a center. A student writes a brief ad seeking the perfect summer. After each student has completed the center and the ads have been edited, have each student copy his ad on a two-inch-wide paper strip. Mount the ads on blank paper to resemble pages from the "classifieds"; then duplicate a class supply for students to read over the summer. Extra! Extra! Read all about it!

adapted from an idea by Tammy Brinkman and Kimberly Martin
San Antonio, TX

Handwriting Art

Wrap up a year of handwriting practice with this unique center activity. Display a message like "Have a wonderful summer!" at the center. Be sure the number of letters in the message equals or exceeds your class enrollment. Then write each letter of the message in the lower right-hand corner of a sheet of blank drawing paper. Store the papers, pencils, and crayons at the center. A student chooses a paper and uses her best handwriting to write a large version of the provided letter near the center of the paper. Then she uses crayons to draw a picture that incorporates the letter and signs her name at the top of the paper. When each student has completed the center, post the resulting student-illustrated message in the hallway for others to read and enjoy!

A. Gilliam—Grs. 3 and 4
Cherrywood Acres School
Niagara Falls, Ontario
Canada

Homophone Hives

Create a buzz in your classroom with these homophone hives. Duplicate on yellow construction paper a desired number of the beehive patterns on page 38. Label each bee's wings with a pair of homophones; then program the hive with a sentence that incorporates one of the homophones. (Insert a blank in the sentence where the homophone should appear.) Laminate the patterns for durability and cut them out. Next use a permanent marker to program the back of each hive for self-checking. Store the cutouts in a resealable plastic bag. Place the bag, writing paper, and pencils at a center. A student copies each sentence on his paper, replacing each blank with one of the provided homophones. Then he flips the cutout to check his work. Now that's a center activity worth buzzing about!

Maureen Casazza
Honesdale, PA

Patterns
Use with "Turkey Transformations" on page 27.

Studying Snacks

Read the directions.
Write the answers.

1. List the snacks in ABC order.

   _____

2. List the snacks from smallest to largest.

   _____

3. Which snack is the heaviest? _____

4. Which snack is the longest? _____

   How long is it? _____ inches

5. On the back of this paper, write a sentence describing your favorite snack.

Patterns
Use with "Homophone Hives" on page 35.

Arts & Crafts

Arts & Crafts

Pretty As A Picture

With a little creativity, it's easy to design a pretty frame for a special snapshot. The resulting handiwork makes a great gift for Grandparents Day or for parents who have just purchased school photos.

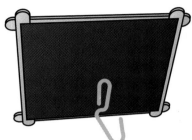

Materials For One Picture Frame:
one 3 1/2" square of black poster board
4 wooden craft sticks
one 8" length of narrow ribbon or yarn
1 large metal paper clip
fine-tipped markers
craft glue
1 student photo

Steps:
1. Glue the four craft sticks around the perimeter of the black square as shown. Allow drying time.
2. Use fine-tipped markers to decorate the wooden sticks.
3. Glue the student photo in the center of the resulting frame.
4. Fashion a bow from the ribbon length. Glue the bow to the frame.
5. To make a stand for the frame, pull the inner piece of the paper clip forward until it is perpendicular to the rest of the clip.
6. Glue the resulting paper-clip stand to the back of the black square.

Barbara Foster—Gr. 2, Carpenter Elementary, Deer Park, TX

Apple Baskets

Weave these personalized apple baskets into your back-to-school plans. To begin, fold a 9" x 12" sheet of construction paper in half (to 9" x 6"). At the end opposite the fold, cut away a 1" x 8" strip from both thicknesses as shown. Then, keeping the paper folded and starting at the fold, cut a series of one-inch strips, stopping approximately one inch from the open ends. Unfold the resulting loom and weave seven or eight one-inch construction-paper strips in the loom. When all the strips are woven, glue the ends of each woven strip in place. To personalize the basket, trace and cut out the letters needed from construction paper. Glue the letters in a pleasing arrangement on the woven basket. Next cut five apple shapes from red paper. Glue the apple cutouts near the top of the basket; then label each one with a self-describing adjective. Attach green leaves and brown stems to the apples if desired. Display the completed projects on a bulletin board titled "A Bushel Of Good Apples!"

adapted from an idea by Teri Eklund—Gr. 2
Walker Elementary, Springdale, AR

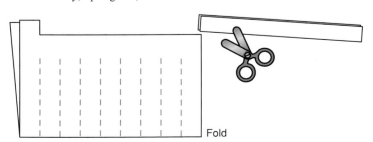

Fold

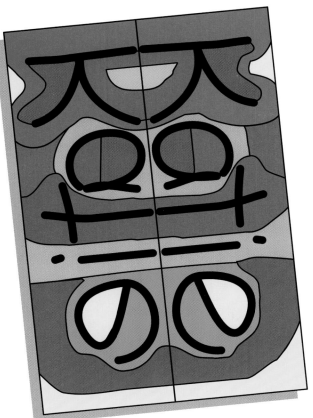

Hidden Names

What's in a name? A very interesting design! To begin this project, fold a 12" x 18" sheet of white construction paper in half lengthwise. Unfold the paper. Then, pressing heavily, use a black crayon to write your first name on the fold line. Refold the paper, keeping your name to the inside. Repeatedly rub your hand firmly across the paper to create a second crayon image of your name. Unfold the paper and use a black crayon to trace over the transferred letters. (See the illustration.) Next use crayons or tempera paint to create a colorful design around the writing. Display these one-of-a-kind name posters for all to enjoy and decode!

Back-To-School Bookmarks

Make reading a top priority this year with personalized bookmarks! To make a bookmark, trace and cut out the beginning letters of your first and last names from colorful paper. Next cut two 4" x 9" rectangles from clear Con-Tact® covering. Peel the backing from one rectangle. Arrange the letter cutouts on the adhesive; then sprinkle the adhesive with colorful glitter, confetti, or small paper punches. Peel the backing from the second rectangle and align the rectangle—adhesive side down—atop the project. Trim the edges of the resulting bookmark to create a preferred shape. If desired, punch a hole in the top of the bookmark and tie a loop of yarn through the hole.

Jo Fryer, Kildeer Countryside School, Long Grove, IL

Colorful Crayons

Create a rainbow of color and promote class unity with these jumbo crayons! As a prelude to the project, discuss the meaning of the phrase "It takes every color to make the rainbow." Help students understand how this phrase applies to their classroom, their community, and their world. Then begin the project with a 6" x 18" piece of white construction paper and a supply of colorful tissue-paper squares. Using diluted glue and a paintbrush, "paint" the tissue-paper squares onto the paper, overlapping the squares as you cover the rectangle. When the rectangle is completely covered, set it aside to dry. The following day trim a 4" x 6" piece of construction paper to resemble the point of a crayon and glue it to one end of the tissue paper–covered rectangle. To the opposite end glue a 2 1/2" x 6" piece of construction paper. Then personalize a construction-paper oval (or other desired shape) and glue it to the side of the crayon. Mount the completed projects on a bulletin board titled "It Takes Every Color To Make The Rainbow."

Jennifer Balogh-Joiner—Gr. 2
Franklin Elementary School
Franklin, NJ

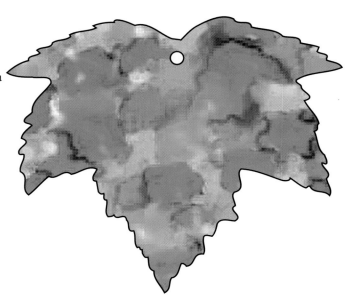

Arts & Crafts

Fall Foliage

Stick with this idea to create a spectacular display of fall foliage! To make a large fall leaf, begin with a ten-inch square of clear Con-Tact® covering. Remove the backing and place the covering sticky side up on a tabletop. Completely cover the sticky surface with torn pieces of tissue paper in assorted fall colors—being sure to overlap the tissue-paper pieces. Use a spray bottle or an eyedropper filled with water to dampen the tissue paper, which makes the colors bleed. Let the project dry overnight; then remove the backing from a second ten-inch square of clear Con-Tact® covering and align the covering atop the tissue paper. Cut a large leaf shape from the project. For a spectacular fall display, punch a hole near the top of each leaf cutout and use monofilament line to suspend the shapes from the ceiling.

Tony Johnson—Gr. 3, Danvers Elementary, Danvers, IL

Paper Plate Jack-O'-Lanterns

Serve up plenty of holiday enthusiasm with these jolly jack-o'-lanterns! To make a jack-o'-lantern, sketch large facial features on the bottom of a thin, white paper plate; then carefully cut out the features. (Assist students as needed with this step.) Sponge-paint the bottom of the plate orange. Also sponge-paint the bottom of a second paper plate yellow. When the paint has dried, glue the orange plate atop the yellow plate. Staple a green paper stem and green curling-ribbon vines to the top of the plate. Happy Halloween!

Roly-Poly Owls

Who-o-o-o could resist these adorable paper-bag owls? Use the patterns on page 55 to create tagboard templates for the outer and inner faces, the eyes, and the beak. Use a pencil to trace the outer-face template on brown paper, the inner-face template on black paper, the eye template on green paper (twice), and the beak template on orange paper. Use a black marker to trace over the pencil lines and to add a black pupil inside each eye shape. Cut out and assemble the patterns as shown. Next glue the resulting owl face to the bottom of an unfolded brown lunch bag. Allow drying time; then carefully stuff the lunch bag with crumpled newspaper or scrap paper. Use a black pipe cleaner to securely tie the bottom of the bag. Fashion a talon from each pipe-cleaner end as shown. "Hoot-diggity"! That's a fine-looking owl!

Carrie Tetson Geiger, Gainesville, FL

Tissue-Paper Banners

These colorful tissue-paper banners are a cut above the rest! Begin with a length of tissue paper that measures approximately 10" x 18". To create a casing, fold the top one inch of the tissue paper forward (Step 1); then accordion-fold the tissue at two-inch intervals (Step 2). Cut a series of shapes along one side of the project, taking care to not cut through the casing (Step 3). Unfold the project. Display the colorful banners end-to-end along lengths of suspended string or yarn. To do this, slip the string under the casing; then tape the casing closed (Step 4). With these banners in place, your classroom ambience will be full of cheer—and color!

Ruth Trinidad—Gr. 1, 28th Street School
Los Angeles, CA

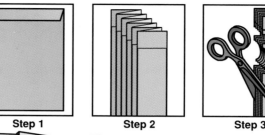

Step 1   Step 2   Step 3   Step 4

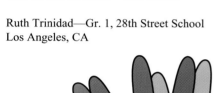

Gobble! Gobble!

This November create a flock of "hand-some" gobblers! To make one of the gobblers, trace the outline of your shoe onto brown construction paper. Also trace the outline of your hand (fingers outstretched) onto sheets of red, blue, purple, orange, green, and yellow construction paper. Cut along the resulting outlines. Position the cutout that matches your shoe's sole so that the heel is at the top and will represent the turkey's head. Glue eyes, a beak, a wattle, and feet cut from construction paper to the turkey body. Stack the hand cutouts; then fan them out to create a colorful set of tail feathers. Glue the feathers to the back of the turkey. Just look at that turkey strut!

Mosaic Placemats

Students will be delighted to add these placemats to their Thanksgiving dinner plans. Cut a supply of one-inch squares from brown, yellow, red, green, orange, and purple construction paper. To make a placemat, trace a large cornucopia-shaped template onto a 12" x 18" sheet of white construction paper. Arrange and glue brown paper squares to cover the horn-shaped basket; then arrange and glue the colorful paper squares to create an assortment of fruit shapes spilling from the basket. Use markers to add a holiday greeting; then sign and date the back of the project. For durability laminate the resulting placemat or cover it with clear Con-Tact® covering. Happy Thanksgiving!

Betsy Ruggiano—Gr. 3, Featherbed Lane School, Clark, NJ

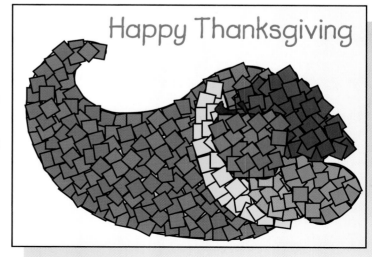

Happy Thanksgiving

Swedish Holiday Fashions

Brighten your holiday festivities with a salute to Sweden's Festival Of Light. To learn more about the customs associated with this December 13 holiday—also known as St. Lucia Day—see page 224. Then have each student make either a "Crown Of Candles" or a "Star-Studded Hat" for your classroom celebration.

Crown Of Candles

This leaf-covered crown of candles is traditionally worn by girls. To make a crown, use the patterns on page 56 to create five green construction-paper leaf shapes and five yellow candle flames. Cut out the patterns. Glue each flame cutout to a 1 1/2" x 4" strip of white construction paper to create a candle; then glue each candle to the straight end of a leaf cutout. Arrange the candle-adorned leaves end-to-end. Glue the pieces together by gluing a leaf tip over the bottom of each of the first four candles (see the illustration). When the glue has dried, size the resulting crown to fit the head of the intended wearer; then staple the crown ends together.

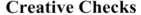

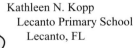

Star-Studded Hat

This cone-shaped hat is traditionally worn by Swedish boys. To make a hat, begin with a semicircle of white bulletin-board paper—diameter approximately 28 inches. Overlap the two corners of the paper until a cone is formed. Size the opening to fit the head of the intended wearer; then paper clip the overlapping edges of the hat rim. Tape the tip of the hat and trim away any extra paper; then remove the paper clip and securely glue the hat seam. Embellish the hat with yellow paper stars (pattern on page 56) and gold glitter.

Kathleen N. Kopp
Lecanto Primary School
Lecanto, FL

Creative Checks

Check this out! Here's a holiday art project that encourages creativity and requires minimal supplies! Begin with a 7" x 10" sheet of 1/2-inch graph paper. Using the lines as your guides, lightly sketch (in pencil) the outline of a desired holiday shape. Color the interior of the shape with markers or crayons; then use a black crayon to outline the shape and desired elements within the shape. Next choose two colors, and alternate between them to color each of the remaining squares on the page. When the page is completely colored, mount it onto a 9" x 12" sheet of colorful construction paper. "Check-tacular!"

Doris Hautala
Washington Elementary School, Ely, MN

Adorable Snow Pals

Even if snow isn't in the forecast, your students will have plenty of frosty fun creating these three-dimensional snow pals! For artistic inspiration, read aloud *Snowballs* by Lois Ehlert (Harcourt Brace & Company, 1995). Then give each child two sheets of 12" x 18" construction paper—one white and one blue. Also make available incrementally sized circle templates for optional student use. A student cuts out and mounts a white construction-paper snow pal onto his blue paper. Then he hole-punches his scrap paper and glues the resulting snowflakes to his project.

At this point, set the projects aside and revisit Lois Ehlert's book, focusing on the variety of snow-pal decorations the illustrator uses. Make plans to decorate the snow-pal projects the following day and invite students to bring from home a variety of decorating items. Also have on hand items like popcorn kernels, popped corn, raisins, buttons, small washers, sunflower seeds, construction-paper scraps, and discarded magazines for student use. Display the decorated snow pals in a hallway for others to admire!

Susie Kapaun
Littleton, CO

Pretty Poinsettia Carryall

If you're into recycling, you're going to love making these colorful carryalls crafted from empty cereal boxes! Trim the top from an empty cereal box; then use tape and yellow paper to wrap the box—leaving the top of the box open. Trim several 2" x 3" red paper rectangles to resemble red poinsettia leaves, and two or more 3" x 4" green paper rectangles to resemble green poinsettia leaves. Glue the cutouts to the front of the paper-covered cereal box; then glue a smattering of yellow hole punches to the center of the resulting flower. To make a handle, hole-punch each narrow side of the carryall. Thread a 30-inch length of red or green curling ribbon through the holes and securely tie the ribbon ends. Pull the doubled-ribbon handle upward; then use a one-foot length of ribbon to tie the two handles together. Curl the ribbon ends. The colorful carryall can be suspended from a doorknob and used to store received greeting cards. Or it can be used as a holiday gift box.

Misti Craig—Gr. 1
Campbellsville Elementary School
Campbellsville, KY

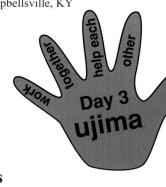

Kwanzaa Trees

These colorful trees remind students and onlookers that Kwanzaa celebrates family *and* seven important principles. To make a Kwanzaa tree, trace the outline of your hand (fingers outstretched) onto red paper seven times. Cut along the resulting outlines; then label each cutout with a different Kwanzaa principle, its meaning, and the day on which it is celebrated. Glue a 3" x 4" black rectangle to the bottom edge of a 12" x 18" sheet of green construction paper; then glue each of the seven hand cutouts to the paper to resemble tree foliage. Use a green glitter pen to add desired details. Cut the green paper away from the tree trunk and shape the tree to your liking. Mount the completed projects with the title "Kwanzaa Is A Time For Family And Growth!"

Arts & Crafts

Freedom Bell

Martin Luther King, Jr., proclaimed that freedom ring throughout the country. These colorful bells are a wonderful reminder of Dr. King's wishes. To make a freedom bell, put dollops of red and white tempera paint on a disposable plate. Partially inflate a small balloon to a size that allows it to be held in one hand. Gently press the balloon into the paint; then press the painted balloon surface onto a 9" x 12" sheet of blue construction paper. For a feathery effect, slightly roll the balloon. Paint the surface of the blue paper using the manner described. When the painted paper has dried, trace a bell-shaped template onto the paper and cut along the resulting outline. Hole-punch the top and the bottom of the painted bell shape. On the blank side of the cutout, write a sentence that describes freedom. Thread a jingle bell onto a length of yarn and tie the yarn ends; then attach the jingle bell through the bottom hole in the project. Through the top hole, thread lengths of red, white, and blue curling ribbon. Tie the ribbon lengths and curl the resulting ribbon ends for a festive look. Display clusters of these freedom bells where air currents will occasionally cause them to move. Let freedom ring!

painting technique by Lona Claire Uzueta—Grs. K–1
Play N Learn
Fairbanks, AK

Happy New Year!

Ring in the Chinese New Year with this impressive class-created dragon! In a large open area that has a washable floor, display a length of white bulletin-board paper. If you plan to have eight student groups working on the project, visually divide the length of paper into seven equal sections and label each one with a different numeral from one to seven. On another length of bulletin-board paper, sketch a large dragon head. Label this section "8." Assign a small group of students to paint each section. Provide the same colors of paint for each group and encourage student creativity. When the paint has dried, cut out the dragon head and trim one end of the long paper length to resemble a dragon tail. For added interest, make a wavy cut along each side of the resulting dragon body. Then glue the dragon head to the dragon body. Display the impressive project in a school hallway. To add a 3-D effect, incorporate a few bends in the dragon. Totally hot!

Phoebe Sharp—Gr. 1
Gillette School
Gillette, NJ

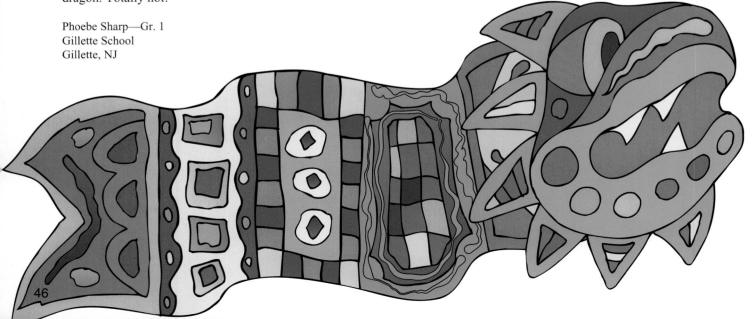

Hearts Aplenty

Get to the heart of your youngsters' creativity with these one-of-a-kind valentine decorations! To begin, use a template to trace four heart shapes on red paper. Cut out each shape. To decorate the hearts, cut four designs from white paper, and glue each design to a different heart. When the glue has dried, fold each heart shape in half, keeping the design to the inside.

To assemble the project, place one folded heart in front of you. Spread glue on the top surface; then align a second folded heart atop the glue. In the same manner, glue the third heart to the second heart, and the fourth heart to the third heart. Then pick up the project, and glue the top and bottom surfaces together. Punch a hole near the top of the project. Thread one end of a length of curling ribbon through the hole and securely tie. Suspend this heartfelt example of creativity for all to see!

Lacy Valentines

Pretty-as-can-be valentines are just a heartbeat away using these easy-to-follow steps.

Materials For One Valentine:
iron, set on low
two 1' lengths of aluminum foil
handheld pencil sharpener
four crayons with their wrappers removed
one 8" heart template
one 8" square of white construction paper
one 10" square of white construction paper
one 9" square of colored construction paper
scissors
glue
hole puncher
pushpin

Steps:
1. Center the 8-inch square of white paper on a length of foil.
2. Sharpen the crayons and spread the crayon shavings over the white paper.
3. Place the remaining length of foil on top of the crayon shavings.
4. Gently iron the top sheet of foil; then carefully remove it.
   (This step must be supervised [or completed] by an adult.)
5. When the crayon has hardened, trace a heart shape on the decorated paper.
6. Cut out the heart shape and glue it in the center of the colored paper.
7. Trim the colored paper to create a heart-shaped border.
8. Glue the project in the center of the 10-inch white square.
9. Trim the white paper to create an irregular heart-shaped border.
10. Use the hole puncher and the pushpin to give the white border a lacy look.
11. Write a desired valentine message on the back of the project.

Arts & Crafts

Heart-Shaped Key Ring

This handcrafted valentine gift can hold the keys to many hearts!

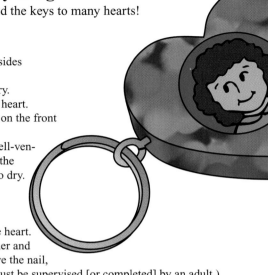

Materials For One Key Ring:
small paper plate
one wooden heart cutout
   (available at craft stores)
various colors of acrylic craft
paint
cotton swabs
paint or permanent marker
one student photo
craft glue
clear acrylic sealer spray
waxed paper
very small nail
hammer
one screw eye
one split key ring
scissors

Steps:
1. Set the heart in the center of the plate.
2. Use cotton swabs to paint the top and sides of the wooden heart. Allow to dry.
3. Paint the back of the heart. Allow to dry.
4. Use the marker to sign the back of the heart.
5. Trim the photo as needed; then glue it on the front of the heart. Allow to dry.
6. Set the project on waxed paper. In a well-ventilated area, spray the top and sides of the heart with clear acrylic sealer. Allow to dry.
7. Spray the back of the heart with clear acrylic sealer. Allow to dry.
8. Repeat Steps 6 and 7 two more times.
9. Twist the screw eye into the side of the heart. (For easy insertion, first use the hammer and nail to gently tap a starter hole. Remove the nail, and twist in the screw eye. This step must be supervised [or completed] by an adult.)
10. Thread the key ring onto the screw eye.

Kristi Gullett—Gr. 2, Peoria Christian School, Peoria, IL

Presidents' Windsock

Herald the arrival of Presidents' Day with these bright and breezy windsocks!

Materials For One Windsock:
template of President Lincoln's profile
template of President Washington's profile
star-shaped template
one 12" x 18" sheet of blue construction paper
three 2" x 18" strips of red construction paper
one 9" x 12" sheet of black construction paper
one 9" x 12" sheet of white construction paper
four 16-inch strips of red crepe paper
four 16-inch strips of white crepe paper
one 36-inch length of yarn
pencil
glue
scissors
hole puncher

Steps:
1. Glue the red paper strips to the blue paper as shown.
2. Trace each presidential profile on black paper.
3. Cut out and glue each profile to the project.
4. Trace several stars on the white paper.
5. Cut out and glue the stars to the project.
6. When the glue has dried, roll the blue paper into a cylinder (keeping the decorations to the outside) and glue the overlapping edges together.
7. Alternating colors, glue the crepe-paper strips inside the lower rim of the project.
8. At the top of the cylinder, punch two holes opposite each other.
9. Thread each end of the yarn length through a different hole and securely tie.

adapted from an idea by Doris Hautala—Gr. 3, Washington Elementary, Ely, MN

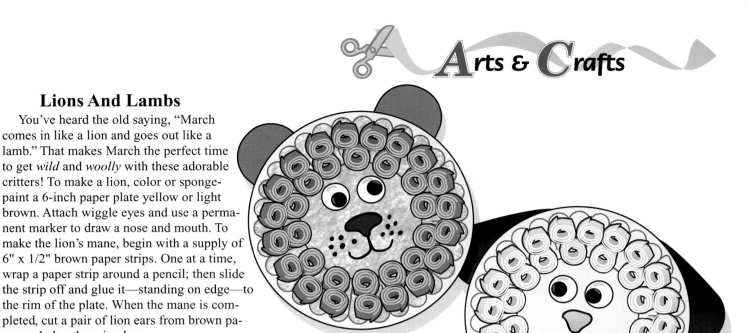

Lions And Lambs

You've heard the old saying, "March comes in like a lion and goes out like a lamb." That makes March the perfect time to get *wild* and *woolly* with these adorable critters! To make a lion, color or sponge-paint a 6-inch paper plate yellow or light brown. Attach wiggle eyes and use a permanent marker to draw a nose and mouth. To make the lion's mane, begin with a supply of 6" x 1/2" brown paper strips. One at a time, wrap a paper strip around a pencil; then slide the strip off and glue it—standing on edge—to the rim of the plate. When the mane is completed, cut a pair of lion ears from brown paper and glue them in place.

To make a lamb, begin with a white 6-inch paper plate. Attach wiggle eyes, draw a nose and mouth, and fashion a woolly coat for the lamb using 6" x 1/2" white paper strips and the technique described above. Cut a pair of lamb ears from black paper and glue them in place. Showcase the furry friends on a bulletin board titled "Watching The Weather" (see page 14).

Leprechaun Look-Alikes

Keep these adorable leprechauns around and you'll have the luck of the Irish at your fingertips!

Materials For One Leprechaun:

one 4 1/2" x 12" piece of green construction paper (body)
one 4" x 8" piece of green construction paper (hat)
one 2" x 8" piece of green construction paper (sleeves)
one 5" skin-tone construction-paper circle (head)
two 2" squares of skin-tone construction paper (hands)
one 2" x 4" piece of white construction paper (bow tie)

one 2" x 6" piece of orange construction paper (hair)
five 1' strips of orange crepe paper
markers or crayons
construction-paper scraps
scissors
glue

Steps:

1. **To make the body,** roll the 4 1/2" x 12" piece of green paper into a cylinder and glue it. Position the seam at the back and glue the top one inch of the cylinder closed. When dry, trim to round each glued corner.

2. **To make the sleeves and hands,** fold in half the 2" x 8" piece of green paper, cut out two matching sleeves, and glue them in place. Stack the skin-toned squares, cut out two matching hand shapes, and glue them in place.

3. **To make the hair, hat, and face,** snip the orange paper into several 1/2" x 2" lengths. Glue the resulting hair to the skin-toned circle. Fold the 4" x 8" piece of green paper in half (to a 4-inch square) and draw half of a hat shape on the paper as shown below. Cut on the outline; then unfold the cutout and add desired decorations. Glue the hat to the top of the circle. Add facial features and glue the resulting head to the top of the body.

4. **To make the bow tie, buttons, and streamers,** cut a bow-tie shape from the piece of white paper, decorate the shape as desired, and glue it in place. Cut out, decorate, and glue several buttons to the front of the body. Glue the crepe-paper strips inside the lower rim of the project.

adapted from an idea by Doris Hautala—Gr. 3
Washington Elementary
Ely, MN

Arts & Crafts

Extraordinary Eggs

Inspire uniquely decorated Easter eggs using this combination technique. To begin, trace an egg shape onto art paper. Inside the egg outline, randomly drip thinned tempera paint; then blow through a drinking straw to transform the paint drips into desired shapes. When the paint is completely dry, use a colored pencil in a contrasting color to completely fill each unpainted area within the egg outline. Cut out the egg shape. Display the egg and others like it on a seasonal bulletin board. Or mount the cutout on a slightly larger piece of contrasting construction paper and trim the construction paper to create a narrow border. The project can be used as a booklet cover for student work, or it can be hole-punched and suspended from a length of monofilament line. "Egg-ceptional"!

Mary Grace Ramos—Gr. 2
Pinewood Acres School
Miami, FL

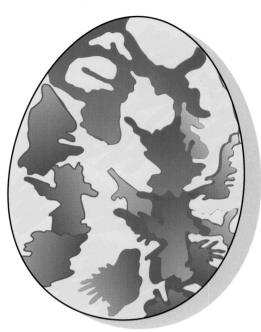

Springtime Baskets

These colorful woven baskets are perfect for delivering springtime, Easter, or May Day surprises! To make a basket, use a ruler and a pencil to divide a 9" x 12" sheet of construction paper into nine 1" x 12" strips. Cut out the strips and lay two aside. Arrange the seven remaining strips side by side; then tape down each end along one edge. Next cut a 9" x 12" sheet of contrasting construction paper into 1" x 12" strips as described above. Set two strips aside, and weave the remaining seven strips in and out of the first set of seven. To assemble the basket, slide the woven strips toward the center of the project; then—one side at a time—gather and staple together the ends of the strips. Use two of the extra strips for handles, stapling them to the basket as shown. How pretty!

Mary E. Morgan—Gr. 1
South Roxana Elementary
South Roxana, IL

Bunny Cups

Hippity, hoppity! Top off your Easter festivities by tucking a few treats into these student-made bunny cups. Start with a Styrofoam® cup or cover a colored disposable cup with white art paper. Attach construction-paper ears, eyes, and whiskers; then secure a pink pom-pom nose in place. Tuck some cellophane grass inside the decorated cup, and it's ready for treats. Everyone will be hopping over to see what these adorable bunnies have delivered!

Symmetrical Masterpieces

Stir up an interest in symmetry with this painting project! Fold in half a sheet of art paper to create a line of symmetry; then unfold the paper. Using colorful tempera paints, create a desired design on one half of the paper. For the best results, stop painting at regular intervals and refold the paper—transferring the colorful design to the other half of the paper. The end result is a stunning piece of symmetrical artwork!

Julia Clark
Maple Street School
Vernon, CT

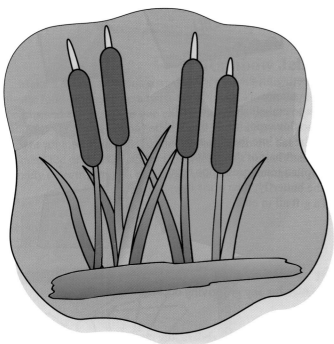

Charming Cattails

All eyes will be on these rustic cattail renditions. In preparation for this project, cut the side panels from large brown paper bags. Cut each panel in half, so that each large bag yields four cattail canvases. To begin, use a template and a fine-tipped marker to trace four cattail spikes onto brown felt. Cut along the resulting outlines; then set the spikes aside. Next trim a brown paper-bag canvas into a desired shape. Use tempera paints to create a blue waterline, green stems and leaves, and yellow cattail tops. When the paint has dried, glue the felt spikes in place. Absolutely breathtaking!

Melanie J. Miller
Nashport, OH

Woven Pop Art

Recycle plastic six-pack rings into unique pieces of pop art! Cut a supply of construction- and wall-paper scraps into six-inch and ten-inch strips of varying widths. First weave the longer strips through the plastic rings; then weave the shorter strips through the plastic rings and the longer paper strips. When the weaving is complete, trim the ends of the paper strips to create a desired look. Glue the weaving to a 6" x 9" rectangle of construction paper that is mounted atop a slightly larger paper rectangle of a contrasting color. This earth-friendly project is perfect for an Earth Day celebration!

Melanie J. Miller

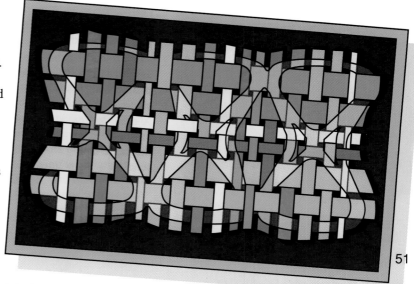

Underwater Seascapes

Whether you're wrapping up an ocean study or investigating coral reefs, make plans to create these colorful underwater scenes. To create the watery backdrop, cover a 9" x 12" sheet of white art paper with a length of plastic wrap. Using blue tempera, paint the portion of the plastic wrap that covers the art paper. Next slide the art paper from beneath the wrap and lay it on the painted surface. Use the palm of your hand to carefully press the paper against the plastic so the paint transfers to the paper. Then peel the paper from the plastic wrap. Set the art paper aside to dry, and dispose of the plastic. When the backdrop is dry, use torn construction paper and construction-paper cut-outs (see the optional fish patterns on page 58) to create a colorful underwater scene.

Melanie J. Miller
Nashport, OH

Stylish Swimmers

Anything goes when it comes to fish fashion—especially when the fish are made from coffee filters! To make a stylish swimmer, submerge a coffee filter in a pan of shallow water; then lay the filter on a paper towel. Next use colorful markers to draw stripes and/or dots on the coffee filter. The colors will bleed, creating a unique design. When the filter is dry, trace a fish shape onto the filter (see the patterns on page 58) and cut it out. Add desired details with a black fine-tipped marker. The fish look lovely displayed in a window. Or they can be incorporated into an underwater scene like the one described above.

For added razzle-dazzle that's reminiscent of the remarkable rainbow fish (from *The Rainbow Fish* by Marcus Pfister), use a silver glitter pen, glue and silver glitter, or glue and a silver sequin to add a small shiny scale to the fish.

Shelley Cignoli—Gr. 1 Teacher Assistant
Jupiter Farms Community Elementary
Jupiter, FL

Magnetic Note Holder

Here's a gift-giving idea that's perfect for Father's Day! Use the hammer pattern on page 58 to create a template; then trace the hammer shape onto a piece of white poster board. Also trace the hammerhead onto black construction paper two times. Cut out the shapes. Glue one black hammerhead cutout to each side of the poster-board cutout. While the glue is drying, use colorful markers to decorate both sides of the handle. Attach a two-inch strip of magnetic tape to the back of the project. Then turn the project over. Write "#1 Dad" in white crayon on the hammerhead, and use craft glue (or a hot glue gun) to attach a wooden clothespin to the handle as shown.

To create notepaper, press a finger onto a brightly colored stamp pad before pressing it onto 4" x 5" sheets of blank white paper. Use colorful fine-tipped markers to transform each fingerprint into a personalized work of art. Then stack and clip the decorated papers to the note holder. How nice!

Linda C. Buerklin—Substitute Teacher
Monroe Township Schools
Williamstown, NJ

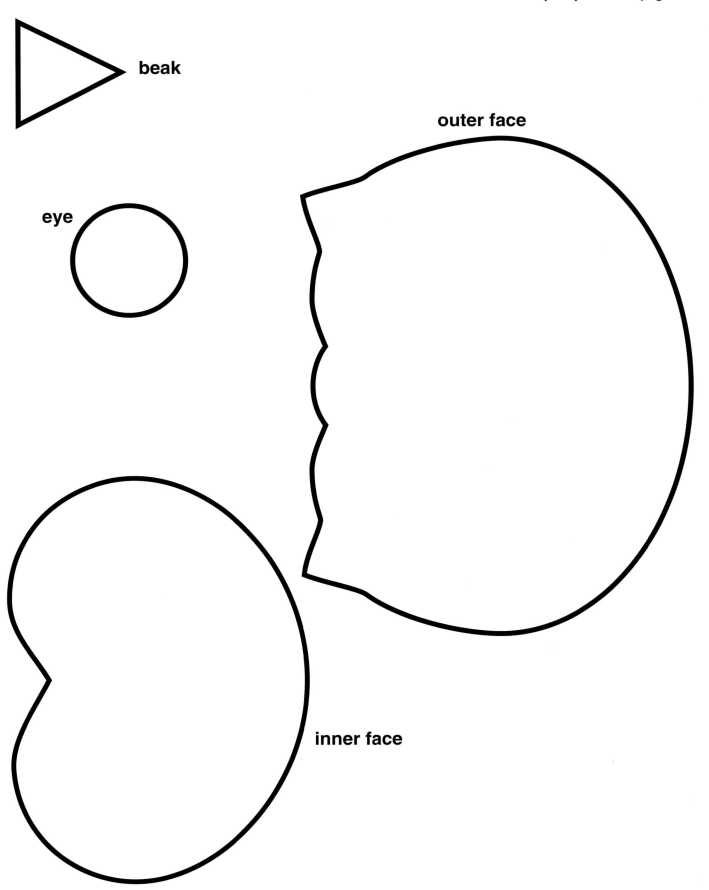

beak

eye

outer face

inner face

Patterns

Use the leaf and candle-flame patterns with "Crown Of Candles" on page 44.

Use the star patterns with "Star-Studded Hat" on page 44.

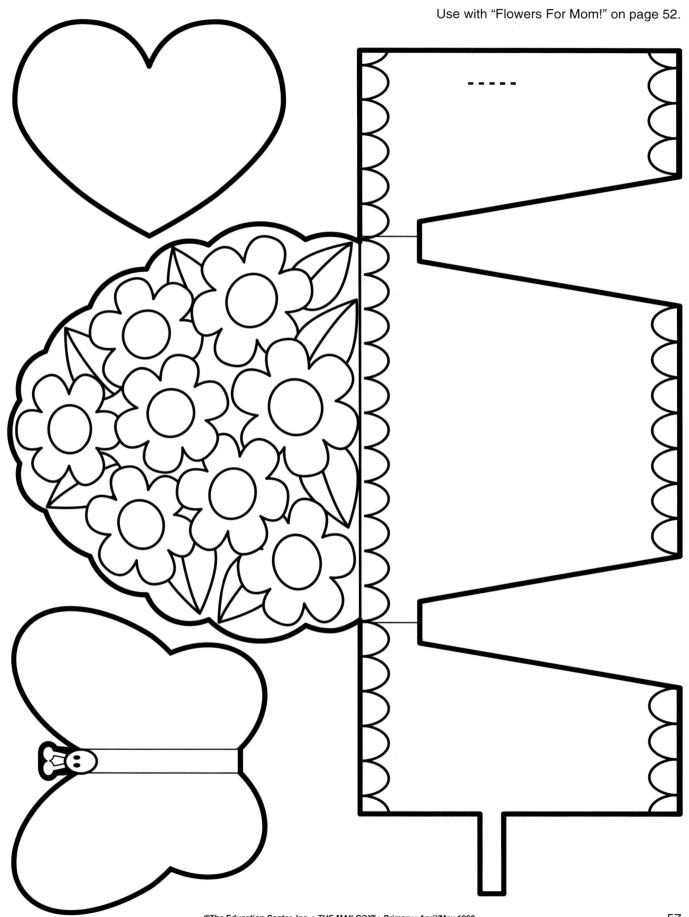

Patterns

Use the fish patterns with
"Underwater Seascapes"
and "Stylish Swimmers"
on page 54.

Use the hammer pattern
with "Magnetic Note
Holder" on page 54.

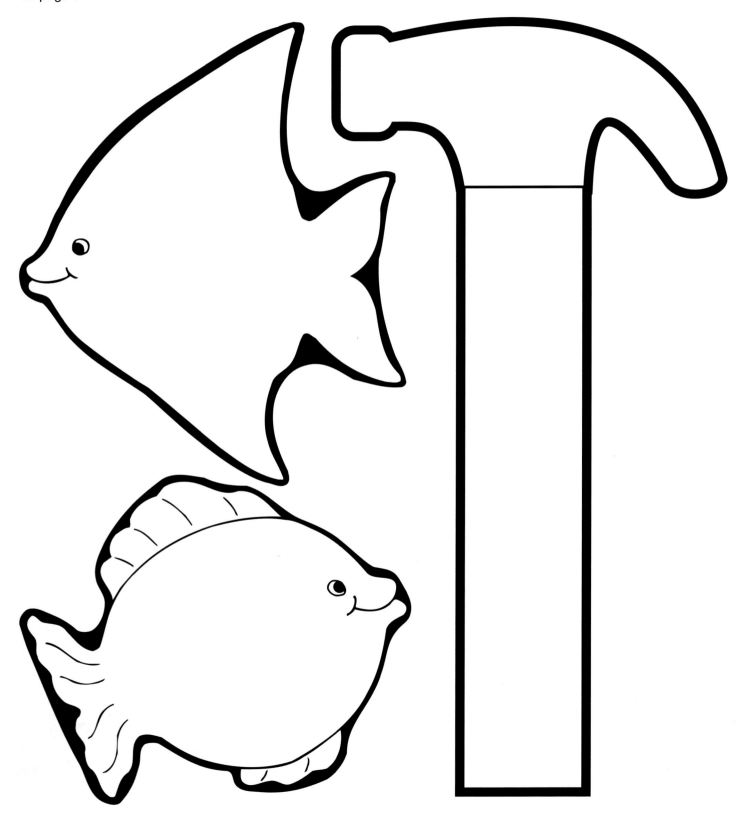

TEACHER RESOURCE IDEAS

Hitting The Road... With Class!

Turn your long-awaited field trip into a five-star learning experience with this collection of teacher-tested tips. All aboard!

A Class Plan

Lengthen the learning experience of your field trip by involving students in its planning stages. Enlist your students' help in brainstorming steps to organize the trip, a list of needed supplies, and so on. Troubleshooting the trip is also an invaluable lesson. To do this, ask students to anticipate problems that might occur during the trip and offer solutions to these problems. In the end, you'll have a well-planned trip and a group of youngsters who are committed to making it a successful experience for everyone involved.

Amy Kallelis—Gr. 3, Sanders Elementary, Smyrna, GA

Investigate Your Destination

Rather than organize a field trip based on the recommendations of others, plan a firsthand investigation of the location. Knowing the ins and outs of a field-trip site not only helps you plan appropriately, but it also gives you additional insight that you can use to enrich the learning experiences of your students.

Susan K. Brighton—Gr. 3, Superior Elementary School Superior, CO

Sparking Interest

To build student enthusiasm and knowledge about an upcoming field trip, prepare a pretrip scavenger hunt. Program a blank tic-tac-toe grid with nine different trip-related activities and give each child a copy of it. Instruct each student to draw an X over every activity she completes and an O over each one she chooses not to complete. To reward students for their pretrip investigations, attach a gold star to the field-trip nametag of each child who earns three Xs in a row. Outstanding!

Debbie Erickson—Grs. 2–3 Multi-Age
Waterloo Elementary School
Waterloo, WI

Going To The Zoo!

Talk to someone who has been to the zoo.	Tell a classmate how your behavior on the field trip will make Ms. Erickson proud.	Draw a map that shows how to get from the school to the zoo.
Write three questions that you hope to ask a zoo employee.	Your Own Idea!	List four items you will need for the field trip.
Draw and color a picture that shows your favorite zoo animal.	Research one zoo animal. Write five facts about it.	List five zoo exhibits you would like to see.

Check It Off

To help ensure that students arrive on the day of the field trip with the items they need, send home a pretrip checklist. Indicate which items are necessary and which ones are optional. Your students' parents will appreciate your forethought, and you'll be one step closer to a successful field trip.

Julie Eick Granchelli, Towne Elementary, Lockport, NY

Lining Up Chaperones

Lining up field-trip chaperones is a perfect task for a parent volunteer. Provide the volunteer with the phone numbers of parents who have expressed an interest, the date and time of the upcoming field trip, a brief outline of what each chaperone is expected to do, and the number of chaperones needed. The parents will enjoy talking with one another, and you'll be free to attend to other field-trip preparations.

Melissa Goldenberg
Oak Hill Elementary
Overland Park, KS

First-Aid Kit

Be prepared for the unexpected! Pack a resealable plastic bag with a variety of first-aid supplies, such as bandages, cotton balls, antibacterial cream, tweezers, gauze, and adhesive tape. Tuck the resulting kit in a tote bag or backpack that you plan to carry. In the event of a minor injury, you'll have just what you need right at hand.

Kimberly D. Nunes-Bufford—Grs. K–2
Jeter Primary
Opelika, AL

Lunch Orders

Distributing a preordered lunch is a breeze when you implement this suggestion! Code a corner of each child's nametag with his lunch order. For example, if a child orders a turkey sandwich and chocolate milk, code his nametag "t/c." A code of "rb/w" could indicate a roast beef sandwich and white milk. This tiny bit of programming can be a field-trip lifesaver!

Sherry Dunn
Billings Elementary
Greensburg, IN

pb/c

Charles

Top-Notch Behavior

Encourage students to be on their best behavior with this positive approach. Before departure, read aloud a list of expected field-trip behaviors; then give each leader a copy of the list and a pencil. Ask each leader to note on her list the positive behaviors that she acknowledges and observes, as well as positive comments directed toward her group by another adult. Periodically check in with each leader to applaud her group's behavior. This positive outlook is sure to deliver top-notch results.

Susan K. Brighton—Gr. 3
Superior Elementary School
Superior, CO

Pretrip Predictions

Before leaving on a field trip, ask students to write in their journals predictions about what they might see and learn on the trip. Then invite students to share their predictions and explain why they might come true. When you return, set aside time for students to talk about the things they saw and learned on the trip, and compare these events to the pretrip predictions that they made.

Julie Eick Granchelli
Towne Elementary
Lockport, NY

Chaperone Guidebooks

Individual guidebooks are a great way to ease the field-trip jitters your chaperones might be experiencing. Compile a booklet of information for each chaperone that includes the name of each adult and the students in his or her group, a schedule for the day, a map of the field-trip destination, a checklist of sights students should see, and guidelines for student behavior. The chances that your chaperones will remain cool, calm, and collected have just been tripled!

Kelly A. Lu—Gr. 2, Berlyn School, Ontario, CA

Field-Trip Groups

Red
Leader: Anita Hall
Students: Max
Rachel
Emma
Roy

Blue
Leader: Frederick Sams
Students: Wendy
Mike
Josh
Lori

Planning Multiple Trips

If you are fortunate enough to take your class on several field trips, here's a tip for you. In a small, inexpensive address book, log the name and address of each field-trip contact person with whom you work. The resulting resource will be invaluable as you plan future trips. In fact you may wish to call each contact person before you close out your classroom for summer break. Booking trips this far in advance will help you secure dates and times that perfectly match your curriculum needs.

Christine A. Bates—Gr. 3
Arlington Christian Academy
Akron, OH

Busy On The Bus

If a lengthy bus ride is required to reach your destination, try this. Prior to boarding the bus, give each child a list of sights that can be seen along the bus route. Younger students can check off each one as they see it. Challenge older students to sequentially number the sights in the order they see them. Students will be so busy watching for upcoming landmarks that the time spent on the bus will fly by!

Julie Eick Granchelli, Towne Elementary, Lockport, NY

Field Books

These individual booklets are the perfect place for students to record their field-trip observations. To make a book, stack several pieces of paper, fold the paper in half, and punch two holes near the folded edge. Next thread a three- to four-foot length of yarn through both holes and securely tie the yarn ends. On the day of the trip, ask each child to personalize the front cover of a field book before he suspends the book from his neck. Provide each chaperone with pencils for her group members. At different points throughout the field trip, ask the chaperones to distribute the pencils so students can record their observations in their field books. When the observations are recorded and the pencils collected, proceed with the field trip. Each student will have a unique collection of notes by the time he returns to the classroom.

Karen Smith—Grs. K–1
Pine Lane Elementary Homeschool
Pace, FL

Lizzy's Field Trip Book

The Zoo
I fed the donkey.

Classy Clipboards

If you require written work to be completed during a field trip, these easy-to-make clipboards are a must! From sturdy cardboard boxes, cut a 9" x 12" rectangle for each student and/or chaperone. Cover each rectangle with colorful Con-Tact® covering and attach a medium-size binder clip to the top as shown. The binder clip holds paper and a pencil too! You can count on youngsters feeling quite important as they carry these classy clipboards with them throughout the trip.

Glorianne Bradshaw—Gr. 1
Valley ElementarySchool
Crystal, ND

Informing Parents

Use the handy forms on page 66 to inform parents of your upcoming field trip and enlist field-trip chaperones.

We love field trips!

Fabulous Field-Trip Possibilities

- **Consider The Ordinary!** Take a city bus into the center of the city. Lead students along a predetermined walking route as you share information about historical buildings and architectural styles. Then take students on a prearranged tour of a downtown hotel, museum, or specialty shop. Students will learn about their community and have a great time too!

  Susan K. Brighton—Gr. 3
  Superior Elementary School, Superior, CO

- **Not Too Fruity!** As a follow-up to your nutrition unit, plan a trip to a large grocery store in your area. It's a great way to introduce students to a variety of fruits, vegetables, meats, pastas, breads, and so on that they may not be familiar with, but that can provide excellent nutrition. Since your youngsters will work up an appetite, follow up this excursion with a healthful snack.

  Kris Wesson—Gr. 1
  Adna Elementary School, Adna, WA

- **Forests Are Fun!** If a trip to your state's Division of Forestry is a possibility, make a phone call to inquire about field-trip opportunities. You may find an economical trip that is packed with learning and fun! (Colleen Proffitt did!)

  Colleen Proffitt—Gr. 2
  Doe Elementary, Mountain City, TN

- **Head To The Park!** A visit to a state or local park is a wonderful wrap-up to a study of plants, weather, or Earth Day. For best results arrange for a park employee or volunteer to speak to your students and provide a tour of the park. Or enlist parent volunteers to lead small-group investigations and discussions at different locations in the park.

  Teresa Flamang—Gr. 2
  Manawa School District, Manawa, WI

- **Enlist An Expert!** There are probably plenty of field-trip possibilities right in your classroom community. Investigate the interests of your students' parents. A parent who is especially interested in history might be pleased to help you plan a trip to a local museum. A geologist or rock hound could help students collect rock samples in a preapproved location and so on! The possibilities are waiting to be explored!

  Susan K. Brighton—Gr. 3

RETURN this portion!

_____ has

Child

my permission to go on the field trip.

_____
Parent's signature

_____
Date

☐ Yes! I would like to accompany the group as a chaperone.

Please call me at _____ .

Dear Parent,

We are planning a trip to _____

on _____ , _____ .
    Day   Date

Your child will need to bring:

- _____
- _____
- _____
- _____
- _____

(Keep this portion of the note as a reminder of the trip!)

©The Education Center, Inc. • THE MAILBOX® • Primary • April/May 1998

RETURN this portion!

_____ has

Child

my permission to go on the field trip.

_____
Parent's signature

_____
Date

☐ Yes! I would like to accompany the group as a chaperone.

Please call me at _____ .

Dear Parent,

We are planning a trip to _____

on _____ , _____ .
    Day   Date

Your child will need to bring:

- _____
- _____
- _____
- _____
- _____

(Keep this portion of the note as a reminder of the trip!)

©The Education Center, Inc. • THE MAILBOX® • Primary • April/May 1998

Note To Teacher: Program a copy of this page with the necessary information; then duplicate one form per student.

AUTHOR UNITS

Tooth Fairy

Written & Illustrated by Audrey Wood
Child's Play (International) Ltd, 1985
Jealous because her brother lost a tooth and she didn't, Jessica tries to trick the tooth fairy with a painted kernel of corn. But, as Jessica finds out, you can't trick the tooth fairy. She also learns that tooth fairies are very forgiving and extremely smart!

Youngsters may say they don't believe in the tooth fairy, but that doesn't mean they'll pass up the chance to put a lost tooth under their pillows—just in case! And the thought of having a tooth displayed in the Hall Of Perfect Teeth is just too good to be true! Follow up this fanciful story by reviewing good dental health habits with your class. Then ask each child to complete a copy of page 73. At the end of the day, send each child home with her tips for keeping healthy teeth and a white kernel of popcorn. Suggest that each child use these two items to retell Jessica's story to a family member. "Loose Tooth Away!"

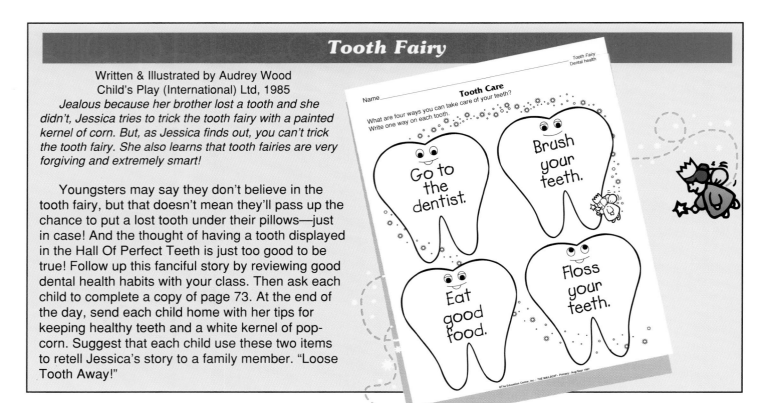

The Little Mouse, The Red Ripe Strawberry, And The Big Hungry Bear

Written by Don and Audrey Wood
Illustrated by Don Wood
Child's Play (International) Ltd, 1993
If a big hungry bear can smell a picked, red, ripe strawberry from a mile away, how is a tiny little mouse supposed to keep his picked strawberry a secret? If hiding it, guarding it, and disguising it won't do, there is another possibility that should work quite nicely!

There's a good chance that this kid-pleasing book will make your youngsters hungry for strawberries! Here's a simple treat that's sure to quench their cravings. To serve between 25 and 30 youngsters, stir two quarts of sliced strawberries into four quarts of strawberry yogurt. Spoon the mixture into individual plastic cups. Then give each child a graham cracker inside a plastic sandwich bag, a serving of strawberry dessert, and a spoon. Remind students about the big hungry bear, and suggest that they disguise their strawberries just in case the bear is nearby. To do this, have each child crumble the cracker inside the plastic bag, then sprinkle the resulting crumbs on top of his strawberry dessert. Invite students to eat their treats, all the while keeping their eyes open for that big hungry bear!

The adorable mouse featured in the book never says a word. But a quick look at the illustrations reveals that the mouse has plenty on its mind! Page back through the book, allowing students to study each double-spread illustration. Ask students to share their ideas for what the mouse might have said each time it was featured. For each page, help the class choose one mouse-related comment. Copy this comment on an individual sticky note. Trim the note to resemble a speech balloon and attach it to the corresponding page in the book. Then reread the book for your students, this time reading aloud the mouse's comments as well as the authors' words.

Weird Parents

Written & Illustrated by Audrey Wood
Dial Books For Young Readers, 1990
This wildly funny and most affectionate story expresses what most youngsters feel about their parents at one time or another—no matter how embarrassing parents can sometimes be, they are still greatly loved.

If you're planning to invite your students' parents to school for Open House or another classroom event, follow up your reading of *Weird Parents* with this activity. Have each child think of one weird thing that an adult in his family does, like singing in the shower, kissing children in public, or wearing totally uncool shoes. Then have each student illustrate a parent or guardian doing something weird. One-sentence descriptions may be added below the illustrations, but no names should be included. Display the completed projects on a bulletin board titled "Our Parents: They May Do Weird Stuff, But We Love Them Just The Same!" Also display Audrey Wood's book nearby. Your visitors are sure to have a good laugh as they peruse this one-of-a-kind attraction.

Students will also enjoy comparing and contrasting the family featured in *Weird Parents* with the prehistoric family from *The Tickleoctopus* (featured on this page). Record the student-generated information on a large Venn diagram that you've drawn on the chalkboard. Next challenge students to write and illustrate stories about a time when these two similar—but uniquely different—families meet. You can count on a batch of really *weird* stories that will *tickle* everyone's funny bones!

Mr. and Mrs. Weird
live in a house
live today
wear silly clothes

human parents
funny
have a son
love their son

wear bones
live in a cave
prehistoric
Ughpaw and Ughmaw

Rude Giants

Written & Illustrated by Audrey Wood
Harcourt Brace Jovanovich, Publishers; 1993
Beatrix the butter maid and Gerda the cow have some colossal problems when two rude giants move close by. But even giants can be taught manners—when their teachers are Beatrix and Gerda!

When youngsters learn that the baby giant is even more rude than its once-rude parents, they'll be flabbergasted! Find out what kinds of behavior your students think could earn the baby this reputation. List their ideas on one half of a piece of bulletin-board paper. Next have the students brainstorm creative ways for Beatrix and Gerda to cure the youngster of each ill manner listed. Write these ideas on the remaining half of the paper. If desired, leave the resulting poster on display and encourage students to write and illustrate reform tales titled "Rude Baby Giant." This would also be a perfect time to inform, discuss, and/or review your expectations concerning classroom manners.

The Tickleoctopus

Written by Audrey Wood & Illustrated by Don Wood
Harcourt Brace & Company, 1994
According to this tale, prehistoric families were downright miserable until a young caveboy named Bup discovered the tickleoctopus. So what is a tickleoctopus? You'll have to read this delightful story to find out!

So what does a tickleoctopus look like? Even though only the long, pink arms of this extraordinary creature are revealed, you can count on your youngsters having some ideas about what the tickleoctopus looks like in its entirety! Provide time for students to either illustrate their creations on drawing paper, or mold them from generous portions of pink play dough. Then, as each child shares his creation with his classmates, ask him to tell how he plans to put his tickleoctopus to use!

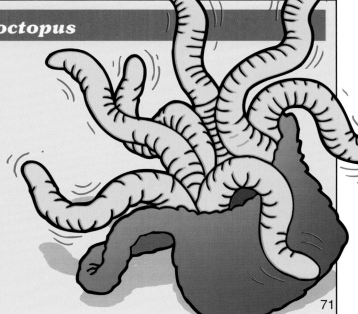

Eric Kimmel
Noted Storyteller And Award-Winning Author

The words of Eric Kimmel can bring knowledge, laughter, and a love of literature into your classroom! Use the information and the activities that follow to extend your students' enjoyment of this author's work.

by Lisa Leonardi

Meet The Author

Award-winning author Eric A. Kimmel is a prolific teller and writer of stories. Born in Brooklyn, New York, in 1946, Kimmel grew up in a culturally diverse neighborhood where most everyone had a story to tell. Kimmel's grandmother, who moved to the United States from the Western Ukraine, was a wonderful source of stories. Brothers Grimm fairy tales also had a major influence on the young Kimmel. In fact, Kimmel was only in third grade when he began perfecting his storytelling techniques and sharing tales with his classmates.

Kimmel's big break as an author came when he was asked to pen a Hanukkah story. The tale, *Hershel And The Hanukkah Goblins,* earned several awards, including a 1990 Caldecott Honor Book award for illustrator Trina Schart Hyman. After 8 previously published books and 15 years of writing experience, this additional recognition set Kimmel's writing career on a firm course. He has since published more than 20 books—many of which have won awards. Kimmel is perhaps most recognized for his adaptations of folktales from around the world. He is hopeful that children will recognize the basic themes that reappear in the stories and will be encouraged to focus on what unites our world, rather than on what divides it.

Kimmel currently resides in Portland, Oregon, with his wife, a dog, two cats, and several fish. When he's not writing or telling stories, he enjoys a variety of activities that include watching birds, riding motorcycles, baking bread, spinning yarn, knitting sweaters, and riding horses. His latest accomplishment is playing the banjo. Now that's a multitalented writer!

contributions by Peggy A. Sharp

Original Stories

Eric Kimmel's original stories are sure to be enjoyed by your youngsters! Pick and choose from this sampling and the related classroom activities.

Hershel And The Hanukkah Goblins
Illustrated by Trina Schart Hyman
Holiday House, Inc.; 1989

On the first night of Hanukkah, Hershel of Ostropol wanders into a village that—thanks to some Hanukkah-hating goblins—doesn't celebrate Hanukkah. Hershel decides to take matters into his own hands and devises plans to rid the goblins from the village's haunted synagogue. Youngsters will hang onto your every word as Hershel manages to outsmart the grumpy goblins and return the spirit of Hanukkah to the village.

On the fourth, fifth, and sixth nights of Hanukkah, Hershel is visited by other fierce goblins. Hershel fools them all, but the reader is not told how he tricks them. Invite each student to create a goblin using a variety of materials, like construction paper, toilet-paper rolls, wiggle eyes, yarn, and pipe cleaners. Once his goblin is finished, have each student write a clever tactic that Hershel could use to banish this goblin from the synagogue. Students will enjoy sharing their creative goblins and tactics with their classmates. *(See page 275 for additional activities related to Hanukkah stories by Eric Kimmel.)*

I Took My Frog To The Library
Illustrated by Blanche Sims
Puffin Books, 1992

When Bridgett visits the library, she brings along her very unusual pets. It's tolerable when Bridgett's frog jumps on the librarian's desk and when the loud laughter of her hyena interrupts storytime. But when her elephant demolishes the library, the librarian strongly suggests that Bridgett leave her pets at home! Like the hyena in the story, your youngsters will laugh out loud at the hilarious animal antics.

Pets are precious, but they can get their owners into some sticky situations! At the conclusion of this story, invite students to describe times when their pets have created problems and explain how they handled the situations. Next have each student write and illustrate a library-related story that features his pet or a pet he'd like to own. Bind the stories into a class book titled "Pet Adventures At The Library." Place the book in the classroom library. For added fun post a sign near the book that prohibits pets from entering your library!

Sharon

One day I took my dog, Hobbes, to my school library. He barked at my friends, chewed on the new library books, and bit the librarian. Hobbes had a great time, but I sure didn't!

One More Original Story
If your students enjoyed *Charlie Drives The Stage,* then it only makes "cents" to follow up with *Four Dollars And Fifty Cents* (Holiday House, Inc.; 1993)—another western tale written by the author!

Charlie Drives The Stage
Illustrated by Glen Rounds
Holiday House, Inc.; 1989

Senator McCorkle has an important meeting with the president! To board the Washington-bound train, the senator must first travel by stagecoach along a route that is so wrought with dangers that only one driver is willing to take the risk: Charlie Drummond. Not avalanches, robbers, or Indians can outsmart or outrun a stagecoach driven by Charlie. The senator quickly learns that Charlie is full of surprises—but not even the senator is prepared for Charlie's final surprise of the trip!

Senator McCorkle is so impressed with Charlie that he intends to tell the president about him—oops, her! Suggest to students that the senator may have been planning to recommend Charlie for a job. Ask students to recall Charlie's strengths and weaknesses. Keeping these characteristics in mind, have students brainstorm jobs that Charlie could do for the president of the United States. List the students' ideas on the chalkboard. Next ask each youngster to choose a job from the list, then write and illustrate a newspaper article that describes how Charlene helps the president. To publish the students' works, mount the projects on a series of newspaper pages. Decorate the front page of the resulting one-of-a-kind newspaper to show the title "The Grass Valley Times," the date, and a class byline. Laminate the pages for durability; then place the publication in your class library. Extra! Extra! Read all about her!

The Grass Valley TIMES
Mrs. Leonardi's Class
December 11, 1997

DRUMMOND APPOINTED

Drummond Wins Award From The President

Anansi Stories

Eric Kimmel's retellings of Anansi stories are sure to receive rave reviews from your youngsters! Weave a web of amusement with the following stories and activities.

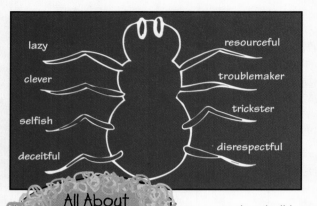

Anansi And The Moss-Covered Rock

Illustrated by Janet Stevens
Holiday House, Inc.; 1988

In this delightful tale of trickery, Anansi the Spider happens upon a strange moss-covered rock that possesses special powers. Anansi realizes he can use the magic of the rock to trick his animal friends. However, Little Bush Deer is onto Anansi's antics and decides to give the trickster a taste of his own medicine!

Anansi is the number-one trickster around! However, it is only Anansi who finds humor in his pranks. Ask students to explain why Anansi's actions are deceitful rather than humorous. To help students analyze Anansi's personality traits, draw the outline of a spider on the chalkboard. Have students brainstorm traits that describe Anansi; then write the traits that are suggested near the ends of the spider's legs.

To extend the activity, have students write sentences describing Anansi's characteristics in rock-shaped booklets. To make a booklet, staple several pages of writing paper between two rock-shaped construction-paper covers. On each booklet page, a student describes a story event that depicts a personality trait of the spider. Then he personalizes and titles the front cover "All About Anansi." If desired have each student glue fabricated moss near the edge of the cover as shown.

Anansi Goes Fishing

Illustrated by Janet Stevens
Holiday House, Inc.; 1992

In this companion tale to Anansi And The Moss-Covered Rock, *lazy Anansi attempts to trick his friend Turtle into catching a fish for him. Unfortunately for Anansi, his plan backfires. Anansi ends up doing all the work and is still left with an empty stomach in the end! Watch this famous trickster get tricked in this comical story that also explains the origin of spider webs.*

The animals that were tricked by Anansi in *Anansi And The Moss-Covered Rock* stand by and watch Anansi get his just rewards in this entertaining sequel. The illustrator has carefully concealed the former Anansi victims behind the river's vegetation. During a second reading, challenge youngsters to locate the animals. Next remind students that both good and bad came from Anansi's failure to trick Turtle. For example, Anansi learns to spin a web; yet he is disgraced in the process. Then encourage students to reflect on Anansi's experiences with this kid-pleasing project. Give each child a 12" x 18" sheet of blue construction paper and eight small fish cutouts: four yellow and four orange. On each yellow fish, a student writes a positive event that Anansi experienced. On each orange fish, he writes a negative event that the spider experienced. Next the student illustrates Anansi and a fishing net on his blue paper; then he glues his fish cutouts around the net as shown.

He was disgraced.

He learned to spin a web.

Another Anansi Tale

If your students enjoyed the first two Anansi retellings by Eric Kimmel, they're sure to love *Anansi And The Talking Melon* (Holiday House, Inc.; 1995). And who knows? The author could be cooking up yet another Anansi tale!

Folktales From Other Countries

The following featured books are just a sampling of the author's retellings of folktales from around the world. Use the provided activities to complement these enjoyable stories.

Baba Yaga: A Russian Folktale
Illustrated by Megan Lloyd
Holiday House, Inc.; 1993

One afternoon Marina's evil stepmother sends her to visit Auntie-in-the-Forest, who is known to all as Baba Yaga, *a very mean and conniving witch. Shaking with fear, Marina sets out to face her unquestionable doom. Along the way she kindly accepts the advice of a friendly frog. Will the frog's advice be enough to save Marina from Baba Yaga?*

At the conclusion of this folktale, emphasize that—just like in the fairy tale *Cinderella*—inner beauty prevails over evil. Ask students to state similarities and differences between Marina and Cinderella, and write their responses on the chalkboard. Then have each student refer to the posted information as she completes a copy of page 78. Conclude this activity by taking a class poll to determine which of these two characters your students like best.

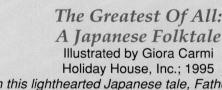

The Greatest Of All: A Japanese Folktale
Illustrated by Giora Carmi
Holiday House, Inc.; 1995

In this lighthearted Japanese tale, Father Mouse searches for the greatest husband for his daughter. In his search he approaches the emperor, the sun, a cloud, the wind, and a wall before he finds a very unexpected—yet very suitable—suitor.

After reading the story aloud, write a student-generated list of story events on the chalkboard. Then divide the class into groups of eight students each. Ask each group member to illustrate a different story character on provided paper, then cut out and glue the character to a craft stick. Invite each group to use its puppets to reenact Father Mouse's search for the mightiest husband. Or challenge each group to create another set of possible suitors for a telling of a similar story. There's no doubt that the greatest of all theatrics will be performed by your students!

An Additional Folktale
Your students are sure to be touched by Eric Kimmel's adapted tale *Sirko And The Wolf: A Ukrainian Tale* (Holiday House, Inc.; 1997). This heartwarming story explains the bond that dogs and wolves share.

Name _____

Two Kind Characters

Think about the two characters shown.

Write words that describe only Marina in her bucket.
Write words that describe only Cinderella in her bucket.

Write words that describe both
Marina and Cinderella in the puddle.

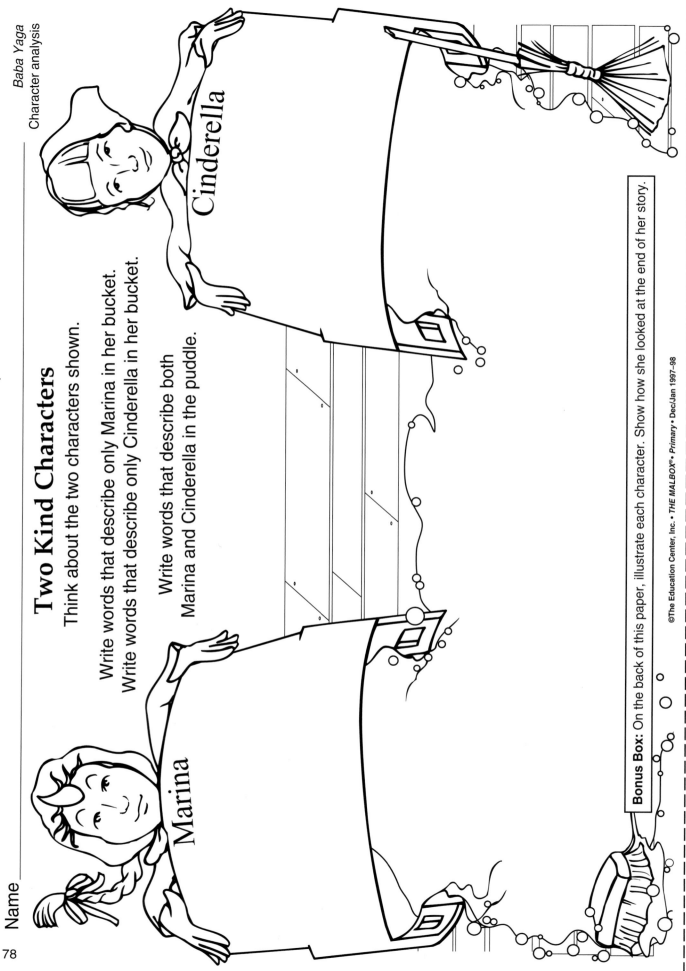

Cinderella

Marina

Bonus Box: On the back of this paper, illustrate each character. Show how she looked at the end of her story.

©The Education Center, Inc. • *THE MAILBOX*® • *Primary* • Dec/Jan 1997–98

Note To Teacher: Use with *Baba Yaga: A Russian Folktale* on page 77.

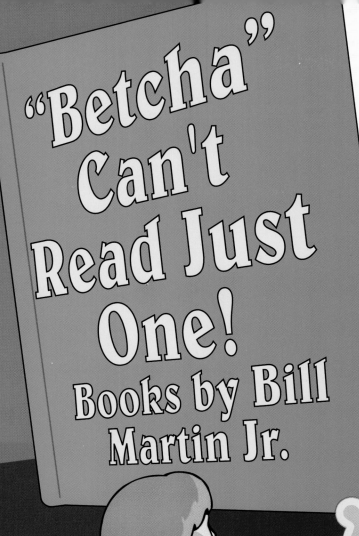

"Betcha" Can't Read Just One!
Books by Bill Martin Jr.

Bill Martin Jr.'s infectious writing style keeps readers coming back for book after book after book. Use this sampling of Bill Martin books and the related activities to nurture your students' love of reading.

by Anne Bustard

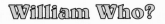

William Who?

Known to most folks as Bill Martin Jr., William Ivan Martin began writing children's books more than 50 years ago. To date he has published well over 100 different titles. That's pretty amazing for a young Kansas boy who struggled to learn to read. Despite Martin's poor reading ability, he managed to proceed through school with a love of books. He credits his storytelling grandmother, his fifth-grade teacher who read aloud to the class twice a day, and his high school drama teacher for instilling in him a love of books, an interest in language, and a desire to read. Martin read his first book—from start to finish—during his freshman year of college. He recalls the experience as "a laborious but glorious undertaking."

Martin's knowledge and passion for books have empowered him to pursue many reading-related careers that include being a teacher, a principal, an editor, a children's textbook creator, a video producer, a lecturer, and a storyteller. As an advocate for reading and teachers, Martin believes in giving children reading experiences that provide ample opportunities for success.

In March 1997, Bill Martin Jr. celebrated his 81st birthday. He resides in Texas and continues to be active in the publishing world.

Brown Bear, Brown Bear, What Do You See?

Written by Bill Martin Jr. & Illustrated by Eric Carle
Henry Holt And Company, Inc.; 1992
A parade of colorful critters traipses across the pages of this most beloved book. The author's engaging and predictable text is magnified by the illustrator's large, colorful collages. What results is an unspoken invitation for listeners to join in on the fun!

After a few oral readings of the book, introduce students to this large-group predictable-pattern game. Sit with your students on the floor in a large circle formation. To play the game, instruct students to repeat the question "Teacher, Teacher, what do you see?" when you touch your ear. Touch your ear; then respond to your students' question as follows: "I see [name of student to your right] wearing [appropriate color word] to the right of me." To continue the game, the student to your right touches her ear. The class asks the original question, substituting the child's name for *Teacher*. The student answers her classmates' question using the established pattern. Continue playing the game in this manner. When each child has taken her turn, conclude the game in a manner that imitates the book's conclusion.

blue

yellow

green

white

wingingly

slowly

knowingly

dizzily

wildly

trrrr-r-r-r-ippingly

The Maestro Plays

Written by Bill Martin Jr. & Illustrated by Vladimir Radunsky
Harcourt Brace & Company, 1996
How does the maestro play? "Singingly," "ringingly," and "wingingly" name a few of the ways! In this book adverbs take center stage as a master of music plays assorted instruments. Dynamic illustrations accompany the action-packed performance. And when the concert is over, claps and bravos fill the pages. Encore! Encore!

Set the stage for the maestro's high-energy recital by introducing students to a variety of instruments and the sounds that they make. Recruit your school's music teacher (or bandleader) to help you with this project. Members of your students' families may also be able to help. When you read the book aloud, alter the tempo and volume of your voice to match those which are conveyed on the book's pages. During a second reading, take time to identify the instruments that are being played and the maestro's talents. Also help students conclude that this *maestro* is a master of music. Then, as an encore, take your students to an unobstructed area like the school gym and read the book a third time. Invite students to *feel* the music from their heads to their toes!

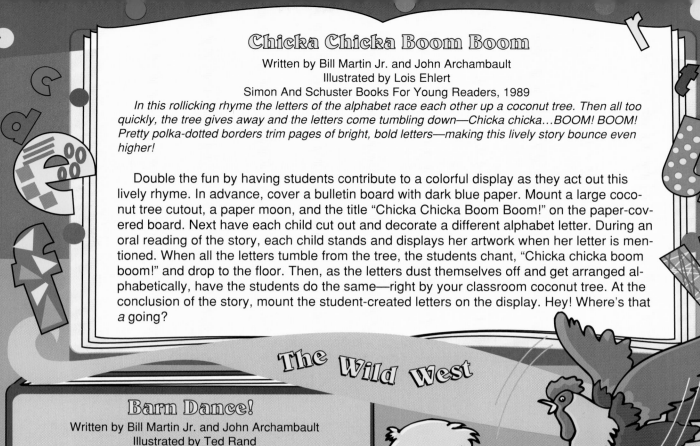

Chicka Chicka Boom Boom

Written by Bill Martin Jr. and John Archambault
Illustrated by Lois Ehlert
Simon And Schuster Books For Young Readers, 1989
In this rollicking rhyme the letters of the alphabet race each other up a coconut tree. Then all too quickly, the tree gives away and the letters come tumbling down—Chicka chicka…BOOM! BOOM! Pretty polka-dotted borders trim pages of bright, bold letters—making this lively story bounce even higher!

Double the fun by having students contribute to a colorful display as they act out this lively rhyme. In advance, cover a bulletin board with dark blue paper. Mount a large coconut tree cutout, a paper moon, and the title "Chicka Chicka Boom Boom!" on the paper-covered board. Next have each child cut out and decorate a different alphabet letter. During an oral reading of the story, each child stands and displays her artwork when her letter is mentioned. When all the letters tumble from the tree, the students chant, "Chicka chicka boom boom!" and drop to the floor. Then, as the letters dust themselves off and get arranged alphabetically, have the students do the same—right by your classroom coconut tree. At the conclusion of the story, mount the student-created letters on the display. Hey! Where's that *a* going?

The Wild West

Barn Dance!

Written by Bill Martin Jr. and John Archambault
Illustrated by Ted Rand
Henry Holt And Company, Inc.; 1986
Here's a toe-tappin', knee-slappin', do-si-doin' fantasy! Summoned by an owl, a young pajama-clad boy slips outside on a moonlit night. The faint sounds of music lead the wide-eyed lad to a most unusual barn dance. Written in rhyme, this high-spirited page-turner gives readers the inside scoop on what farm animals do when their caretakers are sound asleep!

What could be more fun than having your own toe-tappin' hoedown? Plan to play some square-dance music, and if possible enlist the P.E. teacher or a parent volunteer to teach your youngsters a few simple square-dance steps. If dancing is out of the question, make plans to play a game of Scarecrow Says. After all, the fiddle-playing scarecrow does play a significant role in this story. To play this harvest version of Simon Says, students follow only the directions prefaced by "Scarecrow says." Students who miss form a circle around the remaining players and clap their hands to the music. Finish the game by having the circle of students join hands and skip to the right and to the left around the remaining players.

White Dynamite And Curly Kidd

Written by Bill Martin Jr. and John Archambault
Illustrated by Ted Rand
Henry Holt And Company, Inc.; 1986
Ride 'em, Cowboy! Hold on tight as Curly Kidd rides the fiercest bull on the rodeo circuit—appropriately named White Dynamite. Curly's youngster, Lucky Kidd, anxiously watches Curly prepare for and participate in the event—all the while dreaming of one day becoming a bull rider too. Written entirely in dialogue, this western-flavored story and its surprise ending are sure to stir up some excitement in your classroom!

Bull riding is a dangerous sport and Lucky's apprehension about her father's ride is justified. As you page through the book a second time, help students notice people and things that make a bull rider's ride as safe as possible, like special gear, rodeo clowns, cowboys on horses, chutes, and fences. During her father's ride, Lucky Kidd tries to calm her fears by thinking of all the places she'd like to go. If time allows, enlist your students' help in locating several of the places Lucky mentions on a map of North America. Then, for a fun follow-up activity, challenge each child to list eight or more places (in honor of the eight seconds a bull rider must stay on the bull) he would like to visit. Suggest that the students commit their lists to memory so that the next time they feel worried or afraid, they can name these places—just like Lucky did!

81

Knots On A Counting Rope

Written by Bill Martin Jr. and John Archambault
Illustrated by Ted Rand
Henry Holt And Company, Inc.; 1987
In this touching tale a grandfather promises his grandson, Boy-Strength-Of-Blue-Horses, that his love will always surround the boy. As the older man reminisces about the boy's life, the boy—who is blind—is reminded once again of the importance of seeing with his heart.

At the conclusion of this story, ask students to reflect on the relationship that the grandfather and the boy share. Encourage students to name the different ways that the grandfather has influenced the young boy's life. Next find out what childhood stories are important to your students. Ask each student to talk with a family member about a favorite childhood story. If desired, give each child a one-foot length of twine. Instruct the students to add a knot to the rope each time they discuss their stories with their family members. Then, on a designated day, set aside time for interested students to orally share their stories with their classmates.

The Willies

Old Devil Wind

Written by Bill Martin Jr. & Illustrated by Barry Root
Harcourt Brace & Company, 1993
Picture an old creaky house on a dark and stormy night, and you've captured the setting of this dramatic cumulative tale. The rickety mansion slowly comes to life as one object after another joins in making ghostly noises. But when the wind takes its turn, the unsuspecting objects are scattered every which way! Barry Root's dark and moody illustrations perfectly suit the climactic nature of this delightfully eerie escapade.

This story screams out for reader participation! Using the provided chart, write each object and its corresponding sounds on a card. After an initial oral reading of the story, divide the class into ten groups and give each group a programmed card. Provide time for the groups to rehearse their sound effects. Then, during a second oral reading, pause after each object has declared its sound and wait for the appropriate group to provide the sound effect. Ask the entire class to contribute to the wind's ghostly noise. If desired, also pause after each object has been blown away so that the appropriate group can repeat its sound effect. For added fun, redistribute the sound cards to different groups and read the story again—and again and again!

Object	Sound Effect
ghost	"wail, wail, wail, wail"
stool	"thump, thump, thump, thump"
broom	"swish, swish, swish, swish"
candle	"flicker, flicker, flicker, flicker"
fire	"smoke, smoke, smoke, smoke"
window	"rattle, rattle, rattle, rattle"
floor	"creak, creak, creak, creak"
door	"slam, slam, slam, slam"
owl	"hoot, hoot, hoot, hoot"
witch	"fly, fly, fly, fly"

Candle
"flicker, flicker, flicker, flicker"

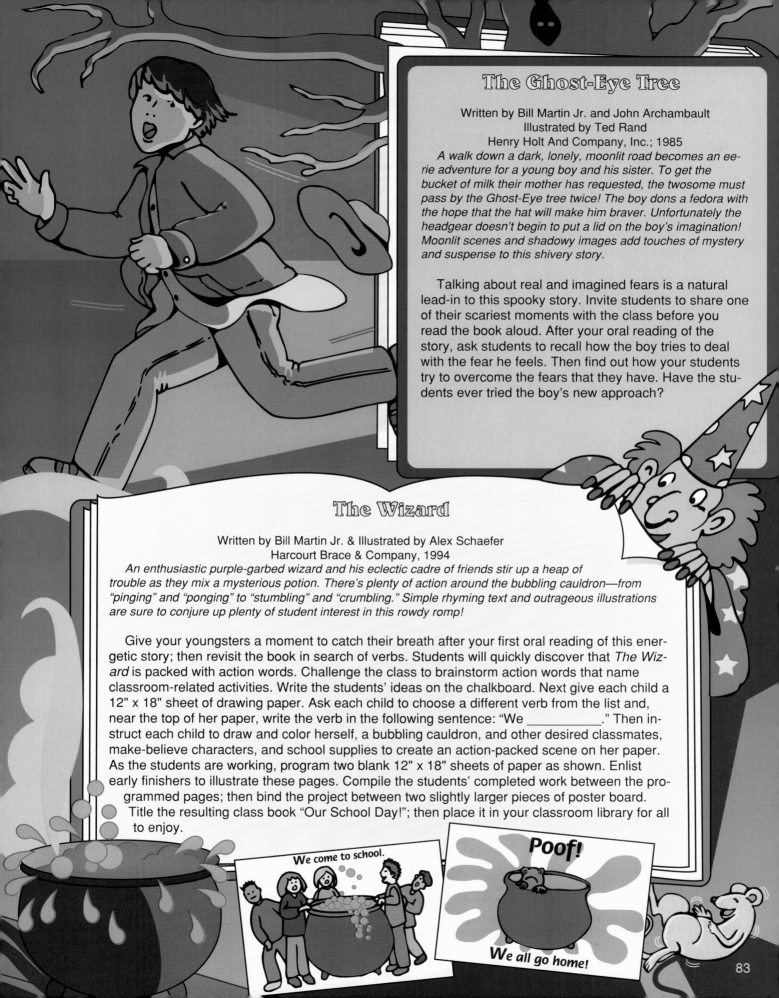

The Ghost-Eye Tree

Written by Bill Martin Jr. and John Archambault
Illustrated by Ted Rand
Henry Holt And Company, Inc.; 1985

A walk down a dark, lonely, moonlit road becomes an eerie adventure for a young boy and his sister. To get the bucket of milk their mother has requested, the twosome must pass by the Ghost-Eye tree twice! The boy dons a fedora with the hope that the hat will make him braver. Unfortunately the headgear doesn't begin to put a lid on the boy's imagination! Moonlit scenes and shadowy images add touches of mystery and suspense to this shivery story.

Talking about real and imagined fears is a natural lead-in to this spooky story. Invite students to share one of their scariest moments with the class before you read the book aloud. After your oral reading of the story, ask students to recall how the boy tries to deal with the fear he feels. Then find out how your students try to overcome the fears that they have. Have the students ever tried the boy's new approach?

The Wizard

Written by Bill Martin Jr. & Illustrated by Alex Schaefer
Harcourt Brace & Company, 1994

An enthusiastic purple-garbed wizard and his eclectic cadre of friends stir up a heap of trouble as they mix a mysterious potion. There's plenty of action around the bubbling cauldron—from "pinging" and "ponging" to "stumbling" and "crumbling." Simple rhyming text and outrageous illustrations are sure to conjure up plenty of student interest in this rowdy romp!

Give your youngsters a moment to catch their breath after your first oral reading of this energetic story; then revisit the book in search of verbs. Students will quickly discover that *The Wizard* is packed with action words. Challenge the class to brainstorm action words that name classroom-related activities. Write the students' ideas on the chalkboard. Next give each child a 12" x 18" sheet of drawing paper. Ask each child to choose a different verb from the list and, near the top of her paper, write the verb in the following sentence: "We _____." Then instruct each child to draw and color herself, a bubbling cauldron, and other desired classmates, make-believe characters, and school supplies to create an action-packed scene on her paper. As the students are working, program two blank 12" x 18" sheets of paper as shown. Enlist early finishers to illustrate these pages. Compile the students' completed work between the programmed pages; then bind the project between two slightly larger pieces of poster board.
  Title the resulting class book "Our School Day!"; then place it in your classroom library for all to enjoy.

We come to school.

Poof!

We all go home!

APPLAUSE FOR ANGELA SHELF MEDEARIS

Usher your youngsters into the diverse world of Angela Shelf Medearis. From historical picture books to ghost stories to retellings of African folktales, this talented storyteller opens a window to the rich experiences and contributions of African-Americans. The following pages feature a sampling of the author's outstanding books along with several related classroom activities. Your students are sure to have plenty of applause for Ms. Medearis!

ideas contributed by Anne Bustard, Sharon Murphy, and Donna C. Kester Phillips

MEET THE AUTHOR

Angela Shelf Medearis, born November 16, 1956, has loved books and reading for as long as she can remember! Her father's career in the U.S. Air Force kept her family constantly on the move. But wherever their travels took them, Angela could always find her favorite books and a friendly face at the local library.

Medearis recalls her elementary school teachers praising her writing, but it wasn't until she was 30 years old and had begun to write professionally that the author realized her writing talent. Since then Medearis has published more than 20 children's books. Her writing is perhaps most widely recognized for its focus on African-American heritage. Her interest in history, her sensitivity to culture, and her love and concern for children give her writing a unique appeal that captivates and entertains young readers.

In addition to her writing, Medearis is the founder of and Project Director for Book Boosters. This multicultural, multiethnic program for all grade levels focuses on reading motivation, creative writing, and drama. Medearis also finds time to promote reading and writing by visiting schools and bookstores, and appearing at conferences throughout the country. When Medearis is not on the move, she can be found at home with her family in Austin, Texas.

THE ZEBRA-RIDING COWBOY

Illustrated by María Cristina Brusca
Henry Holt And Company, Inc.; 1992
In this brightly illustrated tale based on a western folk song, a bespectacled, educated fellow is mistaken for a greenhorn by a group of mischievous cowboys. The stranger not only proves his cowboy ability by riding the most ornery horse around, but he also reins in several stereotypes as well. Included in the back of the book is a note from the author that conjures up an image of what the real Old West was like.

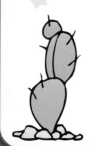

After reading the book aloud, ask students to explain how the cowboys decided that the stranger was a greenhorn. Encourage students to share times they have formed quick opinions about someone or something, only to discover that their opinions were incorrect. Then have each student write and illustrate a story in which he faces—and then over-comes—a situation in which he is misjudged. After students complete their stories, post them on a bulletin board covered with discarded newspapers. Then add the title "Special Edition: Overcoming Quick Judgments," the date, and a class byline to the board. A lot can be learned by reading these stories hot off the press!

Danny — We won!

Yesterday the teacher divided the class into two teams for our math fact game, but no one wanted me on his team. They said I would make a mistake and make the team lose a point. Instead I earned five points for them. Now everyone wants me on his team!

ANNIE'S GIFTS

Illustrated by Anna Rich
Just Us Books, Inc.; 1994

As a member of a musically talented family, Annie longs to play an instrument. But it doesn't matter which instrument Annie chooses, or how hard she tries to play it, the result is always the same—total disaster! Discouraged, yet determined, Annie never loses sight of finding her special talent. And in the end, she realizes that her special talent has been obvious to everyone but her!

Angela Shelf Medearis knows firsthand what it's like to grow up in a musically talented family and not be musically inclined. The inspiration for this heartwarming tale is a childhood memory! At the conclusion of the story, invite students to share their special talents. To do this, have each youngster trace a paper-doll template like the one shown onto construction paper, decorate the shape to resemble himself, and cut it out. Next have each student cut a heart shape from a two-inch square of construction paper, then personalize and label it with his special talent(s). To assemble his project, a student accordion-folds a 3/4" x 2 1/2" strip of paper; then he glues one end of the folded strip to the back of his heart cutout and the other end to the front of his self-likeness. Showcase the completed projects where others can take note of your multitalented youngsters!

THE SINGING MAN

Illustrated by Terea Shaffer
Holiday House, Inc.; 1995

In this adaptation of a West African folktale, a young man is banished from his village when he chooses to become a musician—an occupation that the elders say is unacceptable. With just a few coins in his pocket, a jug of water, a package of food, a flute, and a passion for music, the young man sets out to follow his dream. It is not until years later that others come to understand the wisdom of his choice.

Construction workers build homes, stores, offices, and hospitals.

As a prereading activity, play a variety of musical selections for your students' listening pleasure. Find out how each piece of music makes them feel. Then share the following quote from the story: "Yams fill the belly and trade fills the pockets, but music fills the heart." Ask students what the quote might mean. Then read the story aloud. At its conclusion invite students to summarize the story and further explain the meaning of the quote. Lead students to realize the importance of everyone's dreams for the future.

Next ask students what occupations their dreams for the future hold. List their responses on the chalkboard. Have each student choose a different career from the list, illustrate it on drawing paper, and write one sentence that explains the importance of the occupation at the bottom of his page. Bind the projects into a class booklet titled "Outstanding Occupations," and place it in the classroom library for all to enjoy.

POPPA'S NEW PANTS

Illustrated by John Ward
Holiday House, Inc.; 1995

What do you do with a brand-new pair of plaid pants that are six inches too long? If you're Poppa, you ask someone to hem the trousers for you. And that's exactly what he does. But all Poppa hears are excuses, so he tosses his pants over the back of the rocking chair and decides someone will get to them in time. In this hilarious mix-up in which confusion reigns, Poppa's new pants finally get hemmed…and hemmed…and hemmed!

For a fun follow-up to the story, have each student publish a story about a pair of lucky trousers! To make a pants-shaped booklet, a student trims a 9" x 12" sheet of construction paper to resemble a pair of pants. Then, using her cut-out as a template, she traces and cuts out a second pair of construction-paper pants and three or four pairs of writing-paper pants. Next she writes her story on the lined pages and decorates the construction-paper covers as desired. Finally she staples the lined pages in sequential order between the decorated covers. For an eye-catching display, use clothespins to suspend the stories from a length of clothesline.

My Lucky Pants
My aunt Marie gave me my lucky pair of pants. They were a birthday present. I knew they were the first lucky I was the day I wore them.

TOO MUCH TALK

Illustrated by Stefano Vitale
Candlewick Press, 1995

Who ever heard of a talking yam? Neither the farmer nor the fisherman in this African folktale. And certainly not the village chief! But hearing is believing, and when the chief's royal chair chirps in, there's no more doubting that a yam can talk. Full of hubbub and hullabaloo, this retelling is an irresistible invitation for young listeners to join the fun!

No doubt your youngsters will giggle at the humorous conclusion of this story! After a first reading, have each student write "Oh, that can't happen!" on one side of a speech bubble cutout and "Oh, yes it can!" on the other side. Then have each child tape a craft stick to her resulting story prop. As you reread the story, invite students to display the corresponding quote at the appropriate times.

Follow up your second reading of the story with this class book project. On the chalkboard write a student-generated list of possible talking objects. Have each child choose a different object from the list. Then, near the center of a sheet of drawing paper, he illustrates the object, a likeness of himself, and a family member or friend. To complete the page, he inserts three speech bubbles—one per illustration. In his speech bubble, he exclaims that the object shown talks. He shows his friend or family member exclaiming, "Oh, that can't happen!" and the object chiming in with, "Oh, yes it can!" On the back of his paper, he illustrates a humorous follow-up scene. Bind the completed pages between two construction-paper covers and add the title "Just Too Much Talk!"

THE ADVENTURES OF SUGAR AND JUNIOR

Illustrated by Nancy Poydar
Holiday House, Inc.; 1995

In four easy-to-read chapter stories, the everyday adventures of two young friends are described. From shooting hoops to baking cookies to buying ice cream, the two friends enjoy each other's company. The friendship is an interracial one, but to these two friends, they couldn't be more alike. Students will relate to the activities and easily see themselves in roles these characters represent.

Try this fun follow-up activity for "The New Neighbors"—a story in which the two friends explain the origins of their names. Have each student write his first name and his nickname on individual index cards. (If a student does not have a nickname, he may choose one that he feels is appropriate.) Then, for a family-centered homework activity, ask students to interview their parents to find out more about their names. Instruct each student to record his parent's response for each name on the back of the corresponding card. When the cards are returned, collect the nickname cards and set them aside for later use. Then invite each student to share what he learned about his first name.

For a nickname-related activity, place the nickname cards in a container. One at a time, draw a card and read the name aloud. Then use the information on the back of the card to give students a clue or two about the classmate who bears this nickname. Each child who makes a guess must qualify his guess by explaining why he thinks the nickname being discussed fits the classmate he is suggesting. Return the cards to the students as their nicknames are revealed. Sharing your own nickname is sure to please the crowd!

Hector

I was named after my grandpa. He likes to garden. He has a big heart.

Tiger

My dad started calling me Tiger when I was a baby. He said I was loud! I think it is a good nickname for me now because I can run very fast!

THE GHOST OF SIFTY SIFTY SAM

Illustrated by Jacqueline Rogers
Scholastic Inc., 1997

To win a $5000 reward, a chef named Dan agrees to spend the night in a haunted house. Dan feels certain he's clever enough to outsmart the resident ghost, Sifty Sifty Sam. But when old Sifty shows himself, Dan can't keep himself from trembling with fear. In the end, it's not Dan that Sifty is interested in—it's Dan's cooking! Moonlit scenes and shadowy images dance across the pages of this rollicking rhyme.

Talking about real and imagined fears is a natural lead-in to this spooky story. Invite interested students to tell their classmates about one of their scariest moments. Then dim the lights and read the story aloud. As a follow-up to the story, pair students and challenge each twosome to write a recipe for a one-of-a-kind fish batter that Sifty Sifty Sam is sure to love. Have each pair write its recipe and fish-frying instructions on a large fish cut from bulletin-board paper. Display the projects around the room. There's something fishy going on around here!

First-Class Fish Batter

Ingredients:
flour   soda pop   catsup
salt   onions   lemon juice

Directions:
Mix the ingredients in a big bowl. Use the same amount of each. When the fizzing stops, dip the fish in the batter. Then fry the fish until it is very, very crunchy.

Pattern

Use with *Animals Born Alive And Well* on page 90.

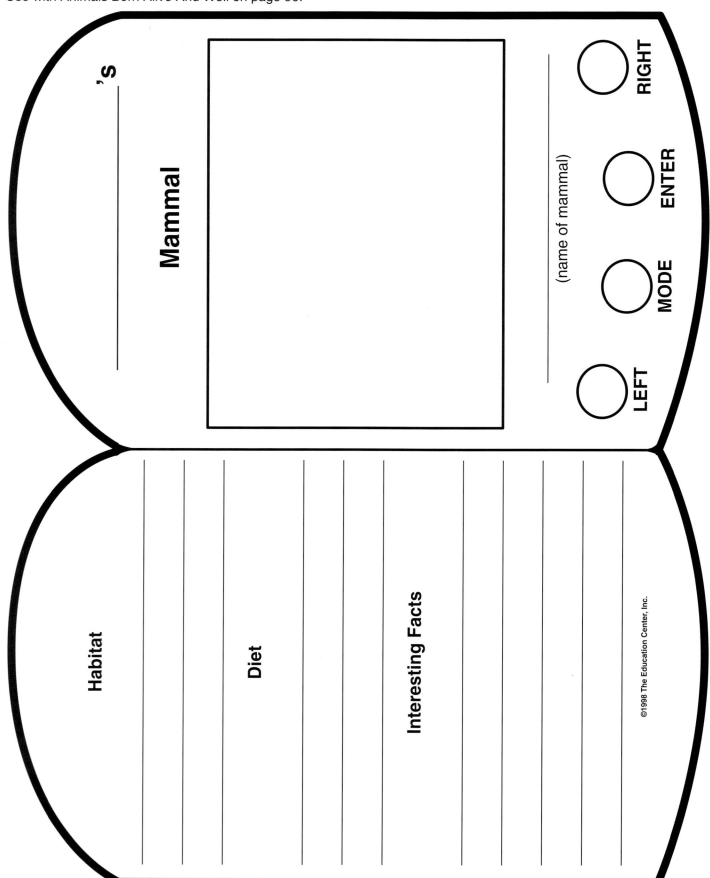

_____'s

Mammal

(name of mammal)

RIGHT

ENTER

MODE

LEFT

Habitat

Diet

Interesting Facts

©1998 The Education Center, Inc.

Rave Reviews For Ruth Heller

No one makes nonfiction more appealing to children than Ruth Heller! Whether she's investigating color, parts of speech, plants, or animals, she presents the facts in a kid-pleasing style. Her secret: plenty of poetic verse, a dash of humor, and endless eye-catching illustrations. Use this collection of activities to introduce students to an amazing author and illustrator *and* an intriguing genre. No doubt both subjects will receive rave reviews from your youngsters!

ideas by Jill Hamilton, Lisa Leonardi, and Sharon Murphy

● Meet The Author ●

As a child Ruth Heller loved to read, draw, and color. And as an adult, she loves the same three things! Born in Canada on April 2, 1924, Heller was around the age of 11 when she moved to the United States with her family. She loved art throughout elementary, junior high, and high school; studied painting and art history in college; and returned to college to study drawing and design when her two sons were in school. Soon after, she was designing gift wrap and creating newspaper ads, posters, puzzles, and coloring books. While at an aquarium researching tropical fish for a coloring book, Heller got the idea for her first nonfiction picture book: *Chickens Aren't The Only Ones*. After several years of searching for an interested publisher, her book was published in 1981, and she's been writing and illustrating children's books ever since. To date Heller has published more than 18 nonfiction picture books—all in rhyme. Heller believes that rhyme helps children learn new facts and sophisticated vocabulary. She purposefully keeps her writing brief and plans for her illustrations to convey as much information as possible.

Heller currently resides with her husband in San Francisco. In addition to creating children's books, the author visits schools and presents at conferences for teachers and librarians. She also enjoys spending time with her family, working crossword puzzles, swimming, playing tennis, and cooking. For more information about Ruth Heller, read her autobiography *Fine Lines* (from the Meet The Author series published by Richard C. Owen Publishers, Inc.; 1996).

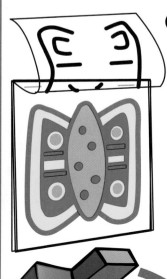

● Color ●

The Putnam & Grosset Group, 1995

Abracadabra! Here is just what you need to investigate the colorful pages of any book! Rhyming text, brilliant illustrations, and transparent overlays inform young readers that only four basic colors are needed to print any color in the world!

Improve your youngsters' understanding of the four-color printing process with this colorful follow-up activity. For easy management, plan to have students complete the activity at an art center under adult supervision. To begin, a student uses a yellow marker to draw and color a simple design on a five-inch square of white paper. Then he aligns a five-inch square of laminated film (or clear cellophane or acetate) atop the paper and staples the top edges. He then uses a magenta (pink or red) permanent marker to add desired color to his drawing. Next he aligns and staples a second square of laminated film atop the project and uses a cyan (blue) permanent marker to embellish his work. Finally he staples a third layer of laminated film atop his project and uses a black permanent marker to add final details. As each layer of color is added, the student witnesses additional colors being created.

● Chickens Aren't The Only Ones ●

The Putnam & Grosset Group, 1993

Why do chickens get all the credit for laying eggs when birds, reptiles, amphibians, insects, and fish lay eggs too? Discover the size, shape, and quantity of eggs laid by several oviparous creatures in Ruth Heller's first published book.

After an oral reading of this "egg-ceptional" book, challenge students to name egg-laying animals. Divide your class into five groups and designate a recorder in each one. Give each recorder a colorful marker and a large egg cutout that you've labeled with one of the following categories: *Birds, Reptiles, Amphibians, Fish, Insects.* Then, for two or three minutes, have each group brainstorm egg-laying animals for its recorder to list on the cutout. Next have each group rotate to a different cutout along a predetermined route. Instruct each group to read the animals listed on the new cutout, then brainstorm additional names for the group's recorder to add to the list. Repeat the activity as described until every group has had the opportunity to brainstorm and list egg-laying animals for each of the five categories. Then collect the eggs and post them in a prominent classroom location. If desired post a sixth egg on which you have written the title "Mammals" and the names of the only two egg-laying mammals: "spiny anteater" and "duckbill platypus." Then, under your students' direction, attach a small egg-shaped sticker beside each correctly listed *oviparous* animal on each of the six egg cutouts.

Birds

bluebirds
owl
turkey
hen
parrot
peacock
duck
pelican
cardinal
goose
robin
blue jay

sparrow
seagull
woodpecker
eagle
penguin
toucan

● Animals Born Alive And Well ●

The Putnam & Grosset Group, 1993

In this informative sequel to Chickens Aren't The Only Ones, *Heller fascinates her readers with a menagerie of mammals. From the largest whale to the tiniest shrew, students are introduced to more than 80 different mammals—some wild, some tame, and some prehistoric!*

Beep! Beep! Buzz! Join the electronic-pet craze with this fun follow-up activity. At the conclusion of this book, write a student-generated list of mammals on the chalkboard—at least one per student. After each child has chosen a different mammal to research, have him write his name and the name of his mammal on a white construction-paper copy of page 88. To complete the research portion of the project, the student describes his mammal's habitat and diet, and writes two or more interesting facts about the animal on the provided lines. Then he draws and colors a picture of the mammal in the box. To assemble the project, he cuts along the bold lines, folds the resulting cutout in half along the thin line, and glues the two halves together as shown. Next he hole-punches the top of the project, threads a length of yarn through the hole, and securely ties the yarn ends. A student can wear his project around his neck or tie it to his bookbag. Whichever the case, students are sure to enjoy sharing their mammal reports with their classmates. And you'll have a trendy activity that doesn't require batteries or make unwanted electronic noises!

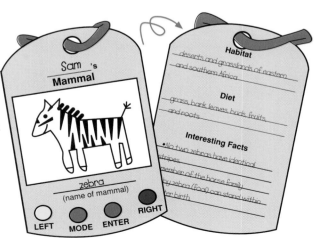

Sam___'s
Mammal

zebra
(name of mammal)

LEFT   MODE   ENTER   RIGHT

Habitat
deserts and grasslands of eastern
and southern Africa

Diet
grass, bark, leaves, buds, fruits,
and roots

Interesting Facts
• No two zebras have identical
stripes.
• member of the horse family
• baby zebra (foal) can stand within
___ after birth

The Reason For A Flower

The Putnam & Grosset Group, 1992

Blossoming with information, this book examines the importance of flowers in nature. Breathtaking illustrations support an ample crop of plant-related vocabulary. This close-up look at blooms is sure to germinate plenty of interest in the plant world.

Candy from a flower? Most likely, your youngsters will be amazed by the different products that stem from flowers. Before you share this book with your students, gather classroom quantities of several products that can be traced to blooming plants, like cotton balls, popped corn, pasta pieces (uncooked), coffee beans, tea bags, rubber bands, paper scraps, twine, chocolate chips, pieces of cork, dried bread or croutons, and straw. (Each child will need six different plant products.) Then, at the conclusion of the book, have students complete the following flower-making project:

To make a flower like the one shown, a student cuts a petal shape from each of six 3" x 5" construction-paper rectangles and a leaf shape from each of two 2" x 4" construction-paper rectangles. Then he glues his six petals, a three-inch paper circle, a ten-inch paper stem, and his leaf cutouts onto a 12" x 18" sheet of construction paper to resemble a flower. When the glue has dried, he writes "Six Reasons For A Flower" in the flower's center and labels each petal with the name of a different plant product. Finally he glues a sample of each product on the corresponding petal. There's little doubt that this project will receive two thumbs-up from your youngsters—green thumbs, that is!

Once your youngsters have explored blooming plants, they'll be eager to learn about those plants that do not bloom. Ruth Heller's book, *Plants That Never Ever Bloom* (The Putnam & Grosset Group, 1984), is the perfect teaching tool!

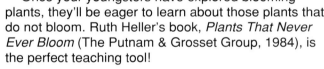

How To Hide An Octopus And Other Sea Creatures

The Putnam & Grosset Group, 1992

One in a series of books about camouflage, this undersea selection features several fascinating creatures that appear to be playing hide-and-seek with readers. Delightful illustrations demonstrate how the appearances of some animals change with their surroundings, and how others rely on special patterns or colors for camouflage. It's a revealing look at the secrets of the undersea world!

For a fun follow-up to this story, have students apply their knowledge of undersea camouflage to create their own clever underwater scenes. To begin, a student draws a sea creature on colorful wallpaper or gift wrap, and cuts it out. Then she glues this cutout to a sheet of light blue construction paper and uses crayons or markers to create a background scene that camouflages the creature. Mount the students' undersea scenes on a bulletin board titled "Hide-And-Seek Beneath The Sea." Students will have a grand time trying to find their classmates' camouflaged creatures.

If your students enjoyed this book, they're sure to enjoy other books in Ruth Heller's How To Hide series:

- *How To Hide A Polar Bear And Other Mammals*
  The Putnam & Grosset Group, 1994

- *How To Hide A Butterfly And Other Insects*
  The Putnam & Grosset Group, 1992

- *How To Hide A Meadow Frog And Other Amphibians*
  The Putnam & Grosset Group, 1995

- *How To Hide A Parakeet And Other Birds*
  The Putnam & Grosset Group, 1995

- *How To Hide A Crocodile And Other Reptiles*
  The Putnam & Grosset Group, 1994

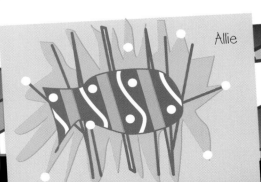

When Ruth Heller made a promise to write a book about each part of speech, she became a teacher's best friend! The following books—each accompanied by a classroom-tested idea—are from the author's Parts-Of-Speech series.

A Cache Of Jewels And Other Collective Nouns

The Putnam & Grosset Group, 1998

In this informative book, Ruth Heller uses a bevy *of beautiful illustrations to portray a* clutch *of collective nouns!*

Delight your brood with this gem of an activity. After an oral reading of the book, write a phrase on the chalkboard that includes a collective noun. Then invite students to provide additional phrases that feature collective nouns, and list their ideas. Next give each child a white construction-paper copy of the treasure-chest pattern on page 94. To complete the project, a student writes and illustrates a different collective-noun phrase in each numbered section of the pattern. Then he cuts on the bold outer lines, carefully cuts along the short dotted line, and glues the two resulting cutouts together where indicated. While the glue is drying, he folds forward the top and bottom sections of his project along the thin lines and uses crayons or markers to decorate the blank surfaces to resemble a treasure chest. Then the student accordion-folds the project along the remaining thin lines and inserts the tab into the slit as shown on the "Finished Project." Be sure to set aside time for youngsters to share their completed projects with their classmates.

1. army of ants
2. fleet of ships
3. string of pearls
4. school of fish

Many Luscious Lollipops: A Book About Adjectives

The Putnam & Grosset Group, 1992

"An ADJECTIVE's terrific when you want to be specific." Through imaginative text and lively illustrations, Ruth Heller presents an array of adjectives that are sure to delight your young audience and educate them too!

Courtney

Adjectives can describe any number of nouns or pronouns; but for this kid-pleasing follow-up activity, each student must describe a very special noun: herself! To begin have each student trace both of her hands on a sheet of skin-toned paper, then cut out the shapes. Next instruct each youngster to write a different, self-describing adjective on each finger and thumb of her cutouts. To complete the project, she uses desired arts-and-crafts supplies—like fabric scraps, construction paper, yarn, markers, crayons, and glue—to create a likeness of herself on a 12" x 18" sheet of construction paper. Then she glues her hand cutouts to the project as shown.

To extend the activity, collect the completed projects, read aloud the adjectives each student wrote, and challenge the class to identify this classmate. Then showcase the projects in the school hallway where others can see your *super, wonderful,* and *talented* students!

Kites Sail High: A Book About Verbs

The Putnam & Grosset Group, 1988

Open the cover of this book, and you find a wonderful world of verbs just waiting to be discovered! From action to linking to tenses to moods, an array of verbs and verb types are highlighted. By the conclusion of this book, your youngsters are sure to agree that verbs are most superb!

Your students' knowledge of verbs is sure to soar with this action-verb activity. At the conclusion of the book, have each student make a list of ten or more actions that he does during a normal day, like *eat, talk, sit,* and *laugh.* (Accept all verb tenses.) Then have each student draw a tic-tac-toe grid on a nine-inch square of white paper. Have each child use a crayon or marker to write his name in the center square. Then, in each of the remaining squares, instruct each student to write a different action verb from his list and create a corresponding illustration. Have each child mount his completed project on a colorful ten-inch square of construction paper; then display the projects on a bulletin board labeled "We're Ready For Action!"

Behind The Mask: A Book About Prepositions

The Putnam & Grosset Group, 1995

So just exactly what is the purpose of a preposition? This playful and eye-pleasing exploration reveals that this part of speech tells us the when, where, and how of things!

What would the English language be like without prepositions? To help youngsters understand the importance of this part of speech in their daily conversations, challenge the class to a game of No Prepositions, Please. Select one student volunteer to begin the first round of play, and whisper the name of a classroom item in this student's ear. The object of the game is for this student to give his classmates clues about the location of the mystery item without naming the item or using any prepositions. If a classmate identifies the mystery item and its location, the class earns a point. If the player names the item or uses a preposition, the teacher scores a point, and the round of play is over. Play the game until the message is clear: prepositions are a very important part of speech!

More Parts-Of-Speech Books

If your students enjoy the books on pages 92 and 93, they're sure to enjoy the other books in this series:

- *Merry-Go-Round: A Book About Nouns*
  The Putnam & Grosset Group, 1992

- *Up, Up, And Away: A Book About Adverbs*
  The Putnam & Grosset Group, 1993

- *Mine, All Mine!: A Book About Pronouns*
  The Putnam & Grosset Group, 1997

- Heller's final book in the Parts-Of-Speech series, *Fantastic And Wow!: A Book About Interjections And Conjunctions,* is scheduled to be published in the fall of 1998.

Tornado

Written by Betsy Byars • Illustrated by Doron Ben-Ami
(HarperCollins Publishers, Inc.; 1996)

The sighting of an August tornado sends family members and Pete, the family farmhand, into the storm cellar. As the group waits out the twister, Pete tells childhood stories about a beloved pooch named Tornado. Pete's entertaining tales curb the family's fears about the storm and about Dad—who was working in the cornfield when the twister appeared. An oral reading of this beginning chapter book is sure to be enjoyed by all!

ideas by Stacie Stone Davis

Who's Who?

At the conclusion of chapter 1, invite students to examine the illustration on page 4. Ask them to identify the characters in the picture and name the family member who is missing. Then have the youngsters tell what they already know about each character based on what you have read aloud so far. As you begin each of the book's next six chapters, have your students identify who is narrating the chapter. The book actually has two first-person narrators, which may be slightly confusing to young listeners.

Two Tornadoes!

In Pete's first tale (chapter 2), he describes a tornado that he experienced as a child. Ask students how this tornado is similar to and different from the storm that this family is currently waiting out. Then take a class poll to find out if students think they could "smell a storm" like Pete's mother could. Encourage students to explain their viewpoints. Conclude the discussion by having each student create an illustration for the chapter. If desired, reread the seven-page chapter so students can pay close attention to the descriptive details provided by the author. Then display the completed illustrations on a bulletin board titled "Two Tornadoes!"

Turtle Trouble

Tornado's unexpected encounter with a turtle will have your youngsters laughing out loud! At the conclusion of chapter 4, give each child a 12" x 18" sheet of drawing paper. Demonstrate how to fold the paper in half three times, so that when it is unfolded, eight rectangles result. After each student has folded and unfolded her paper, have her write the title "Tornado's Turtle Trouble" and her name in her top left-hand rectangle, then sequentially number the remaining rectangles. Next challenge each student to create a comic strip that tells Tornado's story. For the best results write a student-generated list of story events on the chalkboard for reference. Bind the completed projects between two slightly larger pieces of poster board. Title the class big book "Tornado's Turtle Troubles," and place it in the classroom library for further reading enjoyment.

Picking Pet Names

Even though Tornado and Five-Thirty seem to be unique pet names, each one has a logical explanation. Tornado came to Pete's home during a tornado, and Five-Thirty came to Pete's house every day at five-thirty. Invite students to share the names of their family pets and the explanations that go with the names. Students who do not have family pets can talk about pet names in their neighborhoods, extended families, or previous classrooms. If you're planning to introduce a class pet, this is a perfect time to brainstorm a list of possible names!

The Saddest Day

When Tornado was recognized by his first owners, great joy and deep sorrow were felt by those who loved him. The first owners were overjoyed. Pete was devastated. Discuss with your students the integrity that Pete and his father displayed on that very sad day. Ask students what these actions tell them about Pete and his father. Then ask students if they've ever felt so overwhelmed about something that they felt "nailed down" or unable to move, as Pete did. Invite students to tell about the happy and/or sad events that made them feel this way.

Tornado And The Rooster

At the conclusion of the book, an untold tale about Tornado and a rooster is mentioned. Ask students what they think might have happened in this Tornado tale. On the chalkboard write a student-generated list of story ideas; then have each student write and illustrate his own version of the tale. When all the stories are completed, have students sit in a large circle. Slightly darken the room, and ask students to pretend they are safe inside a storm cellar waiting for a tornado to pass. Then invite each child to share his tale about Tornado and the rooster.

Chapter By Chapter

For a fun culminating project, enlist your students' help in identifying the main event(s) of each chapter in the book. Then, under your students' guidance, write a one-sentence description of each event. Next give each student a construction-paper booklet containing seven blank booklet pages. Instruct each student to write "_____'s Retelling Of *Tornado*" on the front booklet cover and add desired artwork to the front and back covers. To complete the project, each student describes and illustrates seven main events in sequential order—featuring one event on each booklet page. Suggest that each child take her booklet home and use it to retell *Tornado* for her family.

Pam Crane

Tornado's hole was taken over by a cat!

Learning About Tornadoes

To give students a better understanding of tornadoes, read aloud *Tornado Alert* by Franklyn M. Branley (HarperCollins Publishers, Inc.; 1988). This slim paperback explains when, where, and why tornadoes occur. It also tells how to stay safe during a tornado. As a follow-up, have each student put his tornado knowledge to the test by completing a copy of page 98.

97

The Ghost In Tent 19

Written by Jim and Jane O'Connor
Random House, Inc.; 1988

All four boys in tent 19 agree that Ivan the camp counselor loves corny camp stuff. So when Ivan spins a tale about a ferocious pirate and some buried treasure, the boys assume it's just one of Ivan's spooky campfire stories—but not for long! Soon the boys are searching for the treasure and making alarming discoveries. This spine-tingling mystery is sure to capture your youngsters' interest, right up to its tenderhearted conclusion.

ideas contributed by Stacie Stone Davis

Camp Tall Pines

Was the rumor true? Could Camp Tall Pines, a presumably ordinary camp on the coast of Maine, be haunted? Add to the suspense of this spooky mystery by having students arrange their desks in a large circle around a mock campfire. To create the campfire, cut flames from yellow and orange paper. Set a lantern-style flashlight on the floor so that its beam will shine toward the ceiling; then tape the flame cutouts around the flashlight. Place a few branches and twigs near the paper flames, and surround the project with a circle of rocks. Prior to each read-aloud session, dim the classroom lights and "light" the campfire.

Tent 19 Tenants

The four boys who bunk together in tent 19 are quite a bunch! At the conclusion of chapter 1, write the boys' names on the chalkboard. Ask students to recall what they've learned about each boy so far. List their ideas below the appropriate names. Reread excerpts from the chapter as needed to create comprehensive lists. Then have each student use the information to make a character flip book. To make the book, fold a 12" x 18" sheet of drawing paper in half (to 6" x 18") and make three equally spaced cuts in the top layer as shown. Then, using the posted information, label and illustrate each resulting flap for a different boy. Under each flap write a brief description of that character's personality. As students work on their projects, invite them to predict what the strange glow in tent 19 might have been!

Sheila Krill

Danny is an average kid, except he gets strange feelings sometimes. He also doesn't like things he can't explain. His best friend is Jed.

Two Different Maps

While eating ice cream at Captain Cone, the boys discover that their place mats feature a replica of Captain Blood's treasure map. When the boys compare this map to the one that Hal drew at the infirmary, they realize that Captain Blood's greatest treasure may be buried under tent 19! Ask students to explain how the boys came to this conclusion. Then put *your* students' map skills to the test with a student-created treasure hunt. Give each child a small treasure (like a pencil, bookmark, or sticker) to hide within the classroom. Next have each child draw a map of the classroom on a sheet of tan paper and mark the location of his treasure with a large X. To give the maps an antique look, have each child carefully tear the edges of his map, then crumple and flatten the map several times. Collect the completed projects and randomly redistribute them to the students. Once you've determined that each student has received a project other than his own, let the hunt begin!

The Greatest Treasure

At the conclusion of chapter 5, the four boys understand the greatness of the treasure that's buried beneath tent 19. Before reading the chapter aloud, invite students to predict what the captain's greatest treasure might have been and explain why. Then follow up your oral reading of the chapter by asking students to talk about the people and things in their lives that they treasure the most. As a wrap-up, have each child complete the activity on page 103.

Moving The Tent

If it weren't for Arthur's quick thinking, tent 19 might not have been moved. As a class discuss why Cubby was at first reluctant to move the tent and why he later changed his mind. Then, on provided paper, have each child write and illustrate a news story about the eerie events that led up to the discovery of John Bloodworth's grave. Mount each student's work on a slightly larger piece of an actual newspaper. Bind the news stories into a class book titled "News From Camp Tall Pines." Place the newsworthy book in your classroom library for all to enjoy.

Camp Brochures

As the story draws to a close, so does summer camp. Take a class vote to find out how many students think they would enjoy Camp Tall Pines. Discuss what makes this camp unique. Next challenge each student to design a brochure that describes the camp. Provide a variety of travel brochures for students to study, and remind the youngsters that a brochure of this type should appeal to both parents and children. Then have each student plan what she will feature in her brochure. If desired, request that each child include a map and a brief camp history on two panels of the brochure. When the students are ready, distribute 9" x 12" sheets of white construction paper. Demonstrate how to fold the paper into thirds to create a brochure. Provide assistance as students fold their papers and design their brochures. When the brochures are completed, set aside time for students to share their work.

Ellen E. Sullivan—Gr. 3, Dudley Elementary School, Dudley, MA

A Shipshape Finish

Wrap up this treasure of a tale with a shipshape project! Each child needs a white construction-paper copy of page 104, a 9" x 12" sheet of white paper, a 12" x 18" sheet of light blue construction paper, a pencil, scissors, crayons or markers, and glue. On the chalkboard write the following five titles: The Funniest Part, The Best Part, The Saddest Part, The Scariest Part, and The Best Character.

To complete the project, a student cuts out the sail pattern on his copy of page 104 and carefully traces the resulting shape on his blank white paper four times. After he cuts out the additional sails, he copies a different title (from the chalkboard) on each sail and writes (and/or illustrates) his ideas on the sails. Next he colors and cuts out the ship's hull, flag, and crow's nest from page 104. Then the student arranges his cutouts on his large blue paper, glues the cutouts in place, and uses crayons or markers to add ship details (like masts and rope ladders) and a background scene. Showcase the students' work on a bulletin board titled "A Treasure Of A Tale!"

Captain Cone's Ice Cream

Read the menu.
Cut out and glue each ice-cream treat by its matching set of coins.

Menu

Walk The Plank .... 47¢

Jolly Roger Soda .... 59¢

Swashbuckling Sundae .... 78¢

Single Cannonball .... 35¢

Aye, Matey Milkshake .... 52¢

Banana Boat Wreck .... 91¢

Dead Man's Float .... 60¢

Treasure Chest $1.00

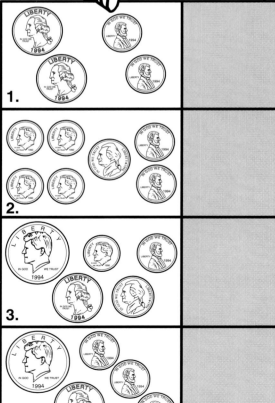

Treasure Chest

Walk The Plank

Single Cannonball

Jolly Roger Soda

Banana Boat Wreck

Dead Man's Float

Aye, Matey Milkshake

Swashbuckling Sundae

Note To Teacher: Use this activity after completing chapter 3.

Name

A Chest Of Treasure

Complete each sentence.

One person I treasure is _____

I treasure this person because _____

_____

Another person I treasure is _____

I treasure this person because _____

_____

Two things that I treasure are _____ and _____

I treasure these things because _____

_____

©The Education Center, Inc. • *THE MAILBOX® • Primary •* Oct/Nov 1997

Bonus Box: Fill this treasure chest with things that you treasure! In each picture frame, illustrate *someone* you treasure. Between the picture frames, draw and color *things* you treasure.

Note To Teacher: Use this activity with "The Greatest Treasure" on page 101.

Patterns

Use with "A Shipshape Finish" on page 101.

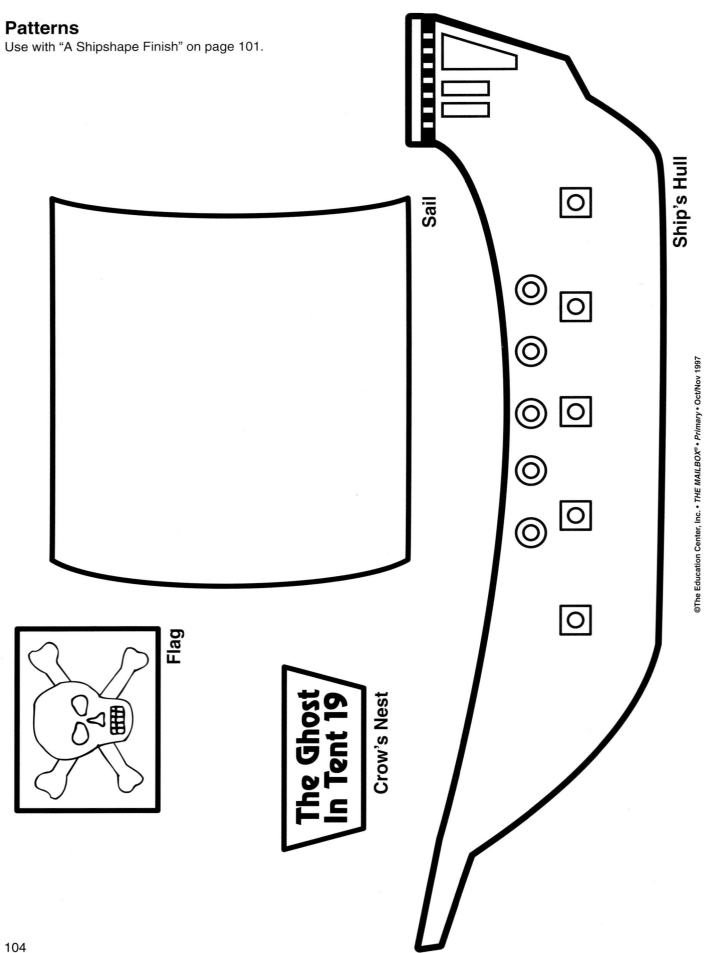

Sail

Ship's Hull

Flag

The Ghost In Tent 19

Crow's Nest

HEY, NEW KID!

Written by Betsy Duffey . Illustrated by Ellen Thompson
(Viking, 1996)

Being the new kid in school is the pits! Just ask Cody Michaels. He'd rather have the chicken pox than enter another third-grade classroom. Then he has a great idea! What if he creates a new and improved version of himself? His classmates will love him, and he'll have a fun time dreaming up his new identity—or so he thinks! This fast-paced, lighthearted story will surely tickle your students' funny bones as it reinforces the importance of being yourself!

ideas by Stacie Stone Davis

CODY'S ANTICS

It won't take long for students to realize that Cody Michaels is no different from any other child—he just wants to fit in. Unfortunately Cody's creation of Super Cody lands him in some *very* tricky situations. Strengthen your students' comprehension and descriptive writing skills by having them chronicle Cody's antics in individual journals. Give each child a construction-paper journal containing at least 13 blank pages—one page per chapter. Then, at the conclusion of each chapter, ask students to summarize what happened in that chapter and predict what will happen in the following one. Don't be surprised when your students beg you to read *just one more chapter!*

EXCUSES, EXCUSES!

Cody is loaded with excuses why he should postpone his first day in his new school. Ask students to recall some of Cody's excuses; then invite them to describe times when they have created silly excuses. Find out if their excuses actually helped the situations at hand or if they only prolonged what the children were trying to avoid. Then ask each child to write and illustrate what he believes to be his most creative excuse to date. After the students have shared their work, bind the projects into a one-of-a-kind class book titled "Room ____'s Best Excuses!" You can count on this book being read time and time again!

Leroy

I told my mom I should wait until next year to go to the dentist. My teeth would be bigger by then and the dentist would do a much better job!

THE TRANSFORMATION

In chapter 2 Super Cody comes to life—and boy, does he! At the conclusion of the chapter, have students complete a copy of page 107. Then take a class vote to find out how many students think it was wise of Cody to invent Super Cody. Encourage discussion among the students.

TIPS FROM DAD

Cody's father is full of helpful advice. The only problem is that his advice often includes a saying or an expression that Cody does not understand. Instead of asking for an explanation, Cody simply pretends to agree. Use this activity to help students understand the advice that Cody's dad shares. Write the sayings from the book on individual paper strips (see the provided list). Each morning post a paper strip and ask students to contemplate its programming. Later in the day, invite students to share their ideas. Lead students to a correct interpretation and write it on the paper strip. When all of the sayings from the book have been explored, invite students to submit additional ones that they would like to learn more about.

Chapter 3
Waste not, want not.
A stitch in time saves nine.
Tomorrow is the first day of the rest of your life.
If at first you don't succeed, try, try again.

Chapter 6
Practice makes perfect.
To be or not to be—that is the question.

Chapter 7
Nothing ventured, nothing gained.

TIMELINES

When the students in Ms. Harvey's class make timelines in chapter 4, Cody thinks his life is boring and short. When you ask your students to make timelines of their lives, they may respond in a similar manner. But after a bit of investigation, they will no doubt discover that their lives aren't so boring after all! To complete this timeline project, a student draws and labels a timeline on a 6" x 12" sheet of paper. Then he titles his timeline and writes one or more facts about each year of his life. Next he mounts his programmed timeline on a 12" x 18" sheet of construction paper. On three-inch squares of paper, the student illustrates six different events that appear on his timeline. Then he glues his illustrations to the project. For added visual appeal, students may wish to color-code their projects like the one shown. Invite interested students to share their work with their classmates. Now *that's* a fun social-studies lesson!

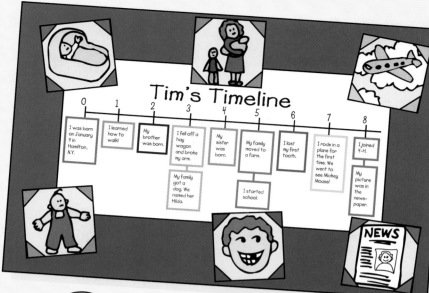

THE SKATING ESCAPADE

No doubt your youngsters will be rolling with laughter after hearing about Cody's skating escapade, which is detailed in chapters 9 and 10. In fact it's perfect material for a comic strip! Have each student fold a 12" x 18" sheet of drawing paper in half three times so that when it is unfolded, eight rectangles result. Then have each student illustrate a comic strip detailing the hilarious events of Cody's skating adventure.

PLANT A SEED; WATCH IT GROW

At the conclusion of the book, the seed that Cody planted in chapter 2 finally sprouts. Ask students how the life of the seed and Cody's experience in his new school are similar. Then guide them to understand that just as the seed needed time to grow and bloom in its new environment, so did Cody. Invite students to share their ideas as to why both the seed and Cody finally bloomed. Then engage students in the following goal-setting project:

First ask each child to set a school-related goal, like becoming a better reader, memorizing multiplication facts, turning in homework on time, or following directions carefully. Then have each student write her goal on the inside of a discarded file folder. Also have each student label a small disposable cup (with drainage holes), partially fill the cup with potting soil, and plant a flower seed in the soil. Store the seed cups on a tray in a sunny classroom location. As students care for their seeds over the next several weeks, have them record in their file folders the steps they are taking to meet the goals they've set. When the seeds begin to sprout, survey the students to find out how many feel they have grown toward meeting their goals, too. As Cody's father might say, "All good things come with time!"

VIRTUAL CODY

If your youngsters enjoyed *Hey, New Kid!*, they'll also enjoy its laugh-out-loud sequel, *Virtual Cody* (Viking, 1997). When Ms. Harvey asks her students to report on the origins of their names, Cody is ecstatic. He just knows he was named after a famous person—perhaps even Buffalo Bill Cody, the legendary rider on the Pony Express. Not so. In fact, when Cody finally learns who (make that *what!*) he was named after, he's ready to crawl under a rock. How can he ever report to his class something that is so embarrassing?

INTRODUCING SUPER CODY!

Read each sentence.
Decide if it describes Cody or Super Cody.
Circle the letter in the matching column.

Cody	Super Cody	
G	L	1. He has a pet emu.
U	T	2. His mother drives a station wagon.
E	J	3. He moved from Kansas.
N	Y	4. He has won many skating trophies.
Z	S	5. He once lived in an igloo.
D	F	6. His father is an F.B.I. agent.
H	E	7. His mother drives a red sports car.
B	W	8. He has a pet cocker spaniel.
P	R	9. His very first word was *encyclopedia*.
O	M	10. He thinks he is boring.

What advice did Cody's mother give him?
For each number, write the circled letter.

___ ___   ___ ___ ___ ___ ___ ___ ___ ___ !
 8   3   4 10   2   9   5   7   1   6

Bonus Box: On the back of this paper, write two sentences that describe you. Draw a yellow circle around these sentences. Then, just for fun, write two more sentences that describe a new, improved you! Draw an orange circle around these sentences.

Let The Good Times Roll!

Think about the story.
Finish each sentence.

The best part of this story is		This story made me think about the time I
	One way that Cody and I are alike is	One way that Cody and I are different is
One thing Cody could teach me is	If I could tell Cody one thing, I would tell him	
One thing I could teach Cody is		I could help a new student feel welcome by

©The Education Center, Inc. • *THE MAILBOX®* • *Primary* • Feb/Mar 1998

108 **Note To Teacher:** Use this activity after completing the book.

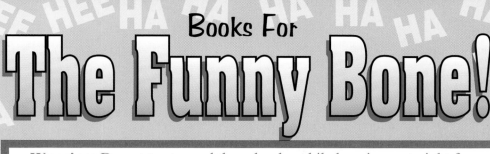

Books For The Funny Bone!

> **Warning:** Do not try to read these books while keeping a straight face. It could be hazardous to your health and to the health of your students.

Hold onto your chair! This collection of laugh-out-loud picture books will have you and your students giggling galore. Whether you're celebrating National Humor Month this April or you're simply looking to enrich your lesson plans with a healthy dose of fun, this collection of entertaining books and activities is just what the doctor ordered!

ideas contributed by Darcy Gruber, April Johnson, Susan Kapaun, Martha Kelly, Kathleen Kopp, Kimberly Malcolm, Cynthia Pfaff, and Jan Ross

The Cow Who Wouldn't Come Down
Written & Illustrated by Paul Brett Johnson
Orchard Books, 1993
When her cow decides to take to the skies, Miss Rosemary tries everything under the sun to lure the cow home. But the heifer is having too much fun to pay much attention to Miss Rosemary's hilarious antics. That is, until Matilda rolls into the barnyard!

At the end of the story, Gertrude the cow is at it again—and this time she's driving the farm tractor! After reviewing with students the clever ways that Miss Rosemary tries to lure her cow from the sky, ask them to brainstorm how she might get the heifer off the tractor. Then have each student write a continuation of the story and publish her work in a cow-shaped booklet.

To make her booklet, the student traces an oval template onto brown paper, white paper, and several sheets of writing paper; then she cuts out the resulting shapes. After she copies her story onto the writing paper, she stacks the story pages in sequential order, places the white oval atop the stack, and staples the entire stack to the brown oval as shown. She then uses construction-paper scraps and markers or crayons to add facial features, ears, and horns to complete her "moo-velous" project.

Truman's Aunt Farm
Written by Jama Kim Rattigan
Illustrated by G. Brian Karas
Houghton Mifflin Company, 1994
A young boy is elated to have received an ant farm for his birthday. But when he sends off for his live ants, what he receives are live aunts! *And that is more than this young boy bargained for!*

In addition to being a great read-aloud, this story is perfect for prompting a review of homophones. To make a directory of homophones for the classroom, have each child illustrate a different homophone pair on art paper as shown. Laminate the projects along with a front cover titled "Homophone Directory" and a back cover. Arrange the projects in alphabetical order; then bind them—followed by a supply of yellow paper—between the two covers. Before you place the directory in the classroom library, explain to students that the directory's yellow pages are where they should list additional homophone pairs that they discover. Remind students to confirm that a homophone pair has not already been illustrated or listed on a yellow page before entering it in the directory. Now that's a resource your students will be eager to get their hands on!

109

Underwear!

Written by Mary Elise Monsell
Illustrated by Lynn Munsinger
Albert Whitman & Company, 1988

This book is all about being silly and having fun! Two fun-loving grassland pals are totally baffled by a buffalo's constant grumpiness. Then they get an idea—about underwear—that even a grumpy buffalo can't resist laughing about.

Underwear, underwear, underwear! Just hearing the word puts a grin on most youngsters' faces. So imagine how they'll feel when you ask them to design an undershirt or a pair of boxers for a chosen animal! To begin have each child label a self-adhesive tag with the phrase "Designed especially for," followed by an alliterated animal name of her own choice, and the words "by [student's name]." Next have each child trace a boxer- or an undershirt-shaped template onto white construction paper, then decorate and cut out the shape. After each child has attached her designer tag to her project, use clothespins to suspend the underwear from a classroom clothesline.

Princess Smartypants

Written & Illustrated by Babette Cole
G. P. Putnam's Sons, 1987

Princess Smartypants is a spunky princess who loves being single and plans to stay that way! However, when a multitalented prince accomplishes each impossible task that the princess sets before him, it looks as if she's met her match. But the princess has one more trick that up until now, she's kept "toadily" to herself.

What could be more fun than trying to outsmart a smarty-pants princess? To set the stage for this activity, inform students that now the princess must accomplish the tasks that they give her in order to stay single. On story paper have each child describe the task that he will ask the princess to perform, then report on and illustrate the result of the princess's efforts. Invite interested students to share their completed projects with their classmates. A class vote may be in order to confirm whether the princess completed enough tasks (more than 50 percent) to stay single!

Not The Piano, Mrs. Medley!

Written by Evan Levine & Illustrated by S. D. Schindler
Orchard Books, 1991

It sounds like a great idea to young Max: going to the beach for the day with his grandmother and her dog. The problem is, will they ever get there?

Mrs. Medley certainly could have used a few pointers on how to pack for a day at the beach! Ask students to name items that they think should be taken to the beach, and write their suggestions on the chalkboard. Then have each child fold a sheet of construction paper in half, trim the four resulting corners, and attach a construction-paper handle to the front and the back of the resulting duffel-bag shape. Next have each child write the title "Packing Pointers For Mrs. Medley" and illustrate a zipper and a beach-related bumper sticker on the front of the bag. Inside the project have each child list five or more beach-packing pointers for Mrs. Medley. After students have completed the projects, challenge them to create additional bags of packing pointers for Mrs. Medley's trips to the zoo, the park, the opera, the circus, and the rodeo. "Yee-ha!"

1. Take a towel and your swimsuit.
2. Take some sunscreen.
3. A hat and a pair of sunglasses are good to take.
4. Be sure to take something to eat and drink.

Packing Pointers
For
Mrs. Medley

To the beach!

Listen Buddy

Written by Helen Lester & Illustrated by Lynn Munsinger
Houghton Mifflin Company, 1995

Buddy, a lop-eared rabbit, leads a life of total confusion! When his parents send him to get squash, he comes home with wash. When his father wants a pen, Buddy brings him a hen. It takes a surprise encounter with a very nasty-tempered varmint to teach Buddy that he can hear just fine—when he listens!

No doubt Buddy's silly antics will have your students thinking in rhymes. To set the stage for a class book-making project, ask students what Buddy might do if his father asks him to grab a *coat* (grab a *boat, goat,* or *note*), sit on a *log* (sit on a *dog, frog,* or *hog),* or eat some *fruits* (eat some *boots* or *suits*). Then ask each child to write a command like "Go feed the dog" at the top of a 6" x 9" sheet of construction paper. On the remainder of his paper, have each student illustrate something Buddy might have done *before* he learned how important it is to listen. Compile the projects into a class book titled "Are You Listening, Buddy?"

Go feed the dog.

Pigsty

Written & Illustrated by Mark Teague
Scholastic Inc., 1994

When Wendell Fultz's mother declares his bedroom a pigsty and tells him he can simply live with the mess, he is tickled pink! Living like a pig is sure to be loads of fun. But wait! Wendell wants to live like *a pig, not* with *a pig and all his piggy pals!*

By working together Wendell and the pigs clean his messy bedroom in one afternoon. Reinforce the benefits of working together with this cooperative-group project. At the end of the activity, each child will have a nutritious snack that resembles Wendell's newfound friends. First inform students how the treat is made (see the provided directions); then divide students into small groups. While each group of students is washing and drying their hands, distribute supplies. Each group will need peanut butter, two knives, and the following materials for each pig it will be making: a small paper plate, one large and one small rice cake, two small candy pieces, two raisins, and two triangular tortilla chips. Then challenge each group to set up an assembly line that utilizes each group member. When all the groups are done making snacks, talk about what the students learned as they munch on the tasty treats they made.

To make a pig:
- Place a large rice cake on a paper plate.
- Spread peanut butter on the large rice cake.
- Press a small rice cake (snout) in place and use peanut butter to attach two raisin nostrils.
- Press two candy eyes in place.
- Press two tortilla-chip ears in place.

If you're looking for additional laughs on the topic of cleaning bedrooms, try these titles:
Clean Your Room, Harvey Moon! • Written & Illustrated by Pat Cummings • Bradbury Press, 1991

When The Fly Flew In... • Written by Lisa Westberg Press & Illustrated by Brad Sneed • Dial Books For Young Readers, 1994

David's Father

Written by Robert Munsch
Illustrated by Michael Martchenko
Annick Press Ltd., 1983

What difference does it make that Julie saw a fork the size of a pitchfork and a spoon the size of a shovel being carried into the new boy's house. He's invited her over for cheeseburgers and milk shakes, and that's just too good an offer to refuse!

Julie is in for a giant-size surprise when she arrives at David's house for dinner. While she and David dine on salad, cheeseburgers, and milk shakes, his father eats 26 snails, 3 fried octopi, and 16 chocolate-covered bricks! You see, David's dad is a giant with some very bad eating habits. For a fun follow-up to the book, ask each child to plan a well-balanced meal that's fit for a giant. Encourage students to rely on their knowledge of the Food Guide Pyramid as they write about and illustrate the foods they plan to serve. Be sure to set aside time for interested youngsters to share their monstrous meals with the class.

Uses For Mooses And Other Popular Pets

Written by Mike Thaler & Illustrated by Jerry Smath
Troll Associates, Inc.; 1994

A moose hat rack? An alligator stapler? An elephant squirt gun? Maybe it's time to consider a new pet! Packed with the impossible, this imaginative paperback is sure to keep students giggling until the very end!

Encourage students to let their imaginations run wild as they conjure up creative uses for a multitude of animals. To begin, write on the chalkboard a student-generated list of animals that do not appear in the book. Next have each student choose a different animal from the list and illustrate a unique use for that animal on provided paper. Then, on a sentence strip, have each student complete the phrase "Imagine if" by describing the illustration he created. Mount each sentence strip with its corresponding picture on a bulletin board titled "Imagine If…"

a pelican delivered the mail.

Purple, Green And Yellow

Written by Robert Munsch
Illustrated by Hélène Desputeaux
Annick Press Ltd., 1997

When Brigid gets carried away with her latest set of coloring markers, no one is safe—not even her dad. Who would dream that colorful markers could land a young girl in such a heap of trouble? Probably most moms and teachers!

At the conclusion of this colorful tale, have students explore their artistic talents with a drawing-and-coloring project. First have each child fold a sheet of drawing paper in half two times, unfold the paper, and number the resulting boxes from 1 through 4. Then, using only a pencil, ask each student to draw himself in Box 1, a pet or a favorite animal in Box 2, a piece of furniture found in his home in Box 3, and a favorite pair of shoes in Box 4. Next have each student use markers (or colored pencils or crayons) to create a colorful variation of each pictured item. Set aside time for interested artists to share their creations. Wouldn't Brigid be impressed!

It's A Spoon, Not A Shovel

Written by Caralyn Buehner
Illustrated by Mark Buehner
Dial Books For Young Readers, 1995

Put your students' manners to the test with this super silly book. Written like a multiple-choice quiz, students choose the most appropriate behavior for each of a variety of animal-related situations. It's a quiz that will have your students laughing out loud!

With a little advance preparation, you can really give your students a good laugh—even beyond what this book is sure to deliver. The day before you plan to read the book aloud, inform students that on the following school day, they will be taking a manners quiz. Encourage them to review their manners with their family members so they will be well prepared. Then, when you read the book, have students write their answer choices on sheets of paper they have numbered from 1 through 20. At the conclusion of the quiz, use the answer key at the back of the book to guide students in checking their papers *and* in finding the letter of each correct answer in its corresponding illustration. Conclude this activity by asking students to tally their correct responses and award themselves a title based on the Manners Code on this page.

Manners Code	
Correct Responses	**Title**
19–20	Master Of Manners
16–18	Prince/Princess Of Politeness
14–15	Behavior Bandit
13 or less	Manners Monster!

My Little Sister Ate One Hare

Written by Bill Grossman & Illustrated by Kevin Hawkes
Crown Publishers, Inc.; 1996

In this story—written in a style similar to "I Know An Old Lady Who Swallowed A Fly"—a young girl ingests a series of bizarre things ranging from ants in underpants to worms and their germs. This book is packed with everything you need for a full-belly laugh!

Because of the predictable pattern of this comical tale, your class can successfully write its own original version. After students have chosen a main character for the story, help them create the first and last story verses (numbers one and ten). Then divide your class into eight groups and assign each group a different number from two through nine. Instruct each group to create a two-line rhyming verse for its number. After you've approved a group's verse, have the group members write and illustrate the verse on provided paper. Ask the group that finishes first to copy and illustrate the first verse of the story, and the group that finishes second to copy and illustrate the last verse of the story. Then mount the ten resulting posters in sequential order on a bulletin board or wall, along with a story title. Over the next several days, lead students in several oral readings of the completed tale. Later compile the posters between two covers to create a book for your class library. You'd better laminate this project if you can—it's sure to be a popular pick among your youngsters!

Our classroom gerbil ate 1 book.
It gulped and smacked and really shook.
Then it grinned.

Inside A Barn In The Country

Written by Alyssa Satin Capucilli
Illustrated by Tedd Arnold
Scholastic Inc., 1995

Rebus pictures add to the fun of this cumulative read-along story. When a tiny mouse squeaks inside a barn, it sets off a chain of events that can only be stopped by a very sleepy farmer.

Your youngsters will be begging to participate in the reading of this silly barnyard story. After an initial oral reading, divide your class into ten groups and give each group a card that you've labeled with a different barnyard animal and the sound, word, or phrase that you'd like the small group to repeat. Then, during a second oral reading, pause to indicate when a group should participate. Ask the entire class to join in when the farmer proclaims, "It's not morning yet; please go back to bed"! For added fun, redistribute the cards to different groups and read the story again—and again and again!

Ten Little Dinosaurs

Written by Pattie Schnetzler & Illustrated by Jim Harris
Accord Publishing Ltd., 1996

Written in rhyming verse, this dinosaur countdown is a scream! If the hilarious antics of the ten different kinds of dinosaurs don't have your students in stitches, the outrageous artwork—which incorporates two enormous, plastic wobbly eyes into every scene—definitely will.

Believe it or not, this superbly entertaining book contains a wealth of factual information! After a just-for-fun oral reading, revisit the book for the purpose of finding out about the ten dinosaurs featured. To do this, read aloud the book's first verse; then flip to the back of the book and read aloud the information about that dinosaur. Then re-read the first verse and enlist your students' help in uncovering the factual information that is hidden there. Investigate each of the ten verses in the manner described, and your young paleontologists will be eager to dig up additional facts about these prehistoric creatures on their own.

Clevell Harris

TEN LITTLE DOCTORS

Make Four Million Dollar$ By Next Thur$day!

Written by Stephen Manes • Illustrated by George Ulrich
A Bantam Skylark Book, 1991

By next Thursday Jason Nozzle plans to be rich, rich, rich! All he must do is *precisely* follow the instructions provided by Dr. K. Pinkerton Silverfish—a leading authority on getting rich quick. It's so simple, what could possibly go wrong? Regardless of the outcome of Jason's get-rich scheme, you can bet *your* bottom dollar that this hilarious read-aloud will have your students grinning from ear to ear!

ideas by Stacie Stone Davis

$$$ Doctor Who? $$$

It won't take long for students to conclude that Dr. K. Pinkerton Silverfish is not an ordinary doctor. Read aloud chapter 1 without revealing the doctor's illustration. At the end of the chapter ask students to recall details about the doctor as you list their ideas on the chalkboard. Then have each child refer to the list as he draws and colors a picture of the doctor on a 6" x 9" rectangle of drawing paper. When the illustrations are completed, reveal the doctor's illustration from chapter 1. Also find out which youngsters agree with Jason's opinion that Dr. Silverfish does not look rich. To encourage discussion on this topic, show students magazine pictures of some of the world's wealthiest people like Bill Gates (Microsoft Corp.), the Walton family (Wal-Mart Inc.), and Ted Turner (Time Warner Inc.). Guide students to understand that although it's easy to have preconceived notions about what wealthy people look like, it is rarely possible to determine a person's wealth based on his or her appearance. At the end of the class discussion, collect the students' illustrations for use with "The Road To Riches" on page 115.

$$ Four Million Bucks! $$

"If only I had a million dollars" may be a phrase your youngsters have said or heard others say. Near the end of chapter 1, Jason rattles off a list of ways that he'd spend not one—but *four* million dollars. Write "$4,000,000.00" on the chalkboard, and give students several minutes to write their own lists of money-spending ideas. Encourage students to consider the needs of others as they compile their wish lists. Then, on provided paper, ask each child to complete and illustrate the sentence "If I had $4,000,000.00, one thing I would do is…" Also give each child a 4" x 9" rectangle of light green construction paper on which to design a four-million-dollar bill. Have each child glue his bill to his completed project; then mount the students' work on a bulletin board titled "Our Four-Million-Dollar Wishes."

$$$$$$$$$$$ Word For Word $$$$$$$$$$$

The outcome of Jason's four-million-dollar pursuit could depend on his ability to accurately follow directions. Put your students' direction-following skills to the test with this ongoing activity. Each morning post a series of four or five different directions for your students to follow at a specified time. A set of directions for ten o'clock might read "Stand up," "Shake your left foot two times," "Sit down," and "Open your writing journal to a blank page." While the class is following the set of directions, state gentle reminders like "Let's see, did the instructions include talking?" and "I'm happy to see that no one has started writing yet." In a few days your youngsters' following-directions skills will be in tip-top condition!

$$$$$$$$$ The Road To Riches $$$$$$$$$

In chapter 2 Jason takes the first step toward becoming a four-millionaire. There's little doubt that youngsters will want to keep an accurate account of Dr. Silverfish's money-making instructions. Who knows? There could be four million bucks in it for each of them too! To make a journal for each child, staple five pages of 6" x 9" writing paper and a blank 6" x 9" front cover to the back of the illustration she drew for "Doctor Who?" on page 114. Suggest that each student write "Steps To Becoming Rich by Dr. K. Pinkerton Silverfish and [student's name]" on the front cover and illustrate herself inside the back cover. Then, beginning with chapter 2, set aside time at the conclusion of each chapter for students to carefully describe every money-making instruction that was introduced.

$$$$ A Happy Ending $$$$

In the final chapter of the book Jason realizes that he will not become a million-aire. At first he is extremely disappointed; however, as he reads Dr. Silverfish's suggestions on how to have fun without spending money, his disappointment begins to fade. Discuss the outcome of the book with your students and find out if they agree with the phrase "Money isn't everything." Then, on provided paper, have each student illustrate herself doing something that's fun and free. Ask each child to write a descriptive caption for her picture; then compile the students' work into a class book titled "Who Needs A Million Dollars?" By golly, Dr. K. Pinkerton Silverfish knows what he's talking about!

$$$$$$$$$$$$$$$$$ More From The Doctor $$$$$$$$$$$$$$$$$$$

One can only imagine what instructions Dr. Silverfish will offer in his next book *Be Famous In A Flash!* Revisit *Make Four Million Dollars By Next Thursday!* for the purpose of identifying its main character and setting, and summarizing the beginning, middle, and ending of the story. Then have students brainstorm ideas for the doctor's next book based on these story elements. When appropriate, distribute copies of page 117. Explain that you would like each student to plan an original instructional-type story. Students who are interested in planning a version of *Be Famous In A Flash!* write this title on their papers. Students who wish to write other instructional-type stories like *Outsmart Your Teacher* or *Win A Popularity Contest* write their chosen titles on their papers. Then each child completes the activity by listing a main character and a setting for his story, and summarizing and illustrating each story part. Invite students to share their creative story plans, or challenge them to use their planning sheets to write, illustrate, and publish full-length stories. Wouldn't Dr. Silverfish be proud!

Get Rich Quick!

Color the paper money. Use the color code.
Explain your answers on the lines.

 Jason is brave. _____

_____

_____

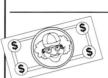 Jason is smart. _____

_____

_____

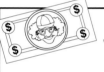 Jason is cool. _____

_____

_____

 Jason is determined. _____

_____

_____

 Jason is foolish. _____

_____

_____

 Jason is curious. _____

_____

_____

©The Education Center, Inc. • *THE MAILBOX* • *Primary* • April/May 1998

116   **Note To Teacher:** Use this activity after completing chapter 4.

Name ______________________________ *Make Four Million Dollars By Next Thursday!*

Story planning sheet

____

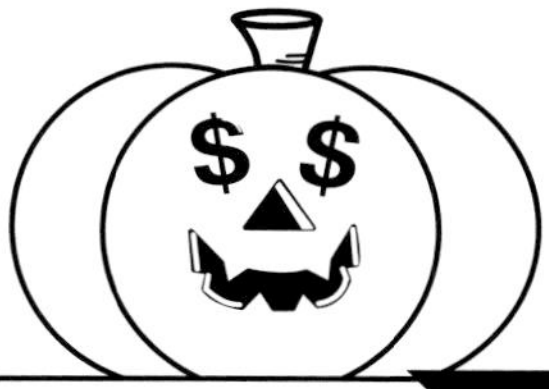

Story Title

Main Character: ______________________________

Setting: ______________________________

The Beginning

____

____

____

____

The Middle

____

____

____

____

____

The End

____

____

____

____

____

Note To Teacher: Use this activity at the conclusion of the book with "More From The Doctor" on page 115.

The Mouse And The Motorcycle

Written by Beverly Cleary

What happens when an inquisitive mouse befriends a medium-size boy who owns a nifty mouse-sized motorcycle? Plenty! Beverly Cleary's heartwarming tale of friendship and suspense is sure to appeal to your students who—at one time or another—have probably wished they could talk with animals, too!

ideas by Stacie Stone Davis

Clevell Harris

Mouse Tales

There are plenty of journal-writing opportunities throughout this delightful chapter book—and what better place for youngsters to complete their writing activities than inside mouse-shaped journals! To make a journal, a student stacks several sheets of circular writing paper on top of a gray construction-paper circle; then he staples the stack at the top. Next he folds the project in half by aligning the bottom half of the stack with the top half of the stack. To decorate his journal, the student glues two construction-paper mouse ears, a pink pom-pom nose, and a wiggle eye in place. For the mouse tail, he bends a pipe cleaner as desired and tapes one end of it inside the cover, near the fold. Then the student uses a crayon to draw a mouth and write his name. Have students pen their thoughts about the story characters, make story predictions, summarize chapters, or create new Ralph-related adventures in their journals. It won't take long for students to determine that Ralph isn't just an ordinary mouse!

Tim

A Late-Night Spin

In chapter 5 Ralph takes Keith's motorcycle for a late-night spin, and quite an adventure unfolds. At the conclusion of the chapter, have students recall the events that took place that night. Then divide students into groups of six and challenge each group to write a late-night adventure featuring the motorcycle-riding mouse. To do this give each group a copy of the story frame on page 120, a pair of scissors, a 9" x 12" sheet of construction paper, pencils, and glue. Ask one member of each group to cut along the dotted lines on the reproducible and distribute the resulting paper strips, keeping the title strip and one additional strip for himself. Next instruct the students to complete the sentences on their strips. Then have each group sequence its story strips and glue them on the construction paper—beginning with the title strip and ending with strip number six. Allow time for the group members to read the story they wrote; then invite one member of each group to read his group's story to the rest of the class. Without a doubt, Ralph will have his share of wacky adventures—and there's a good chance that your youngsters will request this writing activity again!

Ralph's Adventure

1. Last night on the motorcycle, Ralph _went to a restaurant_

2. He saw _owls, pickles, and lots of people_

3. He heard _cows mooing and chickens crowing_

4. The funniest thing that happened to Ralph was _when he rode his motorcycle into the bathroom_

5. The scariest thing that happened to Ralph was _when he rode his motorcycle off the edge of a chair_

6. Ralph kn...

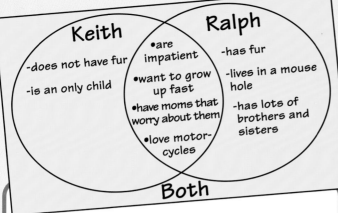

Venn Diagram:

Keith:
- does not have fur
- is an only child

Both:
- are impatient
- want to grow up fast
- have moms that worry about them
- love motor-cycles

Ralph:
- has fur
- lives in a mouse hole
- has lots of brothers and sisters

Forming Friendships

Ralph the mouse and Keith have more in common than a love of toy motorcycles! As a follow-up to chapter 9, draw and label a Venn diagram on the chalkboard that resembles the one shown. Then, under your students' direction, list the similarities and differences that they observe in the two characters. Next have the students evaluate the diagram and offer explanations about why they think the two get along so well.

To extend the activity, ask each youngster to think about a friend with whom she enjoys spending time. Then have each student create a Venn diagram on a sheet of paper that she can use to compare herself to her friend. After the diagrams have been completed, ask each student to determine why this friendship is special. Invite interested students to share their findings with the class.

A Mighty Fine Machine

Vroom! Vroom! Here's an art activity that's sure to get your students' creative wheels turning! Ask each child to choose a favorite motorcycle-related event from the story. Then have each student cut a picture of a motorcycle from a discarded magazine, or color and cut out a copy of the motorcycle pattern on page 312. Ask each student to glue his motorcycle cutout to a sheet of drawing paper and use crayons or markers to draw Ralph riding it. Next the student draws and colors scenery around the motorcycle-riding mouse that depicts the story scene he selected. Finally the student writes a sentence on a paper strip that describes his artwork. Display each illustration with its corresponding caption on a classroom bulletin board titled "Mouse On The Move!" Vroooooom!

Awesome Accomplishments

In chapter 12 Ralph puts his life on the line to find an aspirin for his sick friend. And in chapter 13, he is considered a hero for his brave acts. Ralph feels especially proud when Keith praises him for being a smart and brave mouse. Ask students to think of times when they have felt especially proud. Then challenge each child to describe and illustrate the accomplishment for which he feels most proud. Ask each student to title his work so that it resembles Beverly Cleary's title and includes his accomplishment or deed (like "Ashley And The Spelling Bee" or "Samuel And The Snake"). Collect the completed projects. Next title a sheet of poster board "Look What We've Done!", add a decorative border, and laminate the poster. Display the poster at students' eye level in the hallway outside your classroom door. Each day showcase two or three different stories on the poster. Continue featuring stories until every student's work has been on display. Who feels proud now?

Riding With Ralph

Put each youngster in the driver's seat with this review activity! Pair students and give each twosome a copy of the gameboard on page 122, a penny, and two game markers. Instruct the student pairs to play the game by following the provided directions.

To extend the activity and expose students to more than one classmate's book-related ideas, have the students play the game with a variety of partners. To do this, have the students trade partners on your signal. (For easy management establish a rotation system.) After several rounds of play, serve the students a snack of peanut-butter sandwiches or cookies in honor of Ralph.

There's More!

If your youngsters enjoyed *The Mouse And The Motorcycle,* they'll also enjoy the sequels: *Runaway Ralph* and *Ralph S. Mouse.* There's no doubt that Ralph returns as mischievous and brave as ever!

Note To Teacher: Use this activity after completing the book.

Vroooooom!

START

What is one way that you are like Keith?		
What is one way that you are like Ralph?	Which story character do you like the best? Why?	If you saw a mouse, would you talk to it? Why or why not?

Trapped!

Miss One Turn

Do you think Ralph is honest? Why or why not?		
What do you think is the funniest part of the story?	Should Ralph have gone home with Keith? Why or why not?	What is one way that you are not like Ralph?

Do you think Keith is responsible? Why or why not?		

Directions for two players:
1. Place your game markers on START.
2. In turn, flip a penny and move:
   HEADS = 1 space
   TAILS = 2 spaces
3. Answer each question in the box.
4. The first player to reach FINISH wins.

What do you think is the scariest part of this story?		
What is one way that you are not like Keith?	Why do you think Ralph and Keith became such good friends?	If you could ask Ralph one question, what would it be?

Would you tell a friend to read this book? Why or why not?		

FINISH

What would you like to say to Beverly Cleary about this book?	If you could change one part of the story, what would you change?	

122

Note To Teacher: Use this activity with "Riding With Ralph" on page 119.

LANGUAGE ARTS UNITS

Getting Started On The "Write" Foot!

Step "write" up to the new school year with this collection of easy-to-implement writing activities! Your students' writing skills will be back in business in no time—and there's no fancy footwork involved!

ideas by Lisa Kelly

The "Write" Foot

Get your students started on the "write" foot with these colorful student-made journals. Use the footprint pattern on page 128 to duplicate a class supply of journal covers. Place the journal covers, 9" x 12" sheets of construction paper, a supply of 4" x 8" writing paper, scissors, and a stapler at a center. To make her journal, a student personalizes and cuts out a journal cover. Next she positions the cutout atop a sheet of construction paper, traces around the shape, and cuts on the resulting outline. Then she staples a supply of writing paper between her two journal covers. Continually keep this center stocked with journal-making supplies so that students can create additional journals as needed. If desired, set aside time each day for students to write in their " 'Write' Foot" journals.

The "Write" Foot!

Name Maggie

Shopping

I like to visit the pet store.

All About Me

An oral reading of *Clive Eats Alligators* by Alison Lester (Houghton Mifflin Company, 1991) is the perfect prewriting activity for an "All About Me" booklet project. The seven characters in this book delightfully model diversity with their varying interests and preferences. At the conclusion of the book, list the eight featured subtitles on the chalkboard. Then give each child a construction-paper booklet containing eight blank booklet pages. Have each child write her name and the title "All About Me" on the front booklet cover, then copy a different subtitle near the top of each booklet page. To complete her booklet, a student writes and illustrates a sentence that describes her personal preference or interest about each featured subtitle. Set aside time each day for several students to share their completed projects with their classmates. If you can find the time, complete and share a booklet about yourself too. Students will enjoy learning about their classmates and their teacher, and you'll quickly learn a lot about your class!

Colorful Counting

Not only can you count on this ten-day journal activity to review number words and color words—it also strengthens question-and-answer skills! Under your students' direction, write the number words from one through ten on a length of bulletin-board paper. In a similar manner, create a list of color words. Post the resulting lists for student reference. Give each child a construction-paper journal that holds ten sheets of story paper. Have each student write her name and the title "Colorful Counting" on the front cover of her journal, then add other desired cover artwork.

To begin the journal activity, write "How many _____?" on the chalkboard. Exhibit one item and ask a student volunteer to orally complete the question. Then ask another volunteer to answer the question, stipulating that the answer must include a number word and a color word. Write the student's answer on the chalkboard. Repeat this procedure several times, using a different item each time. Then ask each student to write, answer, and illustrate the modeled question in her journal. Over the next nine school days, spotlight the numbers two through ten in sequential order. In a few days, the students will be eager to identify their own number sets, allowing you to omit this step in the procedure. Later in the year, repeat the activity—this time relating it to the current theme of study. "How many <u>sloths</u> in the rain forest?"

How many apples?

There are three red apples.

Happy

I was happy on my birthday!

Exploring Emotions

Sometimes youngsters have difficulty identifying the emotions they're feeling. This journal activity invites students to explore and better understand their feelings.

Each child needs a construction-paper journal that contains five or more blank pages. Ask each student to title the front cover of his journal "My Feelings," then personalize it with his name and other desired decorations. To complete a journal entry, introduce an emotion like happy, sad, calm, surprised, or angry. Write the emotion on the chalkboard and demonstrate facial expressions and body language that portray the emotion. Encourage students to talk about times they've experienced this feeling. Next have each child write the emotion at the top of a blank journal page and illustrate a time when he felt this way. Students may also write (or dictate for you to write) about their experiences. Explore a different emotion every few days. When the journals are completed, ask students to continue to store them in their desks. The completed journals can be handy tools for the students (and yourself) when interpersonal conflicts arise.

Handfuls Of Achievements!

This weekly writing activity creates a handy year-round display! Each week ask every student to trace the outline of his hand onto colored paper and cut out the resulting shape. Inside the hand cutout, have the child write his name and one accomplishment from the past school week. After each child has shared his accomplishment with the class, display the students' handiwork on a bulletin board titled "Give Us A Hand!" At the end of each month or grading period, ask your students to join you in applauding the entire class for its outstanding accomplishments. Then remove the hand cutouts from the display and send them home with the students so that the accomplishments can be shared with family members.

I scored 100% on my math test!

Ricki Almo

A Family Affair

Students will find writing about their family members an enjoyable task. And because this writing activity results in a one-of-a-kind project, the task is even more desirable! Each student needs a white construction-paper copy of the paper-doll pattern (on page 129) for each family member, including himself. On each pattern—in the provided box—a student names and describes a different family member. Then the student cuts out and decorates his patterns to resemble his family members. Provide an assortment of arts-and-crafts supplies for decorating that includes crayons; yarn; buttons; and scraps of fabric, construction paper, and wallpaper. Remind students to not decorate over their writing. To assemble his family booklet, a student arranges his decorated cutouts side by side in a desired order. Then, working from left to right, he glues each tab to the adjoining cutout. The student trims off the final tab and his project is complete. Have the students form a sharing circle so that each youngster may introduce his family of cutouts to his classmates. If you're preparing for Open House, be sure to display these one-of-a-kind family projects for your visitors to enjoy!

What A Walk!

I Went Walking, written by Sue Williams and illustrated by Julie Vivas (Harcourt Brace Jovanovich, Publishers; 1989), is a perfect springboard for a beginning-of-the-year writing activity. This easy-to-read picture book chronicles the colorful critters that a small boy encounters while on an innocent stroll.

For an independent writing activity, have each student copy the sentences "I went walking" and "What did I see?" near the top of a 9" x 12" sheet of drawing paper. Instruct each child to illustrate her paper by drawing herself and part of the animal she plans to see. Suggest that the students picture themselves (and the partially hidden animals) in the animals' natural surroundings. Next have each student copy, complete, and illustrate the sentence "I saw a [color] [animal] looking at me" on the back of her paper. Assemble the students' work into a class book titled "We Went Walking." No doubt your students will take a walk to the classroom library to check out this class publication!

If you prefer to follow up your oral reading of *I Went Walking* with a group activity, try this! For each group you will need a length of white paper labeled with the sentences "We went walking" and "What did we see?" As a class, brainstorm places that the students would like to walk, such as a beach, a city, a forest, and a jungle. List the students' ideas on the chalkboard. Next divide the class into groups. After each group has chosen a different place to take its walk, distribute the lengths of paper that you've programmed. Ask the members of each group to use crayons or markers to illustrate their length of paper to show the things they imagine seeing on their walk. Display the resulting artwork for all to see. Older students can write the name of each illustrated item on a blank index card, then tape the cards to their group's artwork near the corresponding illustrations.

126

A hospital in Edina, MN, is where I was born on May 17, 1989.

Beautiful is the word my parents used to describe me.

Alphabet Autobiographies

Teach your students the ABCs of writing autobiographies with this unique approach. At home, have each student research special events from his life; then have him bring his findings to school. On separate sheets of paper, ask each child to write autobiographical sentences that begin with different alphabet letters. Challenge older students to create a sentence for each letter of the alphabet. Then have each child illustrate his pages and design a book cover for his book. To complete his book, a student sequences his pages alphabetically, then staples them between his book cover. Right down to the letter, these autobiographies are a great way for students to record their special memories.

Candy Whelan—Gr. 3, Garlough Elementary
West St. Paul, MN

A Happy Class!

Reinforce happy thoughts with a class "Happy Book." To make this class journal, cut out and staple a supply of circular writing paper between two construction-paper circles. Draw a happy face on the front cover. Program the first page with the title "Our Happy Book" and the current date; then place the journal and a special pen (perhaps one with happy faces on it) at a writing center or other desired location. Near the end of each school day, select a different student to write several sentences in the journal that describe a happy event from his day. Ask each child to sign and date his journal entry. Periodically write happy entries in the journal yourself. Then set aside time every week to read aloud the entries for everyone to enjoy. You'll find that these happy thoughts have a very positive effect on the ambience of your classroom! When the journal becomes filled with happy thoughts, make another one. If desired, make the completed journal available for overnight checkout.

Shirley Smith—Gr. 3, Lincoln Elementary, Huntington, IN

I get a kick out of...

Pam Crane

Staying In Step

Create a colorful character similar to the one shown to keep your youngsters in step with writing all year long!

- For a year-round display, mount the cutout and the title "Staying In Step With Writing" on a bulletin board. Have each student display a favorite piece of published writing on the board. Each month ask students to replace their displayed writing with more current samples.
- For a daily journal-writing prompt, tape the character to the chalkboard and draw a large speech bubble beside it. Each day program the speech bubble with a title, story starter, or other writing prompt. Students may choose to use the provided writing prompt for journal writing, or they may write about a self-selected topic.

The "Write" Foot!

Name _____

129

Getting The Scoop On Writing Reports

Keep your youngsters hot on the trail of report writing with these trustworthy ideas from our subscribers. Who knew that writing reports could be so much fun!

It's All In The Hand

Use this handy approach when teaching students to write simple reports or expository paragraphs. Show students your left palm with your fingers extended and give them the following writing tips. Tell students that first *(point to your left thumb)* a writer must introduce her topic. Next she states at least three facts about her topic *(point to fingers one, two, and three);* then she concludes her report *(point to pinkie finger)* with a summary sentence or a sentence that tells how she feels about the topic. Repeat the presentation, this time asking the students to join you in saying and dramatizing the tips. If desired also have each child cut out a duplicated hand shape that you've programmed with the writing tips and tape the cutout to the corner of her desk. Students will be eager to try out their handy writing tips right away!

Carol Ann Perks—Grs. K–5 Gifted, Comstock Elementary, Miami, FL

Four Facts

Report writing can be as easy as one, two, three, and four! Have each student fold a sheet of paper in half twice, then unfold the paper to reveal four boxes. In each box a student writes one interesting fact about her topic. Next she cuts the boxes apart and arranges the facts in a desired order. (This approach allows the student to rearrange the order of the facts an unlimited number of times.) Then, on a sheet of writing paper, she writes an introductory sentence about her topic, her four facts, and a summary sentence. There you have it—a four-fact report!

Debbie Fly—Gr. 3, Edgewood School, Homewood, AL

Boxed Reports

Any report topic and just about any clean, empty box will do for this creative report-writing project. To begin, a student covers his box with colorful background paper. Then, on white paper cut to fit each side of his box (and the top and bottom if desired), he writes and illustrates his report. For the best results, provide a few writing guidelines like the following: each box report must include a prominent title, the name of the reporter, five or more facts, and two or more illustrations. This creative approach to report writing is sure to bring unique and informative results.

Carol Ann Perks—Grs. K–5 Gifted

Waterfalls, little plants, interesting animals, and lots of rock can be found inside caves.

People who explore caves are called cavers.

Only one person can get in small caves, but large caves can be more than 300 miles long.

Caves were often places of shelter along the Underground Railroad.

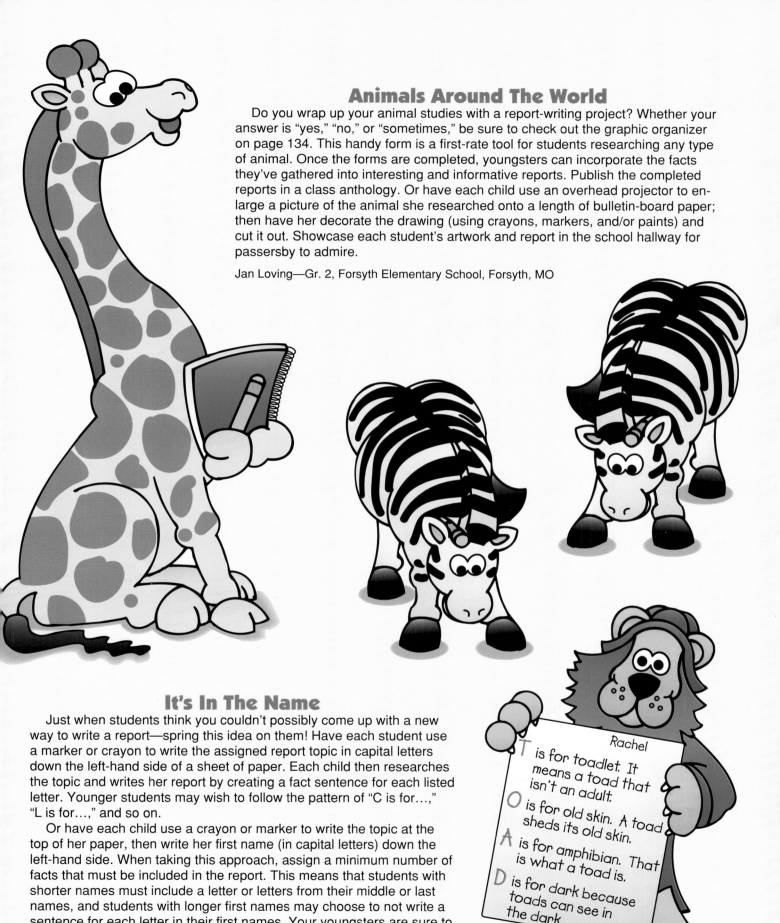

Animals Around The World

Do you wrap up your animal studies with a report-writing project? Whether your answer is "yes," "no," or "sometimes," be sure to check out the graphic organizer on page 134. This handy form is a first-rate tool for students researching any type of animal. Once the forms are completed, youngsters can incorporate the facts they've gathered into interesting and informative reports. Publish the completed reports in a class anthology. Or have each child use an overhead projector to enlarge a picture of the animal she researched onto a length of bulletin-board paper; then have her decorate the drawing (using crayons, markers, and/or paints) and cut it out. Showcase each student's artwork and report in the school hallway for passersby to admire.

Jan Loving—Gr. 2, Forsyth Elementary School, Forsyth, MO

It's In The Name

Just when students think you couldn't possibly come up with a new way to write a report—spring this idea on them! Have each student use a marker or crayon to write the assigned report topic in capital letters down the left-hand side of a sheet of paper. Each child then researches the topic and writes her report by creating a fact sentence for each listed letter. Younger students may wish to follow the pattern of "C is for…," "L is for…," and so on.

Or have each child use a crayon or marker to write the topic at the top of her paper, then write her first name (in capital letters) down the left-hand side. When taking this approach, assign a minimum number of facts that must be included in the report. This means that students with shorter names must include a letter or letters from their middle or last names, and students with longer first names may choose to not write a sentence for each letter in their first names. Your youngsters are sure to have loads of fun using this personalized approach to report writing!

Carol Ann Perks—Grs. K–5 Gifted, Comstock Elementary, Miami, FL

Rachel

T is for toadlet. It means a toad that isn't an adult.

O is for old skin. A toad sheds its old skin.

A is for amphibian. That is what a toad is.

D is for dark because toads can see in the dark.

131

The Three Rs

Nope! It's not what you think! These three Rs stand for "Researching," "Recycling," and "Reporting." For the research portion, a student chooses an animal to investigate. Then, without mentioning the name of the animal, he writes each of his four favorite facts about it on a separate 5" x 7" card. On a 9" x 12" sheet of construction paper, he illustrates and labels the animal. For the recycling portion, the student uses a large recycled grocery bag to create a backdrop for his project. To do this, he cuts away the back and the bottom of the bag; then he flattens the bag, keeping the blank side up. He glues one fact card in each corner of the backdrop. He also folds his animal illustration in half and glues it in the center of the backdrop as shown. Then he uses a crayon or marker to write "My Animal Report" and his name on the resulting flap. For the reporting portion, each child, in turn, presents his mystery animal to the class. First he reads aloud the four facts he wrote. Then he accepts an animal guess from three different classmates. If the animal is identified, he shows the class his illustration. If the animal is not identified, the reporter names the animal and then reveals his illustration. Whether you're wrapping up an animal unit, or looking for a unique report-writing opportunity, this project has plenty of kid appeal!

Barbara Cooper—Gr. 1, Tenth Street School, Oakmont, PA

This animal has a really good memory.

This animal only eats plants.

My Animal Report by Zed Zebra

Its baby can weigh 200 pounds or more!

The front teeth of this animal never stop growing.

Bugs In 3-D

Students will go buggy over these insect reports! To begin, each child researches an insect and writes each of four fascinating facts about it on a separate 5" x 7" index card. Next she creates an enlarged three-dimensional replica of the insect. The replica can be crafted in a variety of ways, including forming the bug from salt dough, then painting the dried project; fashioning the bug from modeling clay; or creating the bug from an assortment of arts-and-crafts supplies that might include construction-paper scraps, tissue paper, waxed paper, toilet-tissue tubes, pipe cleaners, and wiggle eyes. To assemble the report, a student mounts her insect on a cardboard or posterboard rectangle that she has labeled with her name and the name of the insect. Then she tapes a fact card to each edge of the rectangle as shown. Display the completed reports around the classroom. Your students will be so proud of their work that you may wish to invite other classes to tour your students' insect gallery. During each tour, have your student reporters stand near their projects so that they can answer any questions that visitors may have.

Rose Zavisca—Gr. 2, South Bend Hebrew Day School, Mishawaka, IN

A dragonfly can eat while it is flying.

Kim R.

A young dragonfly lives in water from one to five years.

It has spines on its legs!

Dragonfly

A dragonfly can fly 60 miles an hour.

Facts About The Famous

Researching famous people is lots of fun; however, sorting out all the interesting facts about a famous person can be overwhelming. The next time you assign a famous person report, program a copy of the graphic organizer on page 135 with one research question or guideline per quadrant; then duplicate a copy for each student. A student writes the name of the person he is reporting on in the circle; then, in each section, he takes notes that correspond to the programming you've provided. This information can then be transformed into a simple report or into a report that includes one paragraph for each quadrant of information gathered. Invite each star reporter to share his completed project with his classmates.

Connie Pinegar—Gr. 3, Mitchellville Elementary, Mitchellville, IA

Tell when this famous person was born.

Write one fact about this person's childhood.

Explain why this person is famous.

Write three interesting facts this famous person.

by

Working From A Web

When your cub reporters are ready to advance from one-paragraph reports to multiparagraph ones, introduce them to a web. Have each child draw a large oval in the center of a blank sheet of paper, then draw four (or more) straight lines extending from it. Have students write a report topic in the oval, then engage them in brainstorming general ideas about this topic. For example, if the report topic is "the ant," general topics might include "body," "homes," "food," "jobs," and "interesting facts." List the students' ideas on the chalkboard; then have each child copy a different general topic from the list onto each line of his web. As each child completes his research, he notes facts about each general topic on his web as shown. When the note-taking is completed, show students how each general topic can be converted into a paragraph by rewriting each general topic as a main-idea sentence and each related fact as a supporting detail. Now there's a report-writing strategy that yields interesting reports *and* a better understanding of paragraphs!

Debbie Erickson—Grs. 2–3, Waterloo Elementary, Waterloo, WI

The Pocket Approach

When students know how to organize their research notes, writing reports becomes a lot more fun! To use the pocket approach, each child needs a tagboard or construction-paper folder. She writes her report topic on the front of the folder; then she opens the folder and glues up to eight library pockets inside, taking care to not glue any pockets over the fold line. Next the student slips a blank card inside each pocket and sequentially numbers each pocket and its card. Before she begins her research, she labels each pocket with a question about the report topic. Then, as she locates information pertaining to each question, she notes it on the corresponding card. When her research is complete, she converts each question into a main-idea sentence, and she uses her notes as supporting details. Take the pocket approach and writing reports becomes easy as pie!

Mary Boehm—Gr. 3, Webster School, Rushville, IL

Calling The Shots

After your youngsters have a few reports under their belts, try this approach to report writing. Begin by asking each child to choose his own report topic. Next have each student write his name and his report topic on an index card. Then, on each of five additional index cards, have him write a different question that he has about his chosen topic. Each youngster researches his topic and writes the answer to each question on the appropriate index card. If desired give each student a few extra index cards on which to record other fascinating facts that he discovers about his topic. When his research is complete, the student proofreads his cards and stacks them in sequential order, placing his personalized topic card on top of the stack. At this point the student chooses between using his index cards to give an oral report or publishing his report on the computer. Or he can do both! You'll quickly learn that the sky is the limit when students report on topics of personal interest!

Sr. Barbara Flynn—Grs. 2–3, St. Ambrose School, St. Louis, MO

Animal:

Physical Characteristics:

(Give details about what the animal looks like.)

Carnivore   Herbivore   Omnivore

(Circle one.)

(Draw and color a picture of your animal.)

Habitat:

Continent:

Food Chain:

Facts reported by _____

Note To Teacher: Use with "Animals Around The World" on page 131.

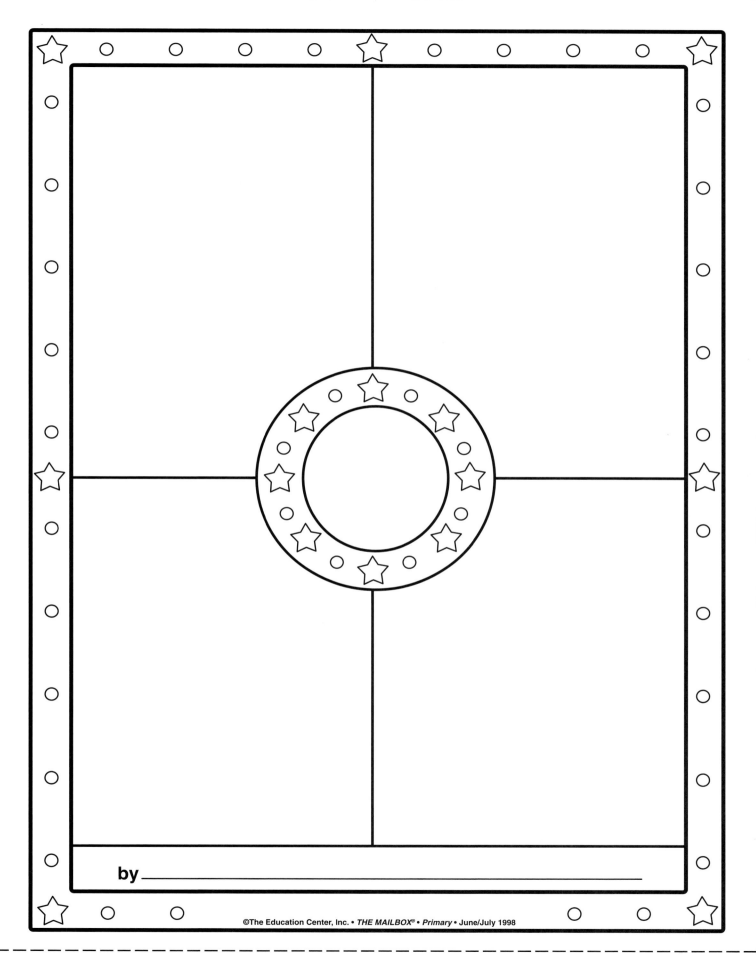

by _____

Note To Teacher: Use with "Facts About The Famous" on page 132.

Parent Letter And Project Guidelines

Use with "A Family Affair" on page 139.

IT'S A FAMILY AFFAIR!
Project Guidelines

1. Please handle every book with care.

2. If a book is damaged, tell your teacher when you return the book.

3. After you have read the book, write your name, the date, and a comment about the book on the paper to the right.

4. Return this bag of materials to the classroom when you are finished reading the book and writing your comment. You may then select another book bag to take home!

Dear Parent,

Your child is participating in our classroom Family Affair Reading Project. The goal of this project is for each child to spend quality time reading together with a family member.

Please take time to enjoy this book with your child. Remember that the books in our classroom library vary in difficulty. Your child will find some books more challenging than others. Do not worry if your child needs help reading a book. It is perfectly fine for you to provide reading assistance. Or you may choose to read the book aloud to your child.

Inside this folder you will find a few simple guidelines for your child to follow. I hope you and your child have a wonderful time reading together!

Sincerely,

A HARVEST OF READING MOTIVATION

You've planted the seed of reading knowledge and you're busy cultivating your students' reading skills. What more could you use? How about a bumper crop of reading motivation? Implement your favorite ideas from this collection and in no time your budding readers will be blooming with reading enthusiasm!

Books And Backpacks

Boost reading enthusiasm and self-esteem with books and backpacks! Each week distribute a backpack to two or three different students. Help each youngster select and place in his backpack a book from the school or classroom library that he would like to read aloud to others. Also place a copy of a parent note in each backpack that explains the following procedure: On Monday and Tuesday evenings, the student practices reading his selected book aloud to his family members. Also encourage each student to gather (or create) story props and to use the props to enhance his presentation of the book. On Wednesday the backpack (containing the book and story props) is returned to school and the student rehearses his book presentation with you. On Thursday the student presents his book to another staff member, and on Friday he chooses to either give his book presentation to his classmates or to another class of his own choice. You can count on reading enthusiasm to soar right along with your students' self-confidence!

Michelle Dunnam—Gr. 2
Haskell Elementary School
Haskell, TX

Literary Door Displays

Get the word out about reading with this schoolwide plan! To begin, ask each class to decorate the outside of its hallway door to spotlight a favorite book. Require that each door decoration include the title of the chosen book. Then, on a predetermined day, ask all teachers to close their hallway doors so that each class of students can take a turn viewing the door displays throughout the school. Students are sure to discover several books that they'd like to read or have read to them! Repeat this schoolwide door-decorating activity as often as you like. To encourage a variety of reading, designate book categories or themes like animal stories, tall tales, fairy tales, nonfiction books, and biographies for future decorating projects.

Andrea Isom Burzlaff—Gr. 3, Coventry School, Crystal Lake, IL
Hope H. Taylor—Gr. 3, Birchcrest School, Bellevue, NE

Mystery Readers

Mystery readers are a foolproof plan for spreading reading enthusiasm! Throughout the year make arrangements for your students' parents and a variety of other community members to read aloud to your class. If desired, provide each reader with a list of suggested literature and request that each guest confirm in advance his or her reading selection to avoid repetitions. On the day that a mystery reader is scheduled to visit, write the words "Mystery Reader" on the chalkboard. Students will anxiously anticipate the mystery reader's visit. With this plan students are exposed to a variety of books and reading styles, and they quickly discover that books are enjoyed by many people!

Krista K. Zimmerman—Gr. 3
Tuckerton Elementary School
Tuckerton, NJ

Bookish Vests

Your youngsters will be dressed for reading success when they wear these student-decorated vests. For each student sew a simple fabric vest or cut a vest from a large paper grocery bag. Personalize the inside of each child's vest; then store the vests for safekeeping. You will also need a supply of patches cut from iron-on Pellon® (for fabric vests) or construction paper (for paper vests). Each time you wrap up a series of activities that relate to a specific book, have each student decorate a patch that highlights the book. To do this a student uses colorful markers to label his patch with the book's title and author, and then he illustrates his favorite scene from the book. If students are decorating fabric vests, collect the completed patches and iron them onto the vests at a later time. Students can glue the paper patches in place themselves. Your students will love wearing these vests and sharing the attached book recommendations with others.

Sandy Greensfelder—Gr. 1
Naples Elementary
Naples, Italy

Reading Through Your State

Promote a love of literature with a state reading campaign! Create a simple outline of your state that shows each county; then duplicate and distribute a class supply of the resulting map. Or enlarge and post one map for the entire class. The goal of this reading project is for students to read their way through their home state. To do this, allow students to color in one county for every 30 minutes (or other designated time increment) of independent reading. The project is complete when the state map is entirely colored. If desired, plan to share interesting facts about each of your state's counties during the campaign. Once your state reading campaign is finished, challenge students to read their way through the United States—state by state. Wow! Reading really *does* take you places!

Karen Hertges—Gr. 3
C. F. S. Catholic Elementary School
Spillville, IA

Reading Can't Be Beat!

March your students into independent reading with this motivational display. Mount the title "Reading Can't Be Beat!" and several colorful music-note cutouts on a bulletin board. Also duplicate a white construction-paper copy of the bookmark pattern on page 140 for each child. Have each student personalize a bookmark, cut out the shape, punch a hole in the top of the cutout where indicated, and tie a loop of yarn through the hole. Use pushpins to display the bookmarks as shown. When a child finishes reading a book, he writes the title and author of the book on his posted bookmark. When all the spaces on his bookmark are filled, he prepares another bookmark and uses a second loop of yarn to connect his two cutouts. Students will enjoy checking out each other's lists for book suggestions, and you'll have a complete record of each student's independent reading efforts. Now isn't that music to your ears?

Linda Madron—Gr. 1
Mary D. Lang Elementary
Kennett Square, PA

CHECK OUT THESE BOOKS
The Missing Fossil Mystery
Author: Emily Herman
Title: The Skates Of Uncle Richard
Author: Carol Fenner
Title:
Author:
Title:
Author:
Title:
Author:
Title:
Author:
Name: Zack Pilley

The Reading Train

Keep your students' interest in reading right on track with this colorful classroom display! Mount an engine cutout and the title "Choo-Choo-Choose A Book To Read!" on a classroom wall. Duplicate a construction-paper supply of the train-car pattern on page 141. Then set aside one or more times per week for students to tell their classmates about the books they've recently read. Each time a student tells the class about a different book, give him a train-car pattern to complete and cut out. Mount the students' completed cutouts end-to-end behind the engine. As your students' interest in reading grows, so will your class train! At the end of the year, dismantle the class train and staple each student's train cars together to create a shape booklet of the books he read during the school year. All aboard for reading!

Robyn Dill—Gr. 1
Northwestern Elementary
Kokomo, IN

Reading Reactions

Reader-reaction cards are sure to pique additional reading interest among your students! Secure a Press-On Pocket to the inside back cover of each book in your classroom library; then slip a lined index card inside each pocket. After reading a book, a student writes his comments about the book on the provided reader-reaction card, then signs and dates the card. To get the project rolling, write a variety of book-related comments on several of the cards. Students will be anxious to read your remarks, read the books you've read, and add their own reactions to the cards. Now that's a surefire way to start a reading epidemic!

Jana Atchley—Education Student
Johnson Bible College
Knoxville, TN

A Family Affair

This year-round reading plan nurtures reading relationships between students and their parents. You'll need to invest some time and energy in the initial preparations, but once the plan is in place it requires minimal effort to manage.

To prepare your book collection, number each book, and then number a large resealable plastic bag to match. Place each book inside its bag. To make an instruction/comment booklet for each of the resulting book bags, fold a 9" x 12" sheet of construction paper in half. Glue a signed copy of the parent letter (page 136) to the front cover; then unfold the construction paper and glue a copy of the project guidelines (also on page 136) to the left-hand side. If desired, laminate the project for durability; then use a brad fastener to secure several pages of blank or lined paper to the right-hand side of the opened booklet. Close the booklet. Number one booklet for each book bag; then seal the booklets inside the book bags.

To create a record-keeping system, duplicate a supply of the reading record on page 141. You will also need student copies of a number list that corresponds to your book collection. To make a check-out folder for each student, attach a copy of the reading record and the number list to a sheet of construction paper, and then fold the construction paper in half as shown. Ask each child to personalize his folder and store it for safekeeping in a designated location.

To check out a book bag, a student writes the bag number and current date in his check-out folder. When he returns the book bag, he records the date of return and circles the corresponding number in his folder. Assist students with this record-keeping procedure until they grow accustomed to it. When a student has filled each space on his reading record, staple a second reading record atop the completed one. Students will enjoy taking books home to share with their parents; parents will enjoy seeing their students' reading skills improve; and you will feel confident that your students are soaring toward reading success!

Linh Tran—Gr. 1
Wallace Elementary, York, PA

Bookmark Pattern

Use with "Reading Can't Be Beat!" on page 138.

CHECK OUT THESE BOOKS!

Title: ______________________________

Author: ______________________________

Title: ______________________________

Author: ______________________________

Title: ______________________________

Author: ______________________________

Title: ______________________________

Author: ______________________________

Title: ______________________________

Author: ______________________________

Title: ______________________________

Author: ______________________________

Name ______________________________

THE READING TRAIN

Name _____

Book Title: _____

Author: _____

Date: _____

©The Education Center, Inc. • *THE MAILBOX* • *Primary* • Oct/Nov 1997

Use the reading record with "A Family Affair" on page 139.

Name _____

MY READING RECORD

Book Number	Date Checked Out	Date Checked In	Book Number	Date Checked Out	Date Checked In

©The Education Center, Inc. • *THE MAILBOX* • *Primary* • Oct/Nov 1997

141

Special Deliveries

From First-Class Pen Pals

Take a fresh look at the learning possibilities that pen pals offer. Whether students correspond across the country or down the hall, or send their messages by postal carriers versus electronically zapping them to their destinations, one thing is clear—the benefits of promoting pen-pal correspondence are enormous. So take a few minutes to read our subscribers' suggestions for ways to foster positive pen-pal relationships. It's a very special delivery that we feel certain you will enjoy!

Prestigious Pals

If you really want to get children fired up for pen-pal writing, try this idea! Survey your class to find out which celebrities interest them the most. Then create a master list of suitable celebrities and their addresses using the following books:

- *The Kid's Address Book* by Michael Levine (Berkley Publishing Group, 1994)
- *The Celebrity Directory, 7th Edition* by Michael Levine (Axiom Information Resources, 1996)
- *The Address Book, 8th Edition* by Michael Levine (Perigree Books, 1997)
- *V.I.P. Address Book Updates* by James M. Wiggins (Associated Media Cos., Ltd.; 1989)

Duplicate the address list for your students. (If desired provide additional copies for youngsters to give to their friends.) Then instruct each student to choose a celebrity from the list, and write and mail a letter to him. Your youngsters will be so thrilled with the responses they receive that they may begin filling up their free time with letter writing!

Iris Blum—Title I Teacher, Legion Park, Houma, LA
Stacey Cashen—Gr. 3 Student Teacher
Ferron Elementary School, Las Vegas, NV

Special Friends

Children who move at midyear can become excellent pen pals. When a student moves away, give him a special note to wish him well and include a stamped, self-addressed envelope. Encourage the student to send you a letter once he is settled. When you hear from the child, ask each student to write a letter to his former classmate. Compile the letters with your letter and send them to the youngster. Students will benefit from the letter-writing experience and you will have provided a positive model of how to keep in touch with a friend.

Cristy Harts—Gr. 2
Southwest Elementary
Pratt, KS

Pen Pals Down The Hall

For a fun and inexpensive writing experience, take these steps to develop an intraschool pen-pal program. Find another teacher in your school who wants pen pals for her students. Place a mailbox or another letter receptacle outside each classroom. Then pair each student with a child from the other class. After writing a letter and addressing an envelope to her pal, a student tucks the letter into the envelope and places it in the class mailbox. Each week assign a different youngster to be your classroom mail carrier. At a designated time each day, the mail carrier stamps each piece of mail with a rubber stamp before she delivers the correspondence to the mailbox of the other class. The mail's here!

Kellie S. Henry—Gr. 3
Kim Harper—Gr. 2
St. Joseph Grade School
St. Joseph, IL

From Batman® With Love

Spark an interest in writing when students pen these mysterious letters. Working with another teacher, pair your youngsters with students in an older class at your school. Keep the pairs a secret from students. Begin the letter writing by asking each older student to write a letter to an unnamed student-partner. Suggest that he include a few questions, so that the response will contain information about the recipient. For added fun have him sign his letter with an unusual pen name like Strawberry, Fred Flintstone®, Batman®, or Barney®. When each younger student has received and read his letter, have him write a letter to his secret pen pal, signing a fictitious pen name. After sending and receiving letters for a few months, combine the classes for a Pen-Pal Party. Youngsters will be all smiles when the secret identities are revealed!

Patsy Higdon—Gr. 3
Cynthia Neal—Gr. 5
Glen Arden Elementary
Arden, NC

Galactic Guy
Glen Arden Elemen
Room 12
Arden, NC 1234

Sister-City Pals

Here's a fun way to select a class with whom your students can correspond. Use an atlas to locate a city with the same name as the town where your school is located. Send a letter to the city's Chamber of Commerce to locate a school there. Then, at that school, contact a teacher of the same grade level to set up student correspondence. The newly paired pen pals will already have something in common: the name of their cities, *and* something to write about—what's happening in their towns.

Cheryl Escritt—Gr. 3, Gibbon Elementary, Gibbon, NE

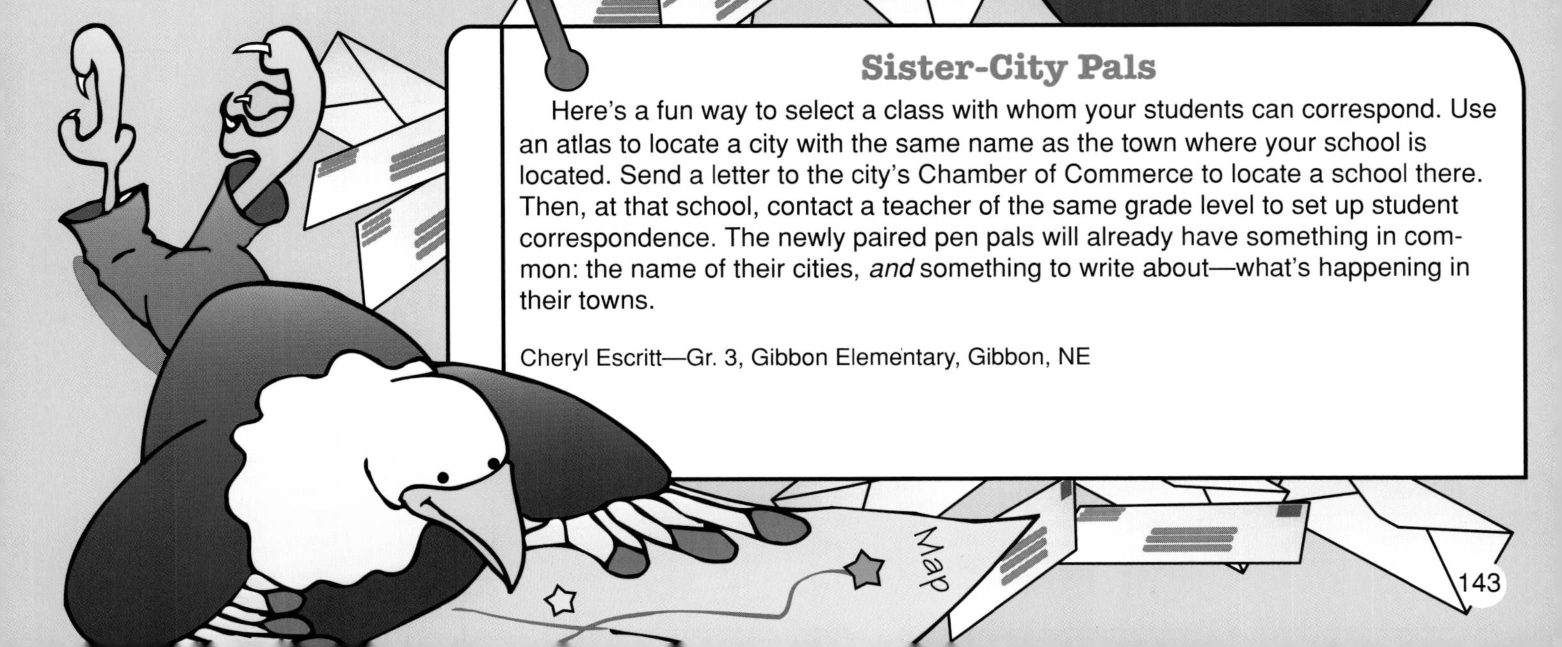

143

Who's That Pen Pal?

Foster descriptive writing skills and stump your students' pen pals with this unique correspondence! Take a picture of each student. When the photos are developed, have each child refer to her snapshot to write a thorough description of herself. Also ask each child to label her letter and the back of her photo with an assigned number. Be sure to create a master list of the number assignments. Collect the photographs and the descriptions; then mail these items along with the master list and a note to the receiving class's teacher. In your note ask that the teacher mount the photos on a bulletin board and distribute the descriptions. Suggest that each child read and reread her pen pal's description until she can guess which photo shows her pal. Using the list you've enclosed, it will be easy for the teacher to verify the matches her students make.

Tina Marsh—Grs. K–5 Gifted Teacher
Jefferson Parkway Elementary
Newnan, GA

About Our School

Looking for a unique way to tell your pen pals about your school? Then this idea is for you! Tell your students that you will be working together to make a special booklet to send to their pen pals. First invite students to brainstorm sentences about their school as you write them on chart paper. Then have each child choose a sentence, copy it onto a sheet of white construction paper, and illustrate it. Collect the completed pages, compile them into a booklet, and drop the project in the mail. Your students' pen pals will proudly display this booklet in their classroom library and perhaps be inspired to reciprocate with a booklet about their school!

Suzanne Kulp—Gr. 2
Harrisburg Academy
Wormleysburg, PA

All About
Harrisburg
Academy
by Ms. Kulp's
Class

News Flash

We interrupt your regularly scheduled pen-pal correspondence to bring you the following videotaped news report. "Good morning, Pen Pals! This is Ryan Lee reporting to you from Silverthorne Elementary School's library. Let's step inside!" For sure, this isn't your typical pen-pal correspondence, but you can't beat it for creating interest between pen pals. Have each student select a school location (such as the playground, office, or computer lab) to be the focus of a news report. Encourage each student to write and rehearse an interesting report about the selected area; then videotape each student on location. Set aside time for your class to screen the completed project before mailing it to your pen pals. Hopefully your pen pals will include a news report in their upcoming correspondence, too!

Valerie A. Hudson—Title I Grs. 1–5
Silverthorne Elementary School
Breckenridge, CO

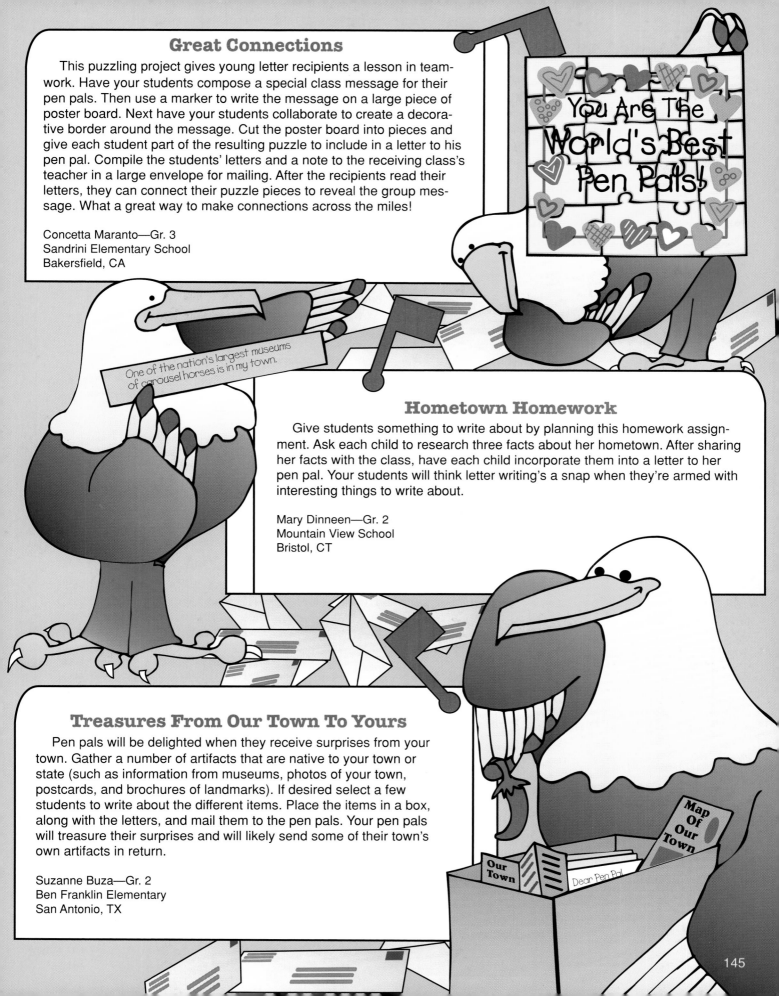

Great Connections

This puzzling project gives young letter recipients a lesson in teamwork. Have your students compose a special class message for their pen pals. Then use a marker to write the message on a large piece of poster board. Next have your students collaborate to create a decorative border around the message. Cut the poster board into pieces and give each student part of the resulting puzzle to include in a letter to his pen pal. Compile the students' letters and a note to the receiving class's teacher in a large envelope for mailing. After the recipients read their letters, they can connect their puzzle pieces to reveal the group message. What a great way to make connections across the miles!

Concetta Maranto—Gr. 3
Sandrini Elementary School
Bakersfield, CA

Hometown Homework

Give students something to write about by planning this homework assignment. Ask each child to research three facts about her hometown. After sharing her facts with the class, have each child incorporate them into a letter to her pen pal. Your students will think letter writing's a snap when they're armed with interesting things to write about.

Mary Dinneen—Gr. 2
Mountain View School
Bristol, CT

Treasures From Our Town To Yours

Pen pals will be delighted when they receive surprises from your town. Gather a number of artifacts that are native to your town or state (such as information from museums, photos of your town, postcards, and brochures of landmarks). If desired select a few students to write about the different items. Place the items in a box, along with the letters, and mail them to the pen pals. Your pen pals will treasure their surprises and will likely send some of their town's own artifacts in return.

Suzanne Buza—Gr. 2
Ben Franklin Elementary
San Antonio, TX

Worth A Thousand Words

When your students write to their pen pals, they'll probably mention classmates—and even you—from time to time. So that the people mentioned in the letters do not remain faceless, use this suggestion. Label a class picture with students' names and your name. Photocopy the labeled photo for each student's pen pal. The next time your students write to their pen pals, have them tuck these photos in the envelopes too.

Carolyn Williams—Gr. 2
North Augusta Elementary
North Augusta, SC

First Row:
Second Row:
Third Row:

Mrs. Williams
Grade Two

Wow!!
He's one
tall dude!

Dear Curtis,
I am 18" tall.
Signed, Sylvester

Celebrity Responses

Engage your students in a graphing activity that has real star appeal. Have each student select a well-known person to write to. (Celebrity addresses can be obtained from the sources listed on page 142.) Ask your class to choose one question for stars to answer, such as "What is your height?" Have each child write the predetermined question on a stamped, self-addressed postcard. (If desired, each student can create his own postcard from cardboard that might otherwise be discarded, such as cereal boxes.) Then direct him to enclose it with a letter explaining that the response will be used in a class assignment. When several cards have been returned to students, begin a class graph to chart the responses.

Ritsa Tassopoulos—Gr. 3
Oakdale Elementary
Cincinnati, OH

A Puzzling Idea!

Looking for a playful way to help your students' pen pals put names with faces? Then this idea is for you! Have a photograph of your class enlarged. Glue the enlargement onto poster board. On the back of the poster board, draw lines to create individual puzzle pieces. Then cut the pieces apart. Enclose the puzzle pieces and the original snapshot in an envelope, along with a letter that identifies each pictured person. Mail the project to your pen pals. The receiving class is sure to have a ball as they refer to the snapshot and piece together whom their new friends are.

Julie Plowman—Gr. 3
Adair-Casey Elementary
Adair, IA

Another Special Delivery!

Just as we promised, we're back with more first-class ideas for fostering positive pen-pal relationships. Thanks again to our subscribers—*our* most cherished pen pals—for sharing their favorite ideas with us!

In The Know

Encourage students to *really* get to know their pen pals with this ongoing activity! Have each child draw a Venn diagram on a sheet of drawing paper and label it with his name, his pen pal's name, and the phrase "How We Are Alike." Suggest that each student store his diagram in his desk for safekeeping. Then—as students learn about their pen pals' likes and dislikes, strengths and weaknesses, and families and friends—they record the information on their diagrams. The project is a fun way for students to learn about their new writing buddies, and it also encourages the students to include questions in their correspondence.

Concetta Maranto—Gr. 3, Sandrini Elementary School, Bakersfield, CA

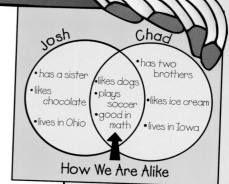

Josh / Chad

- has a sister
- likes chocolate
- lives in Ohio

- likes dogs
- plays soccer
- good in math

- has two brothers
- likes ice cream
- lives in Iowa

How We Are Alike

Front-Page News

Keep students informed about what's going on in their community and in their pen-pals' community with a front-page exchange. Periodically send the teacher of your students' pen-pals the front page from your local newspaper, and ask him or her to do the same for you. Each time a front page arrives, display it along with your local newspaper's front page for the same date. Then, as a group activity, compare and contrast the front-page news and the daily forecasts.

Tammy Brinkman and Kimberly Martin—Gr. 3
Dellview Elementary, San Antonio, TX

Special Deliveries

Simple enclosures can make your students' letters extra enticing to their pen pals. Some easy-to-mail treasures are newspaper clippings, stickers, riddles or jokes, illustrations, homemade puzzles, bookmarks, pressed flowers, and trading cards. Why not make plans today for every student in your class to tuck a special delivery into her next pen-pal correspondence?

Carole Curcio—Gr. 1
Hampton Elementary School, Hampton, NJ

A Pen-Pal Adventure

Strengthen the bonds between your students and their pen pals with a class-created pen-pal adventure. To begin, choose a story topic that can easily incorporate each pen pal as a character. Enlist your students' help in establishing the story's plot; then write a class-created story title and beginning on the chalkboard. Next have each student contribute a sentence for the story that features his pen pal. Record these sentences and a class-created story ending on the chalkboard. Edit the story as a class; then, on provided paper, have each child copy and illustrate the sentence that features his pen pal. While students are working, ask each one in turn to sign a page labeled "Authors and Illustrators." Also enlist

early finishers to copy and illustrate the beginning and ending of the story, and to design front and back book covers.

To assemble the book, enlist your students' help in sequencing the pages; then place the autographed page on top. Bind the pages between the student-created book covers; then carefully pack the project for shipping. You can count on this project receiving rave reviews!

Phoebe Sharp—Gr. 1 Special Education
Gillette School, Gillette, NJ

Mrs. McNeil's Class Trip

by Mrs. Sharp's Class

Math From Mail

After students read and enjoy a batch of pen-pal mail, use the corresponding postmarked envelope(s) to prompt this graphing activity. If your pen-pal letters arrive in a class envelope, create a class graph like the one shown. (If the letters arrive in individual envelopes, individual graphs will be in order.) Then, with your students' help, calculate and graph the number of days it took the correspondence to arrive. Repeat this activity each time a new batch of letters is delivered. Periodically find the average length of time it takes the letters to arrive, and challenge your students to estimate when the letters they send will be delivered to their pen pals. What an easy way to incorporate math into your pen-pal activities!

Concetta Maranto—Gr. 3
Sandrini Elementary School, Bakersfield, CA

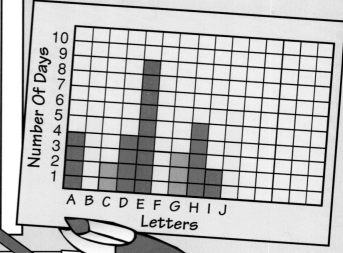

It's A Puzzle!

Your youngsters will have as much fun creating puzzle letters as their pen pals will have piecing them together! To make a one-page puzzle, a student writes his letter on a sheet of white construction paper; then he uses markers to decorate the margins of the completed letter. Next he turns the letter over, draws 10 to 12 large interlocking puzzle pieces, and cuts along the resulting lines. Have each student drop his puzzle pieces into an envelope he has addressed to his pen pal. Most likely the pen pals will reciprocate with similar letters, giving your youngsters the opportunity to piece together some correspondence too!

Sandra Lee—Gr. 1, Wortham Elementary, Wortham, TX

Pictorial Postcard

Add pizzazz to pen-pal correspondence with student-designed postcards. Have each student draw a different scene or landmark from your local community on one side of a blank 4" x 6" card. On the other side, have each child write a note about the landmark, leaving room for a stamp and an address. Mail each card individually at the standard postcard rate, or package them together to send to your pen-pal class. Your students will not only be practicing their writing skills; they'll be learning about local points of interest and refining their artistic talents, too!

Deborah Ross—Gr. 3
Glen Arden Elementary School, Arden, NC

Just The Facts...From A To Z

Here's a letter-writing challenge that's sure to earn your students' stamp of approval! Have each child use crayons or colored pencils to list capital letters from *A* to *Z* down the left-hand side of a sheet of lined paper. Next have each child write a topic she would like to describe at the top of the paper. Topics might include herself, her family, her school, or her community. Then—following the pattern of "A is for...," "B is for...," and so on—she creates a sentence about her chosen topic for each alphabet letter. Have each student tuck her project and a brief letter of explanation in an envelope to her pen pal. The receiving pen pal is sure to get the facts from *A* to *Z* and may even feel compelled to share an alphabetized set of facts in return!

Carol Ann Perks—Grs. 1–5 Gifted
Comstock Elementary, Miami, FL

148

MATH UNITS

THIS MUST BE THE PLACE!

Onesplace • Tensplace • Hundredsplace • Thousandsplace

Fasten your seat belt and cruise into this collection of teacher-tested, place-value activities. As you travel through the unit, you'll see that the activities can easily be adapted to meet the place-value needs of your youngsters. So what are you waiting for? The towns of Onesplace, Tensplace, Hundredsplace, and Thousandsplace await you. Grab your students and hit the road to better place-value skills!

Munchable Math

Warm up students' place-value engines with this tasty activity. Provide each student with a sandwich bag of popcorn or toasted-oat cereal and a napkin. Instruct the students to organize their snacks into groups of tens and ones. Then have each student announce the number of tens and ones she made and the total number of snack pieces she has. Conclude the activity by inviting students to munch on their snacks!

Regina Lykins—Gr. 1
Williamsburg Elementary
Loveland, OH

Place-Value Flip Chart

This handy flip chart is just what your students need to practice place value. To make a tens and ones flip chart, fold an 8 1/2" x 11" piece of colored construction paper in half. Unfold the paper and label the halves "Tens" and "Ones" as shown. Next label ten 4" x 5" white paper cards with the numerals zero through nine. Stack the cards in numerical order and staple the resulting card set in the ones column. Make and staple a second card set in the tens column. Place the resulting flip chart (customized to meet the place-value needs of your students) at a center for students to use with a provided place-value activity. Or assist students in creating individual flip charts. For a large- or small-group activity, announce a number and have each student display the matching number on his place-value flip chart.

Candi DeFran, East River Elementary, Grosse Ile, MI

Thousands	Hundreds	Tens	Ones
0	0	9	5

Barry Slate

Hurry To One Hundred

Here's a place-value game for two players that's a great addition to a math center. To make place-value blocks, laminate several sheets of 1/2-inch graph paper; then cut the papers to create 30 one-square blocks, 30 ten-square blocks, and two 100-square blocks. (See the illustration.) Place the blocks and a pair of dice at the center. To play the game, the first player rolls the dice and collects a matching number of blocks. The second player takes his turn. When a player collects ten *ones,* he trades them for a *ten.* The first player to trade ten *tens* for a *hundred* wins the game! Ready, go!

Sue Volk, Newton, IL

Place-Value Lotto

Beep! Beep! This place-value game is sure to be a whole "lotto" fun! Write any 30 numbers from 0 to 9,999 on the chalkboard. (The numbers should reflect your students' place-value abilities.) Provide each child with a blank lotto board. Instruct him to randomly program each of the 16 squares with a different number from the chalkboard. As students are programming their cards, write the 30 posted numbers on small pieces of paper and place the papers in a container. Also distribute 16 paper markers to each child. To play the game, draw a number from the container and announce each digit's value. (For example, 943 would be announced as nine hundreds, four tens, and three ones.) If a student has the announced number on his board, he covers it. The first student to cover all the numbers on his board announces, "Beep! Beep!" To win the game, he must read aloud the numbers on his board for verification. If desired, award the winning student with a sticker or another small prize.

LOTTO!

2		32	52
92	9	98	61
0	55	27	83
49	36		77

Amy Polcyn—Substitute Teacher
South Lyon Community Schools
South Lyon, MI

I Spy...Numbers!

Play this variation of the traveling game I Spy to reinforce your students' understanding of place value. To prepare for the game, ask students to pretend they're traveling on a large bus to a kid-pleasing destination like a zoo or theme park. Challenge students to name places along the way where they might see numbers. Suggestions may include license plates, highway signs, storefronts, and billboards. Next give each child a sheet of drawing paper on which to illustrate a roadside scene. Require that each scene include a large two-, three-, or four-digit number. (If desired, provide travel magazines and brochures for drawing inspiration.) Collect the completed illustrations.

To play the game, post all (or a portion of) the roadside scenes on the chalkboard. Select one student to secretly choose a posted number. This student begins the game by announcing, "I spy a ___-digit number." The rest of the students try to identify the number by asking yes-or-no questions like "Does the number have a two in the ones place?" or "Is the number greater than 500?" Stipulate that five or more place-value-related questions must be asked before the actual identity of the number may be guessed. The student who correctly names the mystery number chooses the mystery number for the next round of play. Play continues until game time is over.

Elizabeth M. Chappell—Gr. 2
Altura Elementary
Aurora, CO

Beanbag Toss

Who would guess that a beanbag toss could reinforce place-value skills? To create a four-digit gameboard, use masking tape to tape together four colorful sheets of poster board. Label the gameboard sections with place values as shown. Secure the gameboard to the floor and use masking tape to designate a toss line that is about 12 feet from one end. Divide the class into Teams A and B. Have the two teams stand on opposite sides of the gameboard—perpendicular to the toss line. Give a beanbag to each member of Team A.

To begin play, ask each member of Team A to toss his beanbag onto the gameboard (from behind the toss line). Then, with your students' help, count the beanbags that are in each place-value section and identify the four-digit number that Team A tossed. Write this number on the chalkboard. Then give the beanbags to the members of Team B and repeat the process. To determine the winner of the round, flip a penny and award a point to the deserving team: heads = the larger number tossed wins the round, tails = the smaller number tossed wins the round. If both teams toss the same number, award a point to each team. The team with the most points at the end of game time wins.

James R. McCabe—Gr. 3
Gladstone Elementary
Gladstone, OR

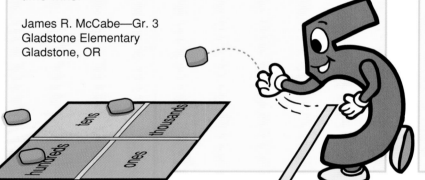

Looking At License Plates

Hit the road with this place-value project! Display a sampling of construction-paper license plates that you have created. Pro-gram the plates to reflect your youngsters' place-value skills. Then ask students a series of questions related to the posted plates like "Which license plate has an even numeral in the hundreds place?" and "Which license plate has less than three tens?" Conclude the large-group activity by enlisting the students' help in arranging the license plates in numerical order from the smallest to the largest numbers.

To extend the activity, ask each student to design a colorful license plate on a 6" x 12" rectangle of drawing paper. Then place the students in small groups and challenge each group to create a predetermined number of place-value questions about its group's license plates. Make plans for each group to present its resulting place-value lesson to the rest of the class!

Elizabeth M. Chappell—Gr. 2
Altura Elementary
Aurora, CO

Bus Bonanza

This unique activity provides busloads of place-value practice! Create three large school-bus cutouts. Label the cutouts as shown and laminate them for durability. Also program a class set of blank cards with numbers from 0 to 999. Write the numbers at the bottom edge of the cards and underline one digit per number. Distribute the numbered cards and ask each child to draw and color a self-portrait on his card. When the drawings are complete, display each bus cutout in a different classroom location. In turn, have each child read aloud the number on his resulting passenger card, identify the value of the underlined digit (ones, tens, or hundreds) and place the card on the corresponding bus cutout. Next have the students gather around the bus cutouts they "boarded" and work together as a group to sequence the passenger cards—placing the smallest number at the front of the bus and the largest number at the back.

Later, laminate and cut out the passenger cards; then place the cards and bus cutouts at a math center for more place-value reinforcement. All aboard!

Elizabeth M. Chappell

Going Places!

Students accumulate travel miles as they play this small-group place-value game! Each group needs a programmed spinner to play. To make a master spinner for duplication, photocopy page 154; then cut out the spinner labels and glue them on the spinner wheel. Program each wheel section with a desired place value (ones, tens, etc.); then duplicate construction-paper copies of the wheel and spinner patterns. Laminate the copies for durability if desired. To assemble the spinners, refer to the directions at the bottom of page 154.

To play the game, divide students into small groups. Each group member needs a sheet of paper and a pencil. Each group needs a die and a spinner. If desired, a calculator can also be provided. In turn, each group member spins the spinner to determine his method of travel and its place value. Then he rolls the die to determine how far he travels. For example, if a student spins a car (with a place value of tens) and he rolls a 6, he travels "six tens," or 60 miles. As soon as the player records his travel miles on his paper, the next player takes his turn. Play continues in this manner. When a player takes his second turn, he records his travel miles and finds the sum of miles he has traveled so far before the next player takes his turn. The first player to travel 200 miles (or another predetermined number) wins the game.

Elizabeth M. Chappell

Making Numbers

This whole-group activity provides plenty of place-value practice. Give each student ten squares of white paper. Have each child label her squares with the numerals zero to nine. To begin the activity, announce two or more different numerals. Instruct each student to use her numeral cards to make the smallest (largest) number possible. If three or more numeral cards are being used, also challenge students to use the numerals to make as many numbers as possible. No doubt students will ask for this hands-on activity over and over again!

Elizabeth M. Chappell—Gr. 2
Altura Elementary
Aurora, CO

Read It!

Place-value practice takes on a new dimension with this partner game. To make the game, duplicate pages 154 and 155 on tagboard. Cut out 33 construction-paper game cards (2 1/2" squares). Label six of the cards "0." Stack these cards facedown on the gameboard (page 155) where indicated. Label the remaining cards with the numerals one through nine—three cards per numeral. Shuffle these cards and place them facedown on the gameboard where indicated. To make a spinner for the game (page 154), program two sections of the wheel with the words "Read It!" Program the remaining wheel sections with the following place values: "ones," "tens," "hundreds," "thousands." To assemble the spinner, refer to the directions at the bottom of page 154. To play the game, the partners (in turn) spin the spinner to determine a place value, draw a numeral card, and place the card on the corresponding gameboard space. A player may stack his numeral card atop another numeral card to make his play. The first person to spin "Read It!" places a "0" card on each open gameboard space and reads the resulting number. If the number is read correctly, the player earns one point; the gameboard is cleared; the cards are sorted, shuffled (as needed), and stacked; and another round of play begins. If a number is read incorrectly, the zero cards are removed and play continues. If all the gameboard spaces are covered before a player spins "Read It!", the player who covers the last gameboard space reads the number for a possible point. The player with the most points at the end of game time wins!

Jacqueline L. Jerke—Chapter 1 Reading And Math
Wynot Public Schools
Wynot, NE

Patterns For Making A Spinner

Use with "Going Places!" and "Read It!" on page 153.

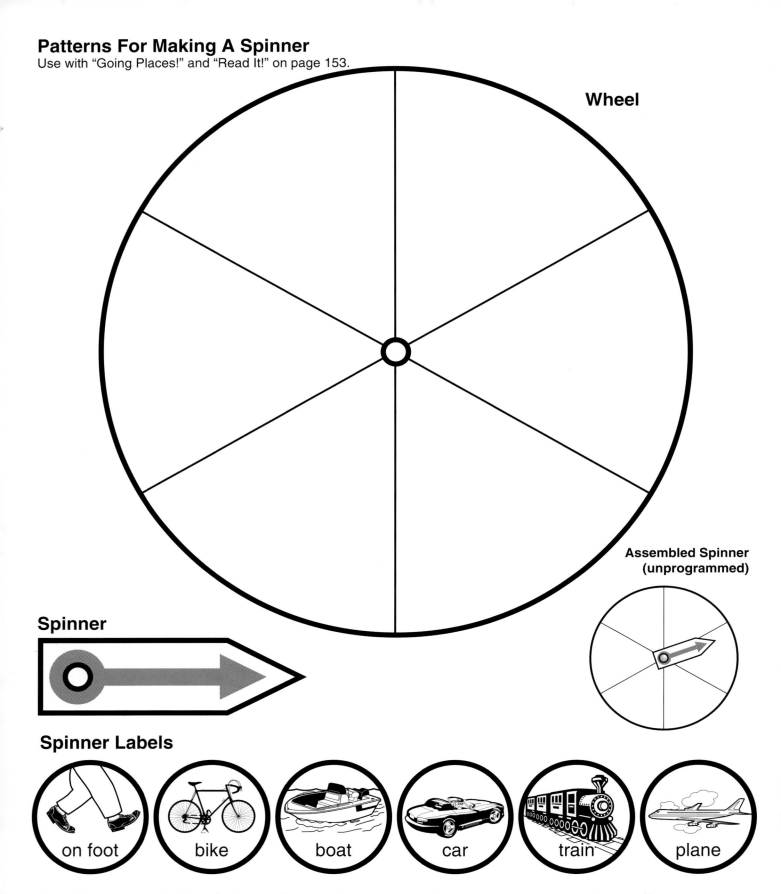

Wheel

Spinner

Assembled Spinner (unprogrammed)

Spinner Labels

on foot   bike   boat   car   train   plane

How To Assemble The Spinner: Cut out the duplicated wheel and spinner patterns. (Be sure to follow the programming directions provided in the corresponding ideas on page 153.) Punch a hole in each cutout where indicated and use a brad to join the cutouts as shown above.

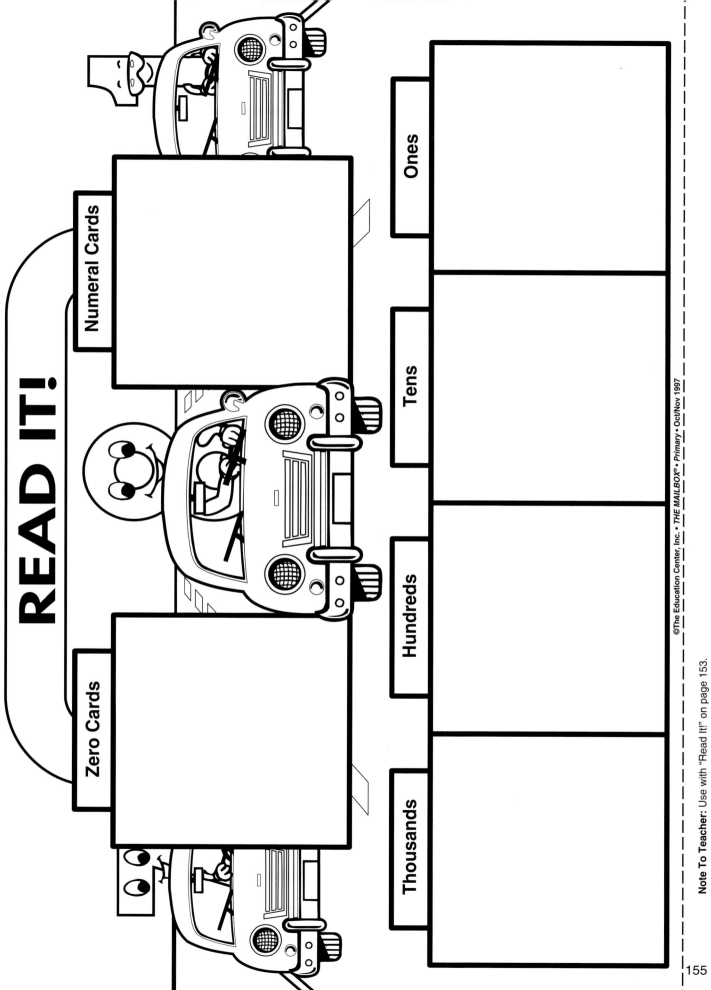

READ IT!

Numeral Cards

Zero Cards

Ones

Tens

Hundreds

Thousands

Note To Teacher: Use with "Read It!" on page 153.

Time Races On!

From slow and steady to fast and furious, this timely collection of activities is just what your students need to race ahead to perfect time-telling skills. So what are you waiting for? There's no time like the present to get started!

GO TURTLE!

Hooray Hare!

King-Size Clock

With this unique clock, interest in time-telling practice will be at an all-time high! In advance spray-paint a clock face that includes numbers, minute markings, and a center dot (to indicate placement of the clock hands) on a solid-color king-size bedsheet. To practice time-telling skills, place the sheet in an open area, and have students sit around the lower half of the clock face. Position a yardstick as the minute hand and a ruler as the hour hand, and ask students to state the time shown. Then invite each student, in turn, to manipulate the clock hands as you announce varying times. When the activity is completed, simply fold the sheet for easy storage. Now that's a king-size idea!

Gina Black—Gr. 2, Remsen-Union Elementary, Remsen, IA

Hop 15 times.
less than a minute: 卌
a minute: |
more than a minute: ||

Draw 20 circles.
less than a minute: 卌 |||
a minute:
more than a minute:

Write the principal's name ten times.
less than a minute:
a minute: |
more than a minute: 卌 ||

Just A Minute

A *minute* is a *minute* is a *minute*—but how long is a *minute?* This partner activity helps students explore the length of 60 seconds. For every two students, create a task card (similar to the ones shown) that features a different activity. First ask students to sit quietly for one minute. Then lead the class in an activity, such as clapping or humming, for one minute. Have students describe how these two minutes were alike and/or different.

Next pair students and give each twosome a task card. On your signal, one partner in each pair performs the activity on the pair's card, while the other partner observes. Announce when one minute is over. Allow time for those students who are still performing to complete their tasks and for each observer to record the outcome of the activity on the pair's task card. Then have the twosomes trade task cards and the partners switch roles for another round of fun. Continue in this manner until each pair has performed each activity. Conclude the lesson by having each twosome total the tally marks in each category on its final task card. After each pair has shared the tallied information with the class, invite students to tell what they have learned about a minute of time. Doesn't time fly when you're having fun?

Susan Majors—Grs. 1–2, Palmer Lake Elementary, Palmer Lake, CO

Individual Timepieces

These individual practice clocks will provide you with instant feedback on your students' time-telling skills. On tagboard duplicate a class supply of open clock-face patterns (if desired, enlarge the clock-face pattern on page 160 for this purpose). Laminate and cut out each clock; then give each child a clock, a wipe-off marker, and a tissue. To begin, announce a time. A student draws clock hands on his clock to show the announced time; then he displays his programmed clock for your approval. A quick glance can assess each student's efforts. Then have each student wipe off the clock hands with his tissue and prepare to reprogram his clock. What a nifty way to provide youngsters with hands-on time-telling practice!

Jill D. Hamilton—Gr. 1, Schoeneck Elementary, Stevens, PA

Pam Crane

Wild And Wacky Wristwatches

Watch out! This interactive bulletin board will have students showing off their time-telling skills! Give each student an index card labeled with a different time. To make a jumbo wristwatch, a student designs a clock face that shows her designated time on a thin, white paper plate. Next she personalizes and decorates two 6" x 18" strips of construction paper to resemble watchbands. Then she glues the watchbands to the paper plate as shown. Encourage students to further customize their watches as desired. Next have each student write her name on the back of her index card. Mount each wristwatch on a bulletin board labeled "Watch Our Wristwatches!" Place the index cards and pushpins in a container near the display. A student matches each digital time on a card to a wristwatch, flips the card to verify her match, and then uses a pushpin to suspend the card near the wristwatch. When the student completes the activity, she returns the pushpins and index cards to the provided container.

Jill D. Hamilton—Gr. 1

Turtle Time

These individual turtle tachistoscopes provide students with practice matching digital and analog times. On construction paper duplicate a class supply of the turtle pattern and the two tachistoscope strips on page 160. Using an X-acto® knife, slit the dotted lines on each turtle. To make a turtle tachistoscope, a student colors his turtle pattern; then he cuts out his turtle and both strips. He programs each clock face to show a different time before he randomly writes the corresponding digital times on the second strip. Then he inserts the strips into the turtle as shown.

To use his tachistoscope, the student adjusts the strips to match. Set aside time for students to exchange and complete their classmates' projects.

Susan Majors—Grs. 1–2, Palmer Lake Elementary, Palmer Lake, CO

Got The Time?

These fashionable timepieces make telling time fun! Duplicate a class supply of the clock pattern (page 160) onto tagboard. Laminate and cut out each clock. Hole-punch the top of each clock; then thread a length of yarn through the hole and tie the yarn's ends. Next divide the cutouts into sets of five and use a wipe-off marker to program each set with a different time.

Each morning randomly distribute the timepieces. Then, throughout the day, incorporate the times shown on the timepieces into your daily activities. For example, request that students wearing the time 6:30 line up first for lunch or that students wearing matching times form small groups. At the end of the week, reprogram each set of five clocks with a different time, and you'll be ready for more telling-time fun the following week.

Jill D. Hamilton—Gr. 1, Schoeneck Elementary, Stevens, PA

Day And Night

Review A.M. and P.M. times with this eye-opening activity. Have each student fold a 12" x 18" sheet of drawing paper in half, then unfold his paper and draw a line down the middle. On the left half of his paper, a student writes an A.M. time and illustrates what he might be doing at that time. On the right half of his paper, he writes a P.M. time and illustrates what he might be doing at that time. Set aside time for interested students to share their projects with their classmates.

Susan Majors—Grs. 1–2, Palmer Lake Elementary, Palmer Lake, CO

7 A.M.   8 P.M.

Time Check!

Reinforce time-telling skills with daily time checks. At five different times during the day, spontaneously declare, "Time Check!" Each child stops what he is doing and writes the time on a paper strip or a duplicated recording sheet. Be sure to make note of the times yourself. At the end of each day, announce the times that should be listed on the students' papers. Now that's easy timekeeping practice!

Diane Balkcom—Gr. 3, Summers Elementary School, Lake City, FL

It's About Time!

This class-book project reinforces that telling time is an important life skill. Challenge students to name occupations that can only be performed by people who can tell time. As you list each child's suggestion on the chalkboard, ask the student to explain his choice. For example, a student might suggest a bus driver who must stay on a time schedule or a nurse who must give patients medicines at designated times. Next have each youngster choose a different occupation from the list. On provided paper have him illustrate himself performing the job and write a sentence or two explaining why he must know how to tell time. Bind the completed projects between two construction-paper covers and title the resulting class book "The Times Of Our Lives!"

Jennie D'Assisi, Richmond Hill, Ontario, Canada

A teacher needs to know when to take her students to lunch.

A coach needs to know how much time is left in the game.

It's A Match!

This large-group game helps youngsters master time-telling skills lickety-split! For every two students, program an open clock card (patterns on page 161) with a different time; then, for each clock card, label an index card with the matching digital time. Laminate the cards for durability. To play, randomly distribute the game cards. Each student reads the time on his game card and searches for the classmate who has the same time. When two students discover that their game cards match, they sit down. After each student has found his match, collect and shuffle the game cards; then play the game again!

Jill D. Hamilton—Gr. 1, Schoeneck Elementary, Stevens, PA

A Line Of Times

Time keeps on ticking with this partner activity! Give each student a copy of the eight open clock cards on page 161. Have each student cut out and program each clock card with a different time; then pair the students and give each pair a 30-inch length of yarn. Each twosome places its yarn in a horizontal line to represent a timeline that starts at 12:00. Then the pair stacks its combined cards facedown. In turn each student draws a clock card and places it in sequential order on the timeline. If a student draws a card with a time that has already been played, he places the card on top of its duplicate. After checking each group's timeline, have students sort their cards, change partners, and repeat the activity. Tick-tock, tick-tock!

Marsha Rogers, Lincoln Elementary School, Ardmore, OK

Timely Journals

Save time each day for students to write in time-related journals. To make a journal for each student, staple a supply of the journal page on page 161 between two construction-paper covers. Each day, a student completes a journal page. To do this she writes a day and/or date, her favorite time from that day, and a reason for choosing that time. She also draws hands on the clock face that show the favorite time she has written about. From time to time, invite students to share their journal entries with their classmates.

Jill D. Hamilton—Gr. 1

My favorite time of the day on **Monday, Dec. 8,** was **3:30**
I liked this time because **my ballet teacher told me I was doing very well.**

Patterns

Use the turtle and tachistoscope strips with "Turtle Time" on page 157.

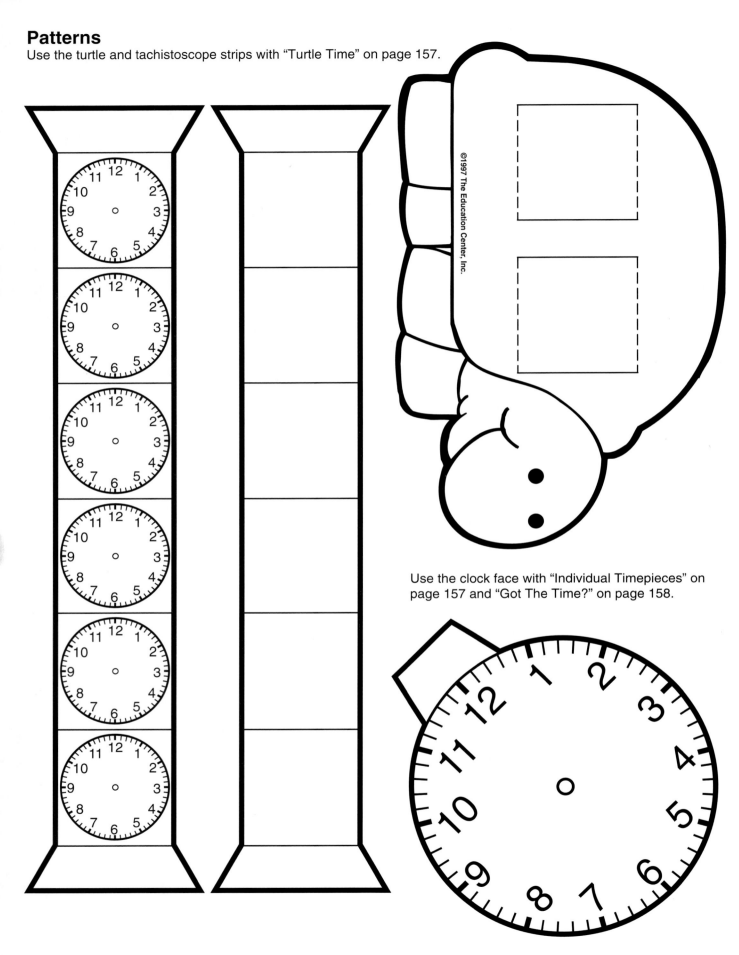

Use the clock face with "Individual Timepieces" on page 157 and "Got The Time?" on page 158.

©1997 The Education Center, Inc.

My favorite time of the day on

_____

was _____.

I liked this time because _____

_____

_____

_____

_____

Note To Teacher: Use the clock cards with "It's A Match!" and "A Line Of Times" on page 159. Use the journal page with "Timely Journals" on page 159.

161

The Numeral Cafe

Scrambled Eggs?

Your youngsters will absolutely love this math-review game—and you will too! Cut out one construction-paper egg for each student plus five more for good measure. Sequentially number the eggs and write a different math problem on each one. Solve each problem on the other side of the egg as shown. Tape one egg—the top only—to each child's desk so that the unsolved problem is showing. Tape the additional eggs to five extra student desks (with chairs) or to a reading table with five chairs.

To play this game, each child personalizes a sheet of paper. On your signal of "Ready," each child stands up and pushes in her chair. On your signal of "Scramble," each child takes her paper and pencil to another desk, copies the problem and its number on her paper, and solves the problem. On your signal of "Check," each student flips the egg and checks her work. Continue play in this manner until students have completed a desired number of problems. Then have students return to their desks. They will have had a great time practicing their math skills, and you won't be faced with a stack of math papers to correct! Now that's a Grade-A math game!

Jeannie Hinyard—Gr. 2, Welder Elementary, Sinton, TX

A Calculated Guess

Sharpen your students' mental-math skills with this quick-and-easy, small- or large-group game. Give each child a laminated card labeled either "Add [numeral]" or "Subtract [numeral]." On the chalkboard write a game numeral that is greater than the greatest numeral shown on a "subtract" card. Select one student to start. This student follows the direction on his card and announces the new game numeral. For example, if the game numeral on the board is 15 and the student's card reads "Add 3," he announces the new numeral 18. The first classmate who, when called upon, correctly identifies the math calculation *(add 3)* takes his turn next. This student then applies his card's direction to the most recent game numeral *(in this case it is 18)*. Play continues in this manner until each child has taken at least one turn or game time is over.

Miriane Krauss—Gr. 3, Bais Yaakov Of Brooklyn, Brooklyn, NY

Add, Subtract, Or Multiply

Here's a partner game that's versatile, practical, and fun for kids. What more could you need? To make a gameboard, program a tic-tac-toe grid with nine numerals; then make a copy for every two students. Pair the children and distribute the gameboards. Each student also needs a blank sheet of paper and a pencil.

To play, announce a math operation: *addition, subtraction, or multiplication.* Then, on your signal, each student refers to the gameboard to create and solve as many math problems as she can. To create an acceptable math problem, the two numbers used must be in boxes that touch horizontally, vertically, or diagonally. When time is called, each student compares her work with her partner's. To earn a point, a student must have created and solved a problem that her partner did not. The partner with the most points wins the game.

adapted from an idea by Debbie M. Darling—Gr. 3
Dolphin Terrace Elementary, El Paso, TX

Roll It!

Mental-math skills are put to the test with this large-group game. In an open area, have students sit on the floor, forming a circle. Announce a number range (like 0–9) and a math operation (addition, subtraction, or multiplication). Give one student a small rubber ball. To begin play, this student declares a number as he rolls the ball to another classmate. This classmate declares a number as he rolls the ball to a third classmate. The third classmate uses the two called numerals and the stated math operation to form an equation. If the student is correct, he begins the next round of play. If he is incorrect, he rolls the ball to a fourth classmate who attempts to provide a correct equation. When a correct answer is given, play resumes as described above. If desired, ask students who answered incorrectly to sit out the next round of play. Continue play until each student has participated at least once. As students become familiar with the game, encourage them to increase its pace. That's when the fun really begins!

Sheila Jessup—Gr. 1, Button Gwinnett Elementary, Hinesville, GA

Tic-Tac-Toe Math

Play this large- or small-group math game in an instant! To make the gameboard, each student draws a tic-tac-toe grid on a piece of paper and writes a different numeral in each game space. Limit students' numeral choices. For example, to review basic addition facts, ask students to use the numerals 0–18 (for basic subtraction facts: 0–9, for basic multiplication facts: 0–50). In turn each child announces a math fact that equals an answer on her gameboard. Every student who has that answer on her gameboard crosses it off. Keep a running list of each math fact given. The first student to cross off three sums (differences, products) in a vertical, horizontal, or diagonal row declares, "Tic-tac-toe!" She then calls out the three answers she has crossed out for your verification. Once a winner of the game has been confirmed, each student quickly draws another gameboard, and play begins again.

Marilyn Webb—Gr. 1, Brookhouse School, Dartmouth,
Nova Scotia, Canada

Pam Crane

163

Math + Poetry = Shel Silverstein

Shel Silverstein's outrageous poems add up to countless opportunities for teaching math-related skills! And what better time to combine math and poetry than in April—Mathematics Education Month and National Poetry Month? Watch the enthusiasm of your youngsters multiply as they giggle their way through the following poems and math activities. The only way to sum it up is *total* fun!

ideas by Lisa Leonardi

A Light In The Attic

HarperCollins Children's Books, 1981

The poems reviewed on pages 164 and 165—"Snake Problem," "Overdues," and "Homework Machine"—are from *A Light In The Attic* by Shel Silverstein.

"Snake Problem"

What do you do when a 24-foot python says, "I love you"? That's the lengthy dilemma facing the child in this love poem.

A 24-foot python is the perfect tool to help your students inch their way toward better measurement skills! After several oral readings of the poem, have each student draw and color a snake on a provided card, then write his name on the card for easy identification. Before asking students to estimate the distance of 24 feet, show them a one-foot paper snake (or a ruler) as a frame of reference. Then lead students into the hallway. On a wall designate the end of an imaginary 24-foot python. Instruct each student to tape his snake card to the wall where he thinks the python's head would be if the snake stretched out to its full 24-foot length. To check the accuracy of your students' estimates, tape a 24-foot length of yarn along the wall. Wow! What a snake!

Students will slither their way to better nonstandard measurement skills with this partner activity! Give each pair of students a one-foot construction-paper python, a pencil, paper, and a variety of manipulatives such as Unifix® cubes, paper clips, craft sticks, and cotton swabs. Have partners measure the length of their python using each type of manipulative and record their findings on the paper as shown. To conclude the activity, have student pairs compare their findings. For older students, multiply the fun by asking them to calculate the number of manipulatives needed to create snakes of various lengths. For example, "If ten small paper clips are needed to make a one-foot python, how many paper clips are needed to make a five-foot snake?"

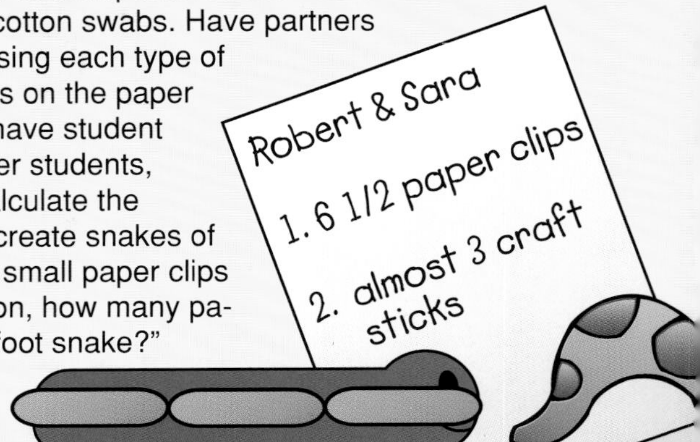

Robert & Sara

1. 6 1/2 paper clips

2. almost 3 craft sticks

"Homework Machine"

The Homework Machine would be the most perfect contraption if only nine plus four equaled three!

Students will be eager to teach this homework machine a thing or two about basic math facts! Copy the poem on chart paper and display it in a prominent classroom location. As you read the poem aloud, have students follow along or read aloud with you. Then enlist your students' help in fixing the homework machine! To begin the repair, tape a blank card over the word *not* (in the next-to-last line of the poem) so that instead of being a not-so-perfect homework contraption, it becomes a perfect one! Also tape a laminated card over each of the two sums, and a laminated sentence strip (or something similar) over the math fact. Next use a wipe-off marker to program each laminated card with the same sum. Challenge students to write on their papers addition sentences that equal the posted sum. After several minutes invite the students to share the sentences they created. Be sure to try out a few of the sentences in the poem. To do this, use your wipe-off marker to program the sentence strip with the desired number sentence. After the poem has been recited, wipe away the number sentence and the strip is ready to reprogram for another oral reading.

For a daily kid-pleasing math challenge, keep the poem on display. Each day reprogram the two laminated cards with a desired numeral and challenge students to write a designated number of math sentences (addition, subtraction, and/or multiplication) that equal the posted numeral. This homework machine works like a charm!

"Overdues"

A library book is found that is long overdue—42 years, to be exact! The question remains whether to return the book or hide it again.

After a few oral readings of "Overdues," this book-related activity is sure to make "cents" at your math center! Check out several books from your school library. Insert an overdue notice with a different fine inside the pocket of each library book. Place the books and a large supply of plastic or paper coins at a center. A student selects a book and uses the coins to pay the fine. Either check students' work or provide a self-checking answer key that lists the possible coin combinations for each fine.

Further challenge students with this large-group activity. Assign a fine, such as five cents, for each day a book is late. Then, using a variety of books, announce a number of days that each book is overdue. Students calculate each book's fine on their papers. Vary the daily fine and the number of overdue days until your youngsters have "fine-ly" paid their dues!

Where The Sidewalk Ends

HarperCollins Children's Books, 1974

The poems reviewed on this page—"Smart," "The Googies Are Coming," and "Band-Aids"—are from *Where The Sidewalk Ends* by Shel Silverstein.

"Smart"

Through a series of trades, a boy takes pride in the fact that after starting off with only a single dollar bill, he ends up with five *pennies. And five is more than one, isn't it?*

This poem provides the perfect opportunity to teach youngsters that more can be less when it comes to coins! Project a transparency like the one shown from an overhead projector. During a second reading of the poem, stop after the first stanza and have a student volunteer place transparent coins on the overhead to show the boy's first money trade. Then enlist the class's help in determining the amount of money lost during the transaction and record this amount in the third column. Repeat this activity after the second, third, and fourth stanzas. After reading the fifth and final stanza, have students calculate the total amount of money the young boy lost. Older students can complete a similar activity on paper. No doubt your students will feel quite *smart* after completing this coin-trading activity!

Money Had	Traded For	Money Lost
		20 ¢

"The Googies Are Coming"

The googies buy children of all different shapes and sizes, and at all different prices. They'll pay 15¢ for dirty ones, 30¢ for clean ones, and only a penny for noisy ones! What a bargain!

After several readings of this money-filled poem, post individual sentence strips showing the price of each type of child the googies want to buy. With your students' help, arrange the strips in descending order based on the prices. Then use the resulting list to enhance your students' problem-solving skills. To do this, give each child a construction-paper booklet of blank paper. Instruct each child to write her name and the poem title on the front cover, then illustrate what she thinks a googie might look like on the back cover. Each morning display a word problem based on the posted list and challenge students to solve the problem in their booklets before the end of the school day. Then, before dismissal, set aside time for the students to compare their solutions with their classmates and make any necessary adjustments. As an added challenge, invite students to submit to you googie-related problems (with answers) for their classmates to solve.

"Band-Aids"

No need to feel sorry for this boy who's bandaged from head to toe! He doesn't have a cut or even a scratch!

This addition activity is just what the doctor ordered! Copy the poem on the chalkboard. To begin, read the poem aloud and have your students determine how many bandages are on the boy's body. Then erase each number word in the poem and replace it with a blank. Have each child use her best penmanship to copy the poem on handwriting paper, inserting a number word from one to five in each blank. Next ask each student to tally the number of bandages the boy is wearing in her version of the poem, and write this number in the lower right-hand corner of her paper. Finally pair students and have each student check her partner's work. Encourage partners to work together to make any needed corrections. Conclude the activity by attaching a colorful bandage to the back of each child's hand or to her work.

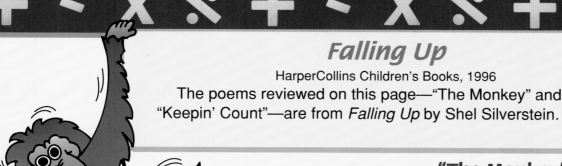

Falling Up

HarperCollins Children's Books, 1996

The poems reviewed on this page—"The Monkey" and "Keepin' Count"—are from *Falling Up* by Shel Silverstein.

2 dogs 8 10 bones.

"The Monkey"

1 monkey who visited a banana 3 (tree) on his way 2 the store got a stomachache from 7 green bananas that he 8. Silverstein's clever substitution of numbers for words makes this poem a delight 4 youngsters 2 read!

Students will go bananas as they try to decipher this intriguing poem! Before sharing the poem with your students, copy it onto chart paper. Cover each numeral with a card that you've labeled with a number sentence that equals the concealed numeral. As you read the poem aloud, have students solve each number sentence and supply the missing numeral. Then, for a fun follow-up, have each student use the same style of writing to pen a sentence for a classmate to read. Your youngsters are cer10 2 have a gr8 time!

"Keepin' Count"

A student is determined to find out how many flies are in Professor Bacar's jar. He counts to three million and seven, but when a fly lady has a fly baby, he has to start counting again!

You can count on students going buggy over this estimation activity! Purchase a bag of plastic flies and a few plastic spiders from a party shop or the Oriental Trading Company (1-800-228-2269). Put the flies in a clear jar (with a lid) and display the jar in a prominent classroom location. Also post a recording chart similar to the one shown. After an oral reading of the poem, ask each student to estimate the number of flies in the displayed jar. Record each student's estimate on the chart; then enlist the students' help in counting the flies. Write this number on the chart too. Return the flies to the jar and use a permanent marker to draw a line around the jar that shows where the flies stop. Then drop a few spiders in the jar and secure the lid. Remind students that spiders eat flies!

After the students have left for the day, remove a noticeable amount of flies from the jar. The following school day, have the youngsters repeat the estimating and counting activities. Encourage the students to study the jar and refer to the chart so they can use the information that they previously gathered. Repeat the activities two or three more times—on different days—until all the flies have been removed from the jar. Not only will your students have polished their estimation and counting skills—they'll also have learned a thing or two about the food chain!

STUDENT	DAY 1 Count: 97		DAY 2 Count: 52		DAY 3 Count:	
	Estimation		Estimation		Estimation	
Sam	509		110			
Amy	23		35			
Jose	45		70			
Kim	150		41			
Alex	92		87			

The answer is definitely 7.

Mind Or Machine

Stage a showdown between mind and machine with this calculator contest. Select one cowhand to operate a calculator, the *machine,* and one cowhand to represent the *mind.* To start the round, state a math fact for the two contestants to solve. The child with the calculator must use it even if he knows the correct answer. The first contestant to announce the correct answer earns a point for either the machine or the mind. Record the point earned on the chalkboard; then continue play as described until every youngster has participated as both the mind and the machine. (Establish a rotation system for easy management.) Your buckaroos may be surprised by the outcome of this race— and who knows? They might even agree that memorizing math facts isn't such a bad idea!

Shari Abbey—Gr. 3, Abilene Elementary School, Valley Center, KS

Add 'Em Up!

Recycle leftover book-order forms with this pardner activity. Pair cowpokes and give each child an unused book-order form to fill out. If desired, designate how many books each cowpoke may order. Then have each youngster total his order using a calculator and record the sum on his order form. Next have each child exchange book orders with his pardner and check the total of his pardner's order for accuracy. The activity is over when the pardners agree that the sum of each of their orders is correct. To extend the fun, have each buckaroo increase his order by a designated number of books and repeat the activity. Or for an added challenge, have the pardners work together to determine a book order that equals a predetermined sum or a sum that is less than (or more than) an approved sum. Yee-ha!

Peg Good—Gr. 2, East Pike Elementary School, Indiana, PA

168

"Cow-culating" Averages

How does a cow know the average temperature of the past five days? He "cow-culates" it! And your buckaroos can too! At a designated time, for five consecutive days, enlist your youngsters' help in reading the outside temperature and recording it on a class chart. After the fifth temperature has been recorded, have each student use a calculator to find the sum of the temperatures. Then instruct the students to divide their sums by 5 to find the average daily temperature. Next ask students how they might find the average temperature over ten days, three weeks, or a month. Then, as a class, make plans to continue reading and recording the temperature for a chosen number of days, enlisting the help of students who live nearby to read the temperature on the weekends. Don't be surprised if your buckaroos get so carried away that they're calculating average temperatures on a daily basis!

Mary Hemp—Gr. 3, Renick R–V School, Renick, MO

Rip-Roaring Riddles

Keep your young cowpokes on their toes with David A. Adler's book *Calculator Riddles* (Holiday House, Inc.; 1995). The answer to each riddle is given as a number sentence. To find the real riddle answer, a student uses a calculator to solve the number sentence, then turns the calculator upside down and reads his answer in the display window. A riddle a day is a great way to reinforce any cowpoke's calculator skills—even your own!

SCIENCE UNITS

The Bone Zone!

If you're looking for the skinny on skeletons, enter the Bone Zone! You'll find a framework of fun activities for reinforcing basic bone facts, literature suggestions, reproducibles, and a ready-to-use centerfold activity. It's a "bone-a fide" way to bone up on bones!
ideas by Jill Hamilton, Catherine Myers-Murphy, and Cheryl Sergi

A Fantastic Framework

Humans would be helpless without their skeletons! To introduce your study of the skeleton, play a game of Simon Says. Engage students in movements that require different parts of the body like touching their toes, clapping their hands, bending their knees and elbows, and hopping. For the final directive, have students pretend to not have skeletons and collapse into limp blobs on the floor. As the students rest, help them conclude that without their skeletons, they would not have been able to make the moves that Simon requested. When it's time for the students to return to their seats, ask them to think about the different bones they are using. When the students are seated, list on the board the bones your students used. The result will be a long list of bones and some insight for you into your students' knowledge of the skeleton.

Them Bones!

Interject a bit of music into your bone study with the following song suggestions!

B-O-N-E-S
(sung to the tune of "B-I-N-G-O")
Once there was a skeleton,
And Bones was his name, oh.
B-O-N-E-S, B-O-N-E-S, B-O-N-E-S
And Bones was his name, oh!

Once there was a skeleton,
And Bones was his name, oh!
B-O-N-E-*(clap)*, B-O-N-E-*(clap)*, B-O-N-E-*(clap)*
And Bones was his name, oh!

(Continue to repeat the verse—each time dropping one more letter from and adding a clap to B-O-N-E-S—until the entire name is clapped.)

The Skeleton Song
(sung to the tune of "Ten Little Indians")
Skull and spine and ribs and hip bone;
Shoulder blades and leg and knee bones;
Elbows, wrists, and toe and ankle bones;
In my skeleton!

(Have students place their hands on each part of the skeleton as it is named.)

Growing Strong Bones

Bones live and grow just like every other part of the body. Explain to students that as their bones grow, they will grow—until their bodies are full-grown. Emphasize that eating calcium-rich foods—like milk, cheese, and spinach—helps to grow strong bones.

To demonstrate how the minerals calcium and phosphorus play an important role in bone strength, perform this simple experiment. Strip the meat from two small chicken or turkey bones, and let the bones dry overnight. The following day pass the bones around the classroom so that the students can feel them. Record the students' observations on one-half of a T-chart as shown. Then place one of the bones in a clear container of water and the other in a clear container of vinegar. Cover the containers and let the bones soak. After four or five days, remove the bones from the liquids and dry them off. Pass the bones around the classroom and have the students describe how the vinegar-soaked bone differs from the water-soaked bone. Record these observations on the T-chart. In conclusion explain that the vinegar-soaked bone softened because the acid in the vinegar dissolved the minerals in the bone. Wow! Those minerals *are* important!

Untreated Bones	Treated Bones
October 13, 1997	October 17, 1997
They feel hard. They are stiff. You can't bend them.	

An Inside Peek

At the conclusion of "Growing Strong Bones" (page 170), students will agree that bones need minerals and nutrients, but they may not agree on how bones get this important nutrition from the food a person eats. Write a student-generated list of suggestions on the chalkboard. Then divide the students into small groups and give each group a portion of a soup bone that a butcher has cut from a larger soup bone. As each group examines the *core* or inside of its bone, reveal that this is where minerals and nutrients are stored. Explain that the nutrients enter bones through a network of blood vessels that brings nutrients and minerals to the bones and takes away waste products. Also reveal that the open spaces in the core are where soft *bone marrow* is stored. Boy, bones are full of surprises!

Plenty Of Backbone

The *backbone* or *spine* is the central support for the skeleton. Have some fun exploring the backbone with this activity. First instruct each child to use one of his hands to feel the bones at the back of his neck. Ask students to describe what they feel *(bumps, knobby bones, etc.);* then explain that these bumps are actually small bones called *vertebrae.* As you inform your students that the backbone contains more than 20 vertebrae, give each student eight or ten pieces of cylinder-shaped pasta (like ziti) and a two-foot length of yarn. Explain that each vertebra in the backbone has a hole in it, and this is where the *spinal cord* (the cord that passes messages between the brain and body) runs. Instruct each child to thread his pasta vertebrae onto his yarn spinal cord. Demonstrate how to securely hold one end of the yarn length in each hand so that the pasta is pressed end-to-end (see the illustration). Have students do the same, then hold their projects vertically.

Next invite the students to use their projects to demonstrate how the spine might look when a person is standing straight, bending over, slouched on a couch, or doing a somersault. Help students understand that if the backbone were a solid bone, the body's movement would be severely restricted. If desired, have each child place his project in a resealable plastic bag for transport home so that later in the day he can demonstrate his newfound knowledge for his family!

A Bone-Building Break

Once students understand the important role that calcium plays in building strong bones, they'll be eager to take a bone-building break! Nourish your students' bones with this calcium-rich treat!

Bone-Building Brew
(makes four 8-oz. servings)

1 cup milk
2 cups fruit-flavored frozen yogurt
1 cup fresh or frozen fruit
Using a blender, thoroughly blend the ingredients; then serve and enjoy!

171

A Protective Case

In addition to being a framework, the skeleton is also a protective case for some of the body's most important organs. The bones in the *skull* protect the brain, eyes, and ears. The *rib cage* protects the heart and lungs. Invite students to feel the bones in their skulls and rib cages as they review the importance of these bones in their daily lives. For a wrap-up, have students put their protected brains to work and complete the reproducible problem-solving activity on page 174!

What bone has a great sense of humor?

The humerus!
by Buddy Bones

What did the rib cage say to the lungs?

"Got you covered!"
by Shelly Ton

What did the foot bone say to the leg bone?

"Stay with me and you'll go places!"
by Cray Nium

Funny Bones

Tickle your students' funny bones with this riddle-writing activity! To begin ask students if they've ever bumped their *funny bones.* Those students who have will agree that it's no laughing matter! Explain that when a person bumps her funny bone, the part affected is a nerve that runs over one end of the *ulna*—one of the forearm bones—and that a strange (or funny) tingling results. Then inform students that the phrase *funny bone* also means "having a sense of humor," and that's the funny bone they'll need for this riddle-writing project!

To complete the writing activity, ask each child to create a bone-related riddle for a class riddle book. Have each child copy his riddle on one side of a provided construction-paper bone cutout, then program the back of the cutout with the riddle's answer and his name. Create bone-shaped front and back covers for the project; then laminate the covers and student-created pages for durability. Hole-punch the book covers and pages; then use a metal ring to bind the pages between the covers. Place the project in your classroom library. Make no bones about it: this funny-bone book is sure to be favored by your students!

To The Bone

Keep your students motivated and informed with this eye-catching bulletin board. Mount the title and character shown. (Consider purchasing a skeleton cutout with movable limbs.) As the class learns the names of bones in the human skeleton, program colorful cards accordingly and ask different students to pin the cards near the skeleton's corresponding bones. Also invite each student to choose a sample of his best work. Display the work samples on the board with personalized, heart-shaped cutouts that the students have created. Invite students to routinely replace their work with more current samples throughout your skeleton study!

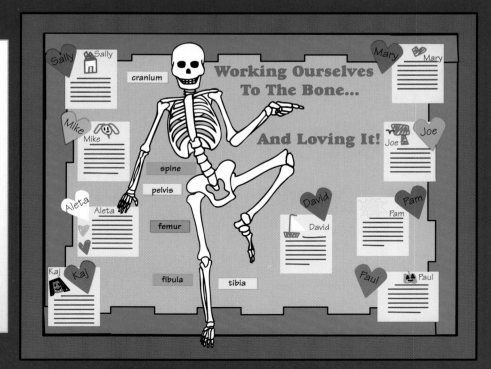

Bony Or Boneless

Who has bones? Students can use their knowledge of skeletons to deduce that all creatures need to have some way of keeping their bodies from collapsing or falling apart. Explain that animals that have backbones (and internal skeletons) are called *vertebrates.* Vertebrates include mammals, reptiles, fish, and birds. Any animal that is not a vertebrate is an *invertebrate.* Invertebrates do not have backbones or internal skeletons, but they do have ways of protecting and supporting their bodies. Challenge your interested students to explore how boneless animals—like earthworms, jellyfish, slugs, and insects—keep their bodies intact.

S
K
E
L
E
T

The leg bone is really two bones. The *fibula* is on the side and the *tibia* is in front.

There are more than 20 bones in each foot! The foot bones grow faster than any other bones in the body.

Boning Up

These student-made skeleton flip books are a fun way for youngsters to bone up on a few bone facts! To make a book, fold a construction-paper copy of page 175 in half so that the programming is to the inside. Crease the fold; then unfold the paper. Cut along each dotted line to the fold; then refold the project. Write the word "SKELETON" on the resulting cover—one letter per flap. To read the flip book, a student opens each flap and reads a fact about the skeletal part shown. No doubt students will be eager to share their newfound knowledge about skeletons with others!

Figuring Out The Femur

The longest bone in the human skeleton is the thigh bone or *femur.* Have each student locate her femur and study its length. Then ask each youngster to estimate in inches the length of this bone. Once the estimates have been recorded, reveal that the length of a person's femur equals one quarter of her total height! To calculate the actual length of her femur, have each child use a calculator to divide her total height in inches by four. (If necessary, enlist the help of a parent volunteer to measure the total height of each child.) Then have each child record the actual length of her femur on a bar graph like the one shown. As an added "bone-us," challenge students to use the resulting class graph to answer a variety of femur-related questions.

Student	Length of Femur (in inches)											
	6	7	8	9	10	11	12	13	14	15	16	17
Zachary												
Elaine												
Dan												
Pedro												
Keesha												
Alan												
Lily												
Buzz												
Juanita												

A Pocketful Of Science

Finding Out About Force

Introduce students to the forces of *push* and *pull* with these hands-on activities.

ideas contributed by Ann Flagg

PUSH

PULL

Activity 1: Push And Pull

You will need:
an open space for student pairs to sit on the floor

What to do:
   Have each child sit on the floor facing a partner. Ask each pair to determine a "Partner One" and a "Partner Two." Then have each student extend his arms in front of him and touch his partners' palms with his own. Instruct each student to push gently against his partner's palms. Next have the students find out what happens when Partner One pushes a little harder than Partner Two, and vice versa. Then allow time for students to further explore the force of push.

Questions to ask:
   1. What force were you using?
   2. What happened when one partner pushed harder than the other one?
   3. What strategy did you use to keep your balance?

Next:
   With pairs sitting in the same positions, have each student extend his arms and grasp his partner's hands. Ask each partner to slowly and carefully lean backward. Instruct Partner Two to gently pull Partner One forward, and vice versa. Then allow time for students to further explore the force of pull.

Questions to ask:
   1. What force were you using?
   2. What happened when one partner pulled the other partner forward?

This is why:

   In the broadest terms, every force can be identified as either a push or a pull. Student pairs experience both of these forces during this activity. When an equal force is exerted by each partner, each student keeps his balance. If one partner exerts a stronger force, the other partner temporarily loses his balance until he exerts a force that equals his partner's.

Activity 2: More About Push And Pull

You will need:

scissors   a bulletin board   a pushpin
scrap paper   a chair

Each student will need:
a pencil   a copy of page 178

What to do:
   To show students that the forces of push and pull are an important part of their daily activities, complete the following demonstrations: use the scissors to cut the paper by pushing the scissor handles together, then pulling them apart; push the pushpin into the bulletin board, then pull it out; push the chair away from you, then pull it toward you.

Questions to ask:
   1. How have I demonstrated the force of push?
   2. How have I demonstrated the force of pull?

Next:
   Divide students into groups of three and give each student a copy of page 178. Have the members of each group brainstorm ways that push and pull are used during the school day and write their findings on their papers. Then ask one member from each group to demonstrate an action that her group listed. Invite other groups to identify the action as a push, a pull, or a combination of the two forces. Continue in this manner until at least one member from each group has demonstrated a different action.

This is why:

   Forces are a part of daily life. Opening or closing a door, and pushing or pulling a pencil to write letters of the alphabet are examples of forces at work. Some forces are very big and other forces are very small. Forces can do lots of things that are very useful to people. They can bend, twist, squeeze, and stretch things. They can also be used to speed things up and slow things down. People can produce large forces, but machines can produce even bigger pushes and pulls.

Activity 3:
A Force That Can't Be Beat!

You will need:
a crumpled sheet of paper   a ruler
a chalkboard eraser   a large, open area
one inflated balloon for every two children

What to do:
Ask three students to stand at the front of the class and face their classmates. Give each student one of the following: the crumpled paper, the ruler, or the chalkboard eraser. Instruct each student to hold her prop in front of her, then—on a signal from you—let go of it. Retrieve the props and repeat the demonstration a second time with three different students.

Questions to ask:
1. What happened when a child let go of her prop?
2. Why do you think all things fall to the ground when they are dropped?
3. Can you think of ways to prevent this from happening?

Next:
Explain that the force of *gravity* pulls most things toward the earth. Then go to an open area, pair students, and give each pair an inflated balloon. Challenge each pair to beat gravity by keeping its balloon from dropping to the ground.

Questions to ask:
1. How did you try to beat gravity?
2. What force were you using?
3. What happened when you did not push your balloon upward?

This is why:

Gravity is a continuous force that affects everything on earth. The force of gravity pulls almost everything in the earth's atmosphere toward the earth. By batting the balloons and attempting to keep them off the ground, students discover that it is impossible to win against gravity, but that gravity can be counterbalanced by the force of push.

Activity 4:
More About Gravity

Each student and you will need:
a 20-inch square cut from   transparent tape
  a plastic garbage bag   a large paper clip
four 30-inch string lengths   scissors

What to do:
Ask students what would happen if they dropped their paper clips. *(The force of gravity would pull them toward the earth.)* Then explain that a miniparachute can be used to decrease the pull created when the paper clip is dropped. Demonstrate each step in making a miniparachute; then have students follow your example.

Step 1: Lay your plastic square flat, trim off one corner of the plastic, and securely tape both ends of one string length to the cutoff surface.
Step 2: Repeat Step 1 at each corner.
Step 3: Pull the string lengths taut.
Step 4: Working as if the eight strands were one, tie a knot in the string at the end that is opposite the parachute; then thread the paper clip onto the resulting loops of string.

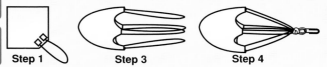

Step 1   Step 3   Step 4

When the projects are finished, have each child grasp the center of the plastic parachute, hold the parachute above her head, and let go of it. Allow time for students to retrieve and drop their parachutes several more times.

Questions to ask:
1. What happens when you drop the parachute?
2. How does the opening of the parachute affect the downward speed of the paper clip?
3. What forces are at work?

This is why:

The parachute creates air resistance. A parachute is an excellent example of the forces of push and pull at work simultaneously. The weight of the paper clip (gravity) pulls it toward the earth, and the push of air pressure created by the opened parachute slows down the paper clip. Because the push of the air pressure created by the parachute is less than the pull of gravity, the paper clip eventually falls to the ground.

Two Mighty Forces!

You use the forces of push and pull every day.
Think about your school day.
List the different ways that you use each force.

500 lb.

PULL

The Force Of...**Push**	The Force Of...**Pull**

Note To Teacher: Use with "Activity 2: More About Push And Pull" on page 176.

Animals In Winter

Have you ever seen a snake in a snowstorm? Or a butterfly in a blizzard? Probably not! Animals cope with wintry weather in a variety of ways. Use this cool collection of activities to enhance your study of animals in winter!

ideas by Jill Hamilton

A Cool Beginning

Begin your investigation into animals in winter with this little ditty. Students will enjoy developing motions to accompany each verse, as well as composing additional song verses. Fa-la-la!

Winter's Coming!
(sung to the tune of "Are You Sleeping?")

Winter's coming;
Winter's coming,
Little bear, little bear.
Time to take a long nap.
Time to take a long nap.
Please don't snore!
Please don't snore!

Winter's coming;
Winter's coming,
Snowshoe hare, snowshoe hare.
Time to change your fur coat.
Time to change your fur coat.
White looks nice!
White looks nice!

Winter's coming;
Winter's coming,
Tiny bird, tiny bird.
Time to migrate southward.
Time to migrate southward.
Flap your wings!
Flap your wings!

Winter's coming;
Winter's coming,
Busy squirrel, busy squirrel.
Time to gather acorns.
Time to gather acorns.
Save your food!
Save your food!

Workers	Sleepers	Tricksters
beavers	groundhogs	snowshoe hares
bees	bears	weasels
pikas	some bats	
deer	frogs	
foxes		

Outwitting Winter

How do animals outwit the most harsh season of the year? In a variety of ways! On a length of bulletin-board paper, draw a three-column chart like the one shown. Lead students to understand that "Sleepers" sleep through all or most of winter, "Tricksters" cleverly camouflage themselves for winter, and "Workers" stay busy all winter long (this category also includes migrators). As students discover how different animals cope with the cold, have them determine as a class which chart heading best describes each animal. Once a decision has been made, write the name of the animal on the chart. You can count on some lively discussions as students attempt to determine the most appropriate column for each animal they study.

The "Bear Facts"

These individual journals are the perfect place for students to record the "bear facts" about animals in winter! On construction paper duplicate student copies of the journal cover on page 184. To make a journal for each child, cut out a duplicated cover, and staple a supply of writing paper between the cut-out cover and a construction-paper back cover of equal size. Have each child personalize a journal and store it in her desk. Also display a variety of books about animals in winter at a center or in your classroom library. As students learn new facts, they write the facts in their journals. Each week set aside time for students to share with their classmates the facts they've discovered. When it's time to wind up your wintry study, students can easily *see* all that they have learned!

Lisa Kelly—Gr. 1
Wood Creek Elementary School
Farmington, MI

179

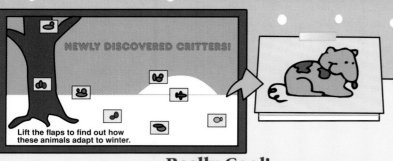

NEWLY DISCOVERED CRITTERS!

Lift the flaps to find out how these animals adapt to winter.

Really Cool!

It's amazing how animals' bodies can help them combat the cold! A *pika* stays warmer because it has a round body, short legs, and small ears. And in addition to a thick coat of fur, a pika also has fur on the bottoms of its feet for warmth! After students have investigated a variety of active winter animals, challenge them to create newly discovered animals that have their own unique ways of adapting to winter. Have each student illustrate his animal on a blank 5" x 7" card, then write how the animal copes with winter on a lined 5" x 7" card. Have each student glue his written description to a large winter scene like the one shown; then have him align his illustration over the description he wrote and use tape to secure the top edge of the illustration to the display. Students will enjoy viewing and reading about these *cool* animals with the extraordinary features!

Hibernation Know-How

Students may initially think that they'd like to *hibernate* through winter! But the thought of missing out on holiday dinners, birthday parties, and other special occasions will probably change their minds! Explain that true *hibernators* (like groundhogs, some bats and squirrels, snakes, frogs, and turtles) fall into a deep sleep and do not awaken (or eat!) until spring. Other animals, like bears and raccoons, also sleep through winter. But these animals sleep more lightly and may wake up on warm winter days and search for food.

Use this fun-to-sing song to teach students about some snoozing animals. For more frosty fun, enlist your students' help in creating additional song verses.

Wintertime Sleepers
(sung to the tune of "There's A Little White Duck")

There's a little brown bear sleeping in a cave,
A little brown bear sleeping in a cave.
He ate and he ate, and he stored up fat.
He may sleep 'til spring; just imagine that!
There's a little brown bear sleeping in a cave.
Sleep, little bear, sleep.

There's a little green frog sleeping in the mud,
A little green frog sleeping in the mud.
She swam to the bottom and she dug right in,
Deep down in the mud where she'll breathe through her skin.
There's a little green frog sleeping in the mud.
Sleep, green frog, sleep.

There's a little groundhog sleeping in a burrow,
A little groundhog sleeping in a burrow.
He crawls from his burrow and he looks around.
If he sees his shadow, he goes back underground.
There's a little groundhog sleeping in a burrow.
Sleep, groundhog, sleep.

Cynthia Payne and Robin Pranga
St. Peters, MO

Cleverly Camouflaged

What do snowshoe hares, weasels, and birds called *ptarmigans* have in common? They all stay active in winter and—turn white! This change of color allows the animals to blend in with their snowy winter surroundings. Making a sliding camouflage card, like the one shown, is a fun and effective way for a student to view this clever winter trick. Give each student a white construction-paper copy of page 182. Instruct each student to color the series of four tree trunks brown, then use brown to color the partial tree trunks and barren trees shown on the smaller card. Next instruct each student to color the remainder of the smaller card, carefully choosing his colors so that the season listed at the bottom of each illustrated column is reflected (for example, the animals would be white in winter and brown in summer). To assemble his sliding camouflage card, the student cuts on the dotted lines and weaves the smaller illustrated card through the trees as shown. By horizontally sliding his smaller card back and forth, the seasons change right before the youngster's eyes!

Peekaboo!

This peekaboo booklet project is sure to make a lasting impression on your youngsters! On the chalkboard write a student-generated list of animals that seek winter shelter underground, at the bottoms of lakes and ponds, in dens, or in caves. Give each child a white construction-paper copy of page 183 and ask him to choose one animal from the list. Then have each student illustrate the animal he chose in the blank space, describe what the animal does during winter on the writing lines, complete the title, and write his name on the provided line. Next have each student cut around his project on the bold lines. Demonstrate how to accordion-fold each end of the project (along the thin lines) as shown in the illustration. Provide assistance with this step as needed.

To make a booklet cover, have each student fold in half a 7 1/2" x 10" sheet of white construction paper, trim the corners of the paper that are not on the fold (cutting through both thicknesses), and unfold the paper. The student then illustrates a desired scene on the resulting oval shape and cuts along the center crease. To complete his peekaboo project, the student aligns and glues each resulting cover to his folded project. Peekaboo!

Elizabeth M. Chappell—Gr. 2
Altura Elementary
Aurora, CO

On The Move!

Some animals survive winter by *migrating* or "traveling to other places in search of food and warmer conditions." When spring comes, these animals return to the homes they left behind. The booklet project on pages 184 and 185 introduces students to five migrating animals. Duplicate student copies of both pages on white construction paper. Distribute page 185. Read aloud each description and invite students to speculate which animal is being described. Then distribute the animal pictures from page 184. Ask each student to color, cut out, and glue each picture in the corresponding box on page 185. To complete the project, a student personalizes the booklet cover, cuts on the dotted lines, stacks the resulting pages beneath the cover, and staples his project together.

Feeding The Birds

Your students are sure to enjoy this unique measurement and graphing project, and so will the birds! In advance nail three disposable, aluminum pie tins to a length of scrap wood (at least three feet long). You will also need three different kinds of birdseed (for example, cracked corn, millet, and black oil sunflower seeds). First ask three students to each measure one cup of a different birdseed and carefully pour the seed into an empty pie tin. Then carefully carry the resulting bird feeder outdoors. If possible position the feeder so that it can be viewed from a classroom window. Before the end of the day, retrieve the feeder and ask three different students to remove and measure the birdseed that remains in each pie tin. Then, on a graph like the one shown, indicate how much of each kind of birdseed *was eaten* that day. The following day, enlist your students' help in refilling each pie tin with one cup of seed, and repeat the process. Encourage students to observe what types of birds and other critters are nibbling on the seeds and to comment on the popularity of the different types of seeds. Continue measuring and graphing the birdseed that is eaten each day for as long as desired. However, make plans to continue feeding the birds (and other visiting critters) until nature's supply of food is once again available.

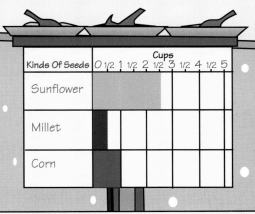

Kinds Of Seeds	Cups										
	0	1/2	1	1/2	2	1/2	3	1/2	4	1/2	5
Sunflower											
Millet											
Corn											

What About People?

As your youngsters become knowledgeable of how animals adapt to winter, they may start to wonder if they do things differently in winter too! Invite students to describe how winter changes their lives, and list their ideas on the chalkboard. Then use these ideas to make a class book titled "People In Winter." To do this, have each youngster copy a different idea from the class list onto a sheet of white construction paper. Then ask each child to illustrate the idea she copied, suggesting that she include herself in her illustration. If Old Man Winter usually brings snow to your area, have students repeatedly dip the eraser ends of their pencils in white tempera paint and dab a flurry of flakes atop their projects. Laminate the completed book pages for durability; then bind them between two student-decorated covers. Display the resulting book in your class library for all to enjoy.

Name _____

Cleverly Camouflaged Critters

(winter)   (summer)   (winter)   (summer)   (winter)   (summer)

Note To Teacher: Use with "Cleverly Camouflaged" on page 180.

A _____

In Winter

by _____

©The Education Center, Inc. • *THE MAILBOX*® • *Primary* • Dec/Jan 1997–98

Journal Cover And Picture Cards

Use the journal cover with "The 'Bear Facts' " on page 179.

The "Bear Facts" About Animals In Winter

Name _____

Use the picture cards with "On The Move!" on pages 181 and 185.

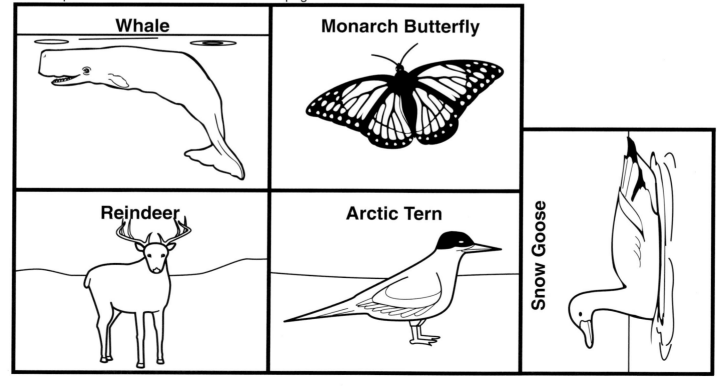

Whale

Monarch Butterfly

Reindeer

Arctic Tern

Snow Goose

Name _____

On The Move!

©1997 The Education Center, Inc.

Glue picture here.

In the winter my food is covered with snow. I must migrate to places where I can find food to eat.

Glue picture here.

I migrate farther than any other bird. I live near the North Pole. Each winter I fly to the South Pole.

Glue picture here.

Snow is part of my name but I still get cold! When winter comes, I fly south to warmer areas.

Glue picture here.

Each fall I gather with many other butterflies just like me. Then we fly south for the winter.

Glue picture here.

My home gets cold in the winter. Sometimes it even freezes! Every winter I swim to warmer waters.

Note To Teacher: Use with "On The Move!" on page 181 and the picture cards on page 184.

A Pocketful Of Science

A Look At Light

Brighten up an investigation of light with these hands-on activities!

ideas contributed by Darcy Brown and Ann Flagg

Activity 1: Straight As An Arrow

You will need:
a flashlight
a piece of chalk
a chalkboard
a candle
matches

Each student will need:
a construction-paper circle
tape
a craft stick
access to a hole puncher

What to do:
From a distance of about five feet, point the flashlight at the chalkboard. Have a volunteer draw a large X on the chalkboard to show where he thinks the flashlight beam will hit. Then turn on the flashlight and discuss the results. Repeat the activity, changing the flashlight angle each time.

Questions to ask:
1. What did you discover about how light travels?
2. Do you think light always travels in a straight line?

Next:
Have each student hole-punch the circle and tape it to the craft stick as shown. Position the candle in plain view; then light it. Dim the room. Ask each student to view the flame by peeking through the hole. Next have each student place his hand between the hole and the flame.

Questions to ask:
1. When could you see (not see) the light? Why?

This is why:

Light travels in a straight line when nothing is in its way. When the light was blocked, it stopped traveling forward. Objects that block light are called opaque.

Activity 2: Following Light

Each small group of students needs:
a container that holds
— three opaque objects that reflect light
— three opaque objects that *do not* reflect light
— a scrap of used laminating film

What to do:
Divide students into small groups and give each group a container of objects. Remind students that they are studying how light travels. Have each group remove its objects and find one object that is different from all the rest.

Questions to ask:
1. Which object is different from all the rest? Why?
2. How are the rest of the objects alike?

Next:
Tell students to set the scrap of laminating film aside, then sort the remaining opaque objects into two groups: those that reflect light and those that do not.

Questions to ask:
1. How can you tell if an object reflects light?
2. How are the objects that reflect light alike?

This is why:

The laminating film is different from the rest of the objects because light passes through it. When light meets an opaque surface, it is reflected or absorbed—or a combination of both. If the surface of an opaque object is rough, any light that is reflected will bounce off in many directions and be very hard to see. But if the surface of an opaque object is smooth and shiny, the light bounces off in just one direction and forms a reflection. A reflection *is an image formed by reflected light.*

Activity 3:
Just Passing Through

Each small group of students needs:
a container of transparent and translucent objects

What to do:
Divide students into small groups and give each group a container of objects. Remind students that they are studying how light travels. Then have each group sort its objects into two like groups.

Questions to ask:
1. How did you sort your objects? Why?

This is why:

Some materials reflect or absorb very little light. Instead they let almost all the light pass through. These objects—like air, water, glass, clear plastic, and used laminating film—are *transparent*, *meaning you can see through them. Some materials are* translucent, *meaning they let some light through. Thin paper (tissue, facial, and waxed), lamp shades, and clouds are examples of translucent objects. You can't really see through them, but you can easily see the light behind them.*

Activity 4:
A Light Trick

Each student will need:
a clear plastic cup
a 6" length of pipe cleaner
water

What to do:
Have each student partially fill her cup with water, then place the pipe cleaner in the cup. Instruct her to bend down and observe the pipe cleaner through the side of the cup.

Questions to ask:
1. How does the appearance of the pipe cleaner change?
2. Do you think the water changed the position of the pipe cleaner? Why or why not?

This is why:

Light travels easily through air because air particles are not very close together. Light cannot travel through water as quickly because its particles are denser. The pipe cleaner appears to be broken because the speed of light changes where the air and water meet. When light passes through a meeting point between two substances (in this case air and water), the change of light speed causes the light rays to change direction. This occurrence is called *refraction.*

Activity 5:
Another Light Trick

You will need:
a penny
clear tape
a shallow, opaque bowl
a table
a pitcher of water

What to do:
Tape the penny in the bottom of the bowl and set the bowl on the table. Invite a small group of students to gather around the table. Ask the students to look steadily at the coin as they carefully step backwards. As soon as they can no longer see the coin, they should stand perfectly still. Then slowly pour water into the bowl. Repeat the demonstration until each student has seen it.

Questions to ask:
1. What did you see?
2. How do you know the penny did not move?

This is why:

The penny could not have moved because it is taped in place. The penny appears to move because when water is poured into the bowl, the light refracts, or changes direction. This makes the penny that was out of sight, suddenly visible. (See the diagram below.)

The Sensational Six
Hands-On Activities For The Food Guide Pyramid

March is National Nutrition Month®, so why not enhance your nutrition unit by serving up a hearty helping of these appetizing Food Guide Pyramid activities? They're the perfect recipe to make your youngsters sizzle with nutritional information and beg for seconds!

ideas by Jill Hamilton and Lisa Kelly

Did You Know?

The U.S. Department of Agriculture developed the Food Guide Pyramid to encourage people to improve their diets. It is based on the USDA's research on what foods Americans eat, what nutrients are in these foods, and how to make the best food choices. The Pyramid is an outline of what to eat each day. A range of servings is provided for each major food group. It is not always necessary to eat the maximum servings suggested. The number of servings that a person needs depends on how many calories her body requires. Almost everyone should have at least the lowest number of servings in each range.

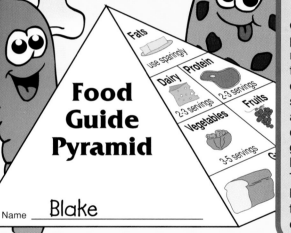

Food Guide Pyramid

Fats use sparingly

Dairy 2-3 servings

Protein 2-3 servings

Vegetables 3-5 servings

Fruits

Name Blake

Personal Pyramids

Get to the point of the Food Guide Pyramid with the three-dimensional project on page 193. Distribute a white construction-paper copy of the Pyramid pattern to each student. As a class, read each food group and the number of recommended servings; then enlist students' help in naming foods from each group. If desired, have students illustrate one food per group. Explain to students that the foundation of the Pyramid—*bread, cereal, pasta, and rice*—should constitute the basis of our diets. Foods at the top of the Pyramid should be eaten proportionately less. When all six groups have been discussed, each student finishes personalizing his Pyramid by completing each sentence and adding his name. Then he cuts out the pattern on the bold lines, folds on the dotted lines, and tapes the tab inside the Pyramid. Encourage students to display their Pyramids on their desks and use them as references during other nutrition activities.

Name

Collect All The Servings!

Gameboard

= one serving

Fats very few servings

Dairy 2–3 servings

Protein 2–3 servings

Vegetables 3–5 servings

Fruits 2–4 servings

Grains

Collecting Servings!

Students will be chomping at the bit to play this self-made center game! To make the game, divide students into six groups and assign each group a different food category. Distribute a stack of discarded magazines, a supply of blank index cards, glue, and scissors to each group. Instruct students to cut out food pictures that represent their assigned categories and glue them on individual index cards. Collect the cards and program the back of each one with the corresponding food group. Laminate the cards for durability; then store them in a decorated lunch bag. Place the bag, crayons, and a class supply of the gameboard (page 194) at a center.

To play the game, each student needs a gameboard. One player removes the food cards, shuffles them, and places them back in the bag. Each player, in turn, draws a card and identifies its food category; then she flips the card to check her answer. If the player is correct, she colors one serving in that category on her gameboard. The student then places the card in a discard pile. If a player gives a correct answer but all the circles for that category are colored, her turn is over. The first player to color all the circles—or servings—on her gameboard wins!

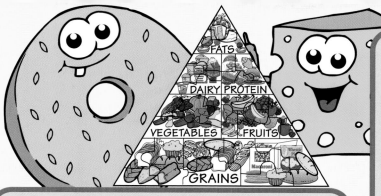

The Fabulous Five

Each of the five major food groups shown on the Pyramid provides nutrients that are needed for maintaining good health. The foods in the sixth group—*fats, oils, and sweets*—are needed for a balanced diet, but contain fewer essential nutrients. After sharing the nutrition notes shown with your students, assign a different food group to each of five student teams. Instruct each team to design a colorful poster that promotes the benefits of eating foods from its assigned food group. Provide the teams with white poster board or tagboard, construction paper, markers, and other poster-making supplies. Set aside time for each team to present its poster and talk about the benefits that its food group can provide. Then display the appetizing projects in the school hallway so others can view the benefits of eating a varied diet.

Pyramid Puzzle

Take the puzzle out of the Food Guide Pyramid with this center activity. Cut a large triangle from poster board. Divide the triangle into six sections to resemble the Food Guide Pyramid; then label each section with its corresponding food group. Enlist students' help in cutting food pictures from discarded magazines. Then glue each picture to its corresponding food group on the Pyramid. Laminate the Pyramid for durability before cutting it into puzzle pieces. Store the puzzle in a resealable plastic bag at a center for hands-on exploration. Encourage students who especially enjoy putting together the class puzzle to make their own Food Guide Pyramid puzzles.

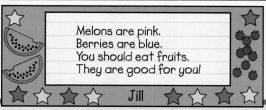

Melons are pink.
Berries are blue.
You should eat fruits.
They are good for you!

Jill

Poetry Placemats

Writing poems about the Food Guide Pyramid is twice as much fun when the poems become placemats! Set the mood by reading aloud a few of your favorite food-related poems. (*Food Fight: Poets Join The Fight Against Hunger With Poems To Favorite Foods* edited by Michael J. Rosen [Harcourt Brace & Company, 1996] is a delightfully entertaining collection of food poems.) Then display sample formats like the ones shown below for students to use as they write their poems. To make a placemat, a student glues her written work to a 12" x 18" sheet of colorful construction paper and adds desired decorations. Laminate the projects for durability. Set aside time for each student to share her prose before she takes her placemat home. Time to set the table!

Nutrition Notes

Grains
- provide the carbohydrates, a body's main source of fuel
- provide B vitamins that are necessary for normal growth
- provide fiber for good digestion
- provide minerals needed for bone formation

Fruits And Vegetables
- provide vitamin A that is necessary for tissue growth and good vision
- provide vitamin C that is necessary for healing and for healthy bones, teeth, and skin
- provide fiber that helps in the digestion process
- provide vitamin E that helps maintain cell membranes

Dairy Products
- provide proteins needed for cell growth and maintenance
- provide minerals needed for bone formation
- provide vitamins that help in digestion and using energy efficiently
- provide calcium that is needed for bone growth and development, muscles, and blood clotting

Protein Foods
- provide building materials of the body called *amino acids*
- aid tissue growth and the maintenance of cells
- provide energy-producing B vitamins
- provide minerals, like iron, that help the blood provide the tissues with oxygen and prevent anemia

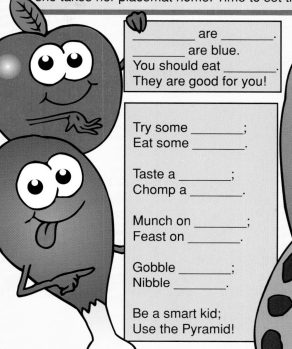

_____ are _____.
_____ are blue.
You should eat _____.
They are good for you!

Try some _____;
Eat some _____.

Taste a _____;
Chomp a _____.

Munch on _____;
Feast on _____.

Gobble _____;
Nibble _____.

Be a smart kid;
Use the Pyramid!

189

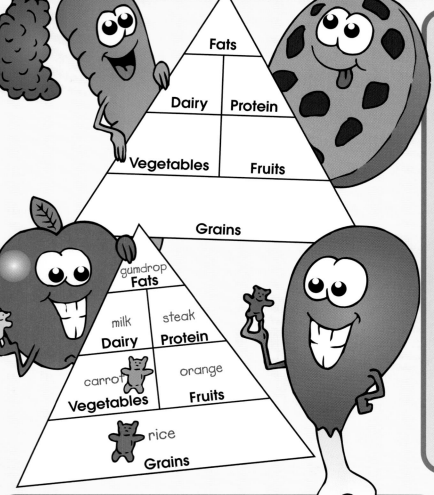

A Ravenous Creature

Set the stage for this nutrition letter-writing activity with an oral reading of "Hungry Mungry" from Shel Silverstein's poetry collection *Where The Sidewalk Ends* (HarperCollins Children's Books, 1974). Hungry Mungry is a child who will eat anything in sight: his extremely large dinner, his parents, the U.S. Army, the universe, and even himself! At the conclusion of this poem, list the *foods* Hungry Mungry ate for dinner on the chalkboard. Ask student volunteers to mark through the unhealthful foods on the list. Then have each student write a letter to Hungry Mungry encouraging him to eat a healthful, balanced diet. Remind students to tell him about the Food Guide Pyramid too. After students complete the letters, mount them on a bulletin board titled "Eat Up This Advice, Hungry Mungry!"

Tasty Lotto

This Food Guide Pyramid game is sure to satisfy your students' appetite for reviewing the food groups. Write a student-generated list of healthful foods on the chalkboard—one food per student. (Be sure foods from each food group are included.) Have each student select a different food from the list, then write its name on one side of an index card and two clues describing it on the other side. Ask that one clue refer to the Food Guide Pyramid. Collect the completed cards and place them in a container. Next give each child a Pyramid-shaped lotto board like the one shown. Instruct him to program each section with a corresponding food from the chalkboard. Also give each student six small, edible snacks to use as markers.

To play the game, draw a food card from the container and read the clues aloud, taking care not to reveal the answer on the back of the card. If a student has this food on his gameboard, he covers it. The first student to cover all his foods announces, "I'm full!" Then he verifies the covered foods by naming them. If time permits have the winning student call the second game. When game time is over, collect the lotto boards for later use and invite students to eat their game markers.

Appetizing Riddles

Add a touch of creative thinking to your Food Guide Pyramid activities with this riddle-writing project. For each student cut a triangle from the front cover of a folded 9" x 12" sheet of white construction paper (see the illustration). To begin, read aloud a food-related riddle book, like *What Am I?: Looking Through Shapes At Apples And Grapes* by N. N. Charles (The Blue Sky Press, 1994), for writing inspiration. Then challenge each student to create a riddle that includes a reference to a food group. Next the child copies his riddle on the front of his construction-paper card. Inside the card he illustrates the answer, making sure that when the card is closed, part of his illustration is seen through the cutout. Allow time for students to share their food riddles with their classmates. If desired, bind the riddles into a class book titled "Food For Thought." Place the book in your classroom library for all to enjoy!

I am sweet.
I have seeds.
I am in the vegetable group.

What am I?

watermelon

Layers Of Nutritional Learning

These student-made Pyramid booklets provide layers of learning! After a student has made his booklet (see the booklet-making instructions), he labels its layers as shown. Then, on each resulting page, he writes and illustrates facts about the corresponding food group. In no time at all, students will be flipping over their unique booklets *and* the Food Guide Pyramid!

To make a layered, Pyramid-shaped booklet:
1. Create one triangle template in each size shown.

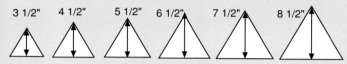

3 1/2"   4 1/2"   5 1/2"   6 1/2"   7 1/2"   8 1/2"

2. On a sheet of 8 1/2" x 11" paper, trace the following triangles: 3 1/2", 5 1/2", 6 1/2".
3. On another sheet of 8 1/2" x 11" paper, trace the following triangles: 7 1/2" and 4 1/2".
4. On a third sheet of 8 1/2" x 11" paper, trace the following triangle: 8 1/2".
5. Cut out each triangle shape.
6. Incrementally stack the cutouts so that the largest triangle is on the bottom and the smallest one is on top. Staple at the top.

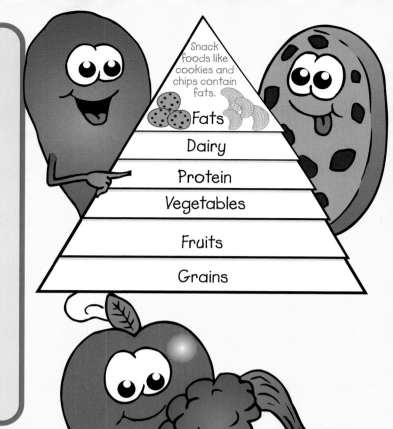

Snack foods like cookies and chips contain fats.

Fats
Dairy
Protein
Vegetables
Fruits
Grains

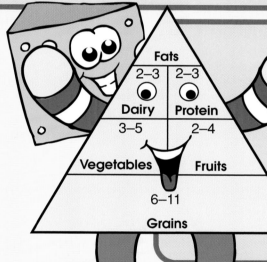

Fats
2–3   2–3
Dairy   Protein
3–5   2–4
Vegetables   Fruits
6–11
Grains

Pyramid Pals

Looking for a unique way for students to promote the Food Guide Pyramid at home? These nifty refrigerator magnets will do the trick! On tagboard duplicate a class supply of the Pyramid patterns on page 192. Have each student color and cut out one pattern; then laminate the cutouts for durability. Next have each student attach a self-adhesive magnet to the back of his cutout. Wiggle eyes can be glued to the front if desired. Encourage students to post their Pyramid pals on their families' refrigerators. No doubt these adorable pals will serve as positive reminders and attract your youngsters to healthful foods!

Nutritious Nibbling

Now that your youngsters have built up an appetite, treat them to a Food Pyramid kebob. This tasty treat reinforces the Pyramid's six groups and their serving sizes. It's a great way to top off your Food Guide Pyramid unit! Because the recipe requires several food items, ask parent volunteers to contribute some of the ingredients if desired. To make a Food Pyramid kebob, slide one of each of these foods onto a shish-kebob skewer in the following order: French bread slice, apple slice, cucumber slice, ham cube, cheese cube, and marshmallow. There you have it: nutrition on a stick!

What A Web Site!

If you have access to the Internet, be sure to check out the web site—http://www.usda.gov/fcs/cnpp.htm—posted by the U.S. Department of Agriculture. This site features information about the Food Guide Pyramid, dietary guidelines, and a resource for nutrition educators. Now that's a site to see!

A Hearty Helping Of Nutritious Literature
Nourish your students' need for literature with servings of these delectable books!

The Edible Pyramid: Good Eating Every Day
Written & Illustrated by Loreen Leedy
Holiday House, Inc.; 1996

Welcome your students to The Edible Pyramid, a restaurant that specializes in delicious and nutritious meals. Using the Food Guide Pyramid, the customers learn the healthful way to eat.

What Food Is This?
Written & Photographed by Rosmarie Hausherr
Scholastic Inc., 1994

In this informative book, questions about particular foods are answered, and basic nutrition is reviewed. There is also a section in the back of the book detailing the Food Guide Pyramid.

This Is The Way We Eat Our Lunch: A Book About Children Around The World
Written by Edith Baer & Illustrated by Steve Björkman
Scholastic Inc., 1995

The lively rhymes in this colorful book take readers on a trip around the world to sample the different kinds of foods that children have for lunch.

The Vegetable Show
Written & Illustrated by Laurie Krasny Brown
Little, Brown and Company; 1995

Escort your students to the Garden Street Theater to see the Greatest Greenest Show on Earth: *The Vegetable Show.* Top performers include String Beanie, Bud the Spud, and Lotta Root.

Oliver's Vegetables
Written by Vivian French & Illustrated by Alison Bartlett
Orchard Books, 1996

While visiting his grandpa who has a wonderful garden, a little boy discovers that life exists beyond french fries.

The Seven Silly Eaters
Written by Mary Ann Hoberman
Illustrated by Marla Frazee
Harcourt Brace & Company, 1997

Each new baby in the Peters household is a fussier eater than the previous one. So what is a mother to do? She's not sure until her children give her a birthday present that solves her problems perfectly!

Patterns
Use with "Pyramid Pals" on page 191. Each child needs one pattern.

Fats
2–3 Dairy
2–3 Protein
3–5 Vegetables
2–4 Fruits
6–11 Grains

Fats
2–3 Dairy
2–3 Protein
3–5 Vegetables
2–4 Fruits
6–11 Grains

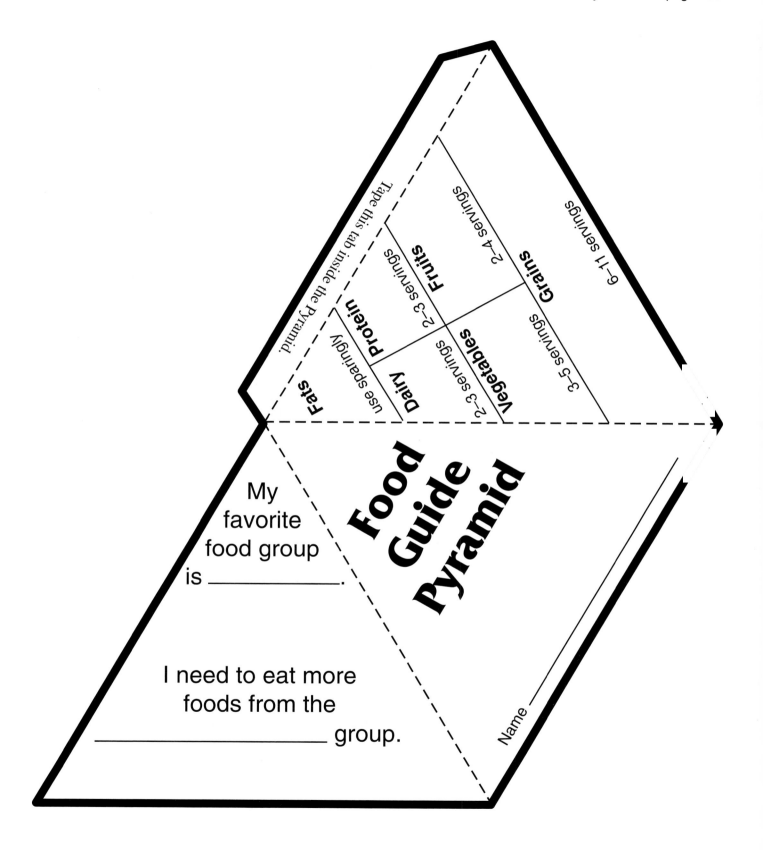

Tape this tab inside the Pyramid

Grains
6–11 servings

Fruits
2–4 servings

Protein
2–3 servings

Vegetables
3–5 servings

Dairy
2–3 servings

Fats
use sparingly

Food Guide Pyramid

My favorite food group is _____.

I need to eat more foods from the _____ group.

Name _____

Collect All The Servings!

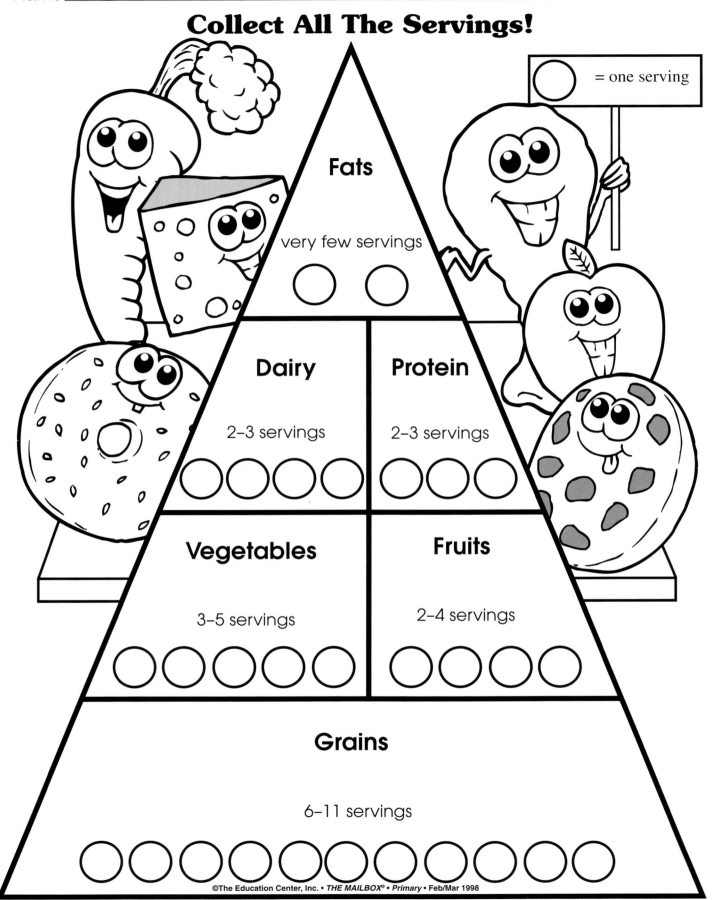

= one serving

Fats

very few servings

○ ○

Dairy

2–3 servings

○ ○ ○ ○

Protein

2–3 servings

○ ○ ○

Vegetables

3–5 servings

○ ○ ○ ○ ○

Fruits

2–4 servings

○ ○ ○ ○

Grains

6–11 servings

○ ○ ○ ○ ○ ○ ○ ○ ○ ○ ○

©The Education Center, Inc. • *THE MAILBOX* • *Primary* • Feb/Mar 1998

Note To Teacher: Use with "Collecting Servings!" on page 188.

Name _____

My Nutrition Notes

Keep a record of what you eat each day.
Draw a tally mark for each serving.

Week Of: _____

Food Group	Monday	Tuesday	Wednesday	Thursday	Friday
Grains 6–11 servings					
Vegetables 3–5 servings					
Fruits 2–4 servings					
Dairy 2–3 servings					
Protein 2–3 servings					
Fats, Oils, And Sweets Use sparingly.					
	◯	◯	◯	◯	◯

How did you do?
Use the Code Box.
Draw a symbol in the circle each day.

Code Box
☆ = I ate the correct number of servings in each food group.
☺ = I ate at least one serving in each food group.
 = I did not eat at least one serving in each food group.

195

Life-Cycle Cards

Use with "Cycles Of Life" on page 201.

Honeybee	Penguin	Ladybug	Spider
pupa	chick	egg	young spider
egg	young penguin	adult	egg
adult	egg	larva	adult
larva	adult	pupa	spiderling

A Circle Of Change

Investigating The Life Cycle

What do humans, maple trees, spiders, and killer whales all have in common? Each has—as does every living organism—a cycle of life. Use this creative collection of activities and reproducibles, along with the centerfold, to investigate the life cycles of several different species.

ideas contributed by Judi Butler, Kathy D. Coffey, Jill Hamilton, Lisa Kelly, Mary Ann Lewis, and Sharon Murphy

The Human Life Cycle

Introduce life cycles with the species your students know best—humans! To begin, review the four stages of the human life cycle—*baby, child* or *teen, adult,* and *senior citizen.* Also plan to read aloud a picture book that illustrates the four stages of human life. (*When Artie Was Little* by Harriet Berg Schwartz [Alfred A. Knopf, Inc.; 1996] is an excellent choice.) Then have each student interview a senior citizen to learn something about each stage of the senior's life. If desired distribute interview questions for students to use. (Encourage younger students to enlist the seniors' help in recording their responses.) Then have each student use the information he has gathered to illustrate the senior citizen's life cycle. To do this, a student folds a sheet of drawing paper into fourths, unfolds it, and labels each section with one of the four life-cycle stages. Then in each section he describes and illustrates an event for that stage of the senior's life. When the projects have been completed, set aside time for students to share their work.

Personalized Wheels

After reviewing the human life cycle, students will be eager to create personalized life-cycle wheels. Ask each student to bring to school a baby photo and a current photo. Duplicate the snapshots before returning them to your students to take home.

To make a life-cycle wheel, each student uses a pencil and ruler to divide each of two paper plates into four equal sections. To make the wheel portion, a student labels the top-right quadrant of one plate "Baby" and glues her baby photo there. Then she rotates the plate one-quarter turn clockwise, labels the top-right quadrant "Child," and glues her current photo there. In a similar manner, she labels the next quadrant "Adult" and illustrates herself as an adult engaged in a desired career. Then she labels the final quadrant "Senior Citizen" and illustrates herself enjoying this stage of life. To make the wheel cover, the student draws a large dot in the center of the second plate where the four lines intersect. Next she cuts away one plate section—leaving the dot intact. She erases the remaining pencil marks and personalizes the plate as desired. Then, using a brad, the student attaches the wheel cover atop the wheel. To share her project with friends and family members, she turns the bottom plate clockwise.

Investigating Butterfly Metamorphosis

From egg to caterpillar to chrysalis to adult, the complete metamorphosis of a butterfly is more than fascinating. Use the following activities to bring to life the four stages of a butterfly's life cycle. Student excitement is sure to soar!

Raising Butterflies

To give your students an opportunity to see firsthand one of nature's most amazing transformations, order a Raise-A-Butterfly kit from Carolina Biological Supply Company (1-800-334-5551). The kit, priced at $19.98, contains five larvae, culture medium, a plastic cage, water and food vials, a climbing mat, and instructions. After setting up the kit, provide students with journals to chronicle the changes they witness.

The Makings Of A Monarch Butterfly

Use these art activities to further extend your students' knowledge of each stage of a butterfly's life cycle. For the best results, complete one art project on each of four different days. Students will be all aflutter over the resulting projects!

Egg: A butterfly's life cycle begins when a female butterfly deposits an egg on the underside of a leaf. Have each student cut out a large leaf shape from green bulletin-board paper and tape a small Styrofoam®-packing-piece egg to the underside of it.

Caterpillar: When a caterpillar, or *larva,* hatches from the egg, the second stage of life begins. The hungry caterpillar munches on the leaf and quickly outgrows its skin. This process, called *molting,* occurs four or five times. To represent this stage of life, have each student create a caterpillar. To do this a student glues together several slightly overlapped black, yellow, and white construction-paper circles; then she glues wiggle eyes and black pipe-cleaner antennae in place. Next she removes the egg from her leaf and punches or cuts several holes in the foliage before she tapes her caterpillar to the cutout. Munch! Munch!

Chrysalis: The third stage of life begins when the caterpillar stops eating and attaches itself to a twig or leaf. Soon its skin molts for the final time and a *chrysalis* (or *pupa*) is exposed. While in the chrysalis, the caterpillar's cells are rearranged and the body structure of an adult butterfly begins to take shape. By the time the butterfly is ready to hatch, the pupa has become translucent. To demonstrate this life-cycle stage, cut two chrysalis shapes from waxed paper for each student. Align both shapes and hole-punch the edges as shown. A student uses a length of yarn to carefully lace the two cutouts together; then she tucks crumpled pieces of black and orange tissue paper inside the project to illustrate the translucent appearance of the chrysalis.

Adult: When a monarch butterfly emerges from the chrysalis, the metamorphosis is complete. To illustrate this final stage, have each student paint a row of six egg-carton cups black for her butterfly's body. To make wings, a student uses black, yellow, and white tempera paint to sponge-paint a 15" x 20" piece of orange tissue paper. When the paint is dry, she gathers together the middle section of the tissue paper to form the wings, secures the paper with a twist-tie, and glues it to the body. Then she inserts two pipe-cleaner antennae.

The Chicken Or The Egg?

So which came first—the chicken or the egg? Crack open the mystery of a chicken's life cycle with this "egg-cellent" project. After a review of the chicken's life cycle, have each student make a fold-out booklet like the one shown. To begin, a student makes three accordion folds in a 5" x 20" strip of white bulletin-board paper to create a five-inch-square booklet. He opens the booklet and writes "The Life Cycle Of A Chicken" and his name on the first page. Then, on the bottom half of each of the next three booklet pages, he describes in sequential order the life-cycle stages of a chicken. He illustrates each stage on the top half of its page. To create the booklet's cover, he glues in place a red construction-paper comb and a yellow construction-paper beak, then uses a crayon to draw eyes. To complete the project, the student tapes a yellow or white craft feather to the back of the booklet. Students will be chirping to share these adorable booklets with their families and friends!

A baby chick hatches from the egg. When it dries off it has short, fluffy, yellow feathers. It can walk, see, eat, and drink.

An adult chicken has a red comb on its head and a red wattle. It has earlobes, too!

Chicken Life Cycle

Stage 1: A hen lays an egg.

Stage 2: A baby chick uses its beak to hatch from the egg. Its damp body dries quickly, leaving it with short, fluffy, yellow feathers called *down*. The chick can walk, see, eat, and drink.

Stage 3: A full-grown or adult chicken has feathers, a comb, a wattle, and earlobes.

From Egg To Alligator

This nifty project reinforces the life cycle of the biggest and most clever of reptiles—the alligator. Share information about an alligator's life cycle. (In addition to the information provided, *The Alligator* by Sabrina Crewe [Steck-Vaughn Company, 1998] is also an excellent resource.) Then have students create a mobile that features an alligator's life cycle. To begin, a student glues four craft sticks to four 4 1/2" poster-board circles to form a diamond shape. While the glue is drying, she colors and cuts out a set of the alligator life-cycle cards found on page 203. She then turns over the diamond shape and numbers the circles clockwise starting at the top (see the illustration). Next she glues the card that shows the first stage of the life cycle in circle 1; then she flips the project and writes a sentence on the back of the circle that describes the stage. She continues in this manner with the three remaining stages. For an informative gator display, hole-punch the top circle of each completed project. Thread a length of yarn through each hole and tie the yarn ends. Then suspend the mobiles throughout the classroom.

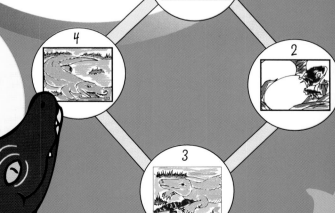

Alligator Life Cycle

Stage 1: The female alligator makes a nest near the edge of the water. After laying her eggs in the nest, she covers them with leaves and twigs.

Stage 2: About two months later, baby alligators hatch from the eggs. They call for help from inside the nest, and the mother alligator uncovers them. They are only nine inches long and they have black bodies with pale yellow stripes.

Stage 3: Baby alligators can swim right away. They live along a mudbank and stay close to their mother until they are two or three. They prey mostly on animals that live in the water.

Stage 4: As an alligator gets older, its stripes fade. Alligators are mature at about six years of age. They continue to grow throughout their lives.

What A Change!

Leapin' lily pads! After a review of the frog's life cycle, be sure to make these individual tachistoscopes with your students! Use the pattern on page 202 to duplicate a class set of tagboard lily pads. On white construction paper, duplicate a class set of the life-cycle cards on page 202 and the tachistoscope strip from page 203. Use an X-acto® knife to slit the dotted lines on each lily pad; then distribute the materials.

To make a lily-pad tachistoscope, a student colors his lily-pad pattern and life-cycle cards; then he cuts out the lily pad, the strip, and the cards. Next he glues the cards in sequential order on the strip and inserts the strip into the lily pad. To make a blossom for the lily pad, he folds a 3 1/2" white circle in half four times before trimming it as shown. Then he unfolds the blossom and glues it to the pad. To use his tachistoscope, the student moves the strip to view the different stages of the frog's life cycle.

Frog Life Cycle

Stage 1: A female frog lays hundreds of eggs.

Stage 2: A tadpole hatches within 3 to 25 days. Hind legs develop on the tadpole. The tadpole's lungs begin to develop and its front legs appear. The tadpole loses its gills and a tiny frog, still bearing a stump of a tail, emerges from the water.

Stage 3: The frog absorbs its tail and can now live out of water.

Watch It Grow

This activity will have your youngsters sprouting new knowledge about the life cycle of a bean plant. Soak a class supply of lima beans (plus a few extras) in water overnight. The following day have each child partially fill a personalized, clear plastic cup with potting soil and plant a soaked bean seed very close to the side of his cup. (Plant the extra seeds in case some students' seeds do not germinate.) Then challenge each student to document the stages of his bean's life cycle with this timeline project. You will need a supply of duplicated timeline cards like the ones shown. To begin the project, have each child document the planting of his bean seed on a timeline card. To do this he writes the date and a brief description of the event on the top half of the card; then he illustrates the event on the bottom half. Give each child a letter-size envelope in which to store this card and future ones. Explain to students that during the next two to three weeks, they must remember to do two things: to lightly water or mist their seed cups so that the soil stays moist, but is not soaked; and to record on individual timeline cards the changes they observe in their seed cups.

When it's time to assemble the timeline projects, a student sequences an even number of timeline cards and glues them along a length of yarn—leaving extra yarn at both ends of the project. Next he glues construction-paper lima-bean cutouts to the backs of the first and the last cards. When the glue is dry, he accordion-folds the resulting booklet. To complete the project, he writes "The Life Cycle Of A Bean Plant" and his name on the front cover; then he fashions a bow from the yarn ends. Now that's a project worth blooming about!

Plant Life Cycle

Stage 1: The seed splits and the primary root is formed.

Stage 2: As the primary root grows downward, the stem breaks through the soil. Additional roots grow from the primary root.

Stage 3: The seed coat drops off.

Stage 4: As the stem grows upward, leaves form.

April 13: I planted a bean seed. I set the cup by the window.

The Life Cycle Of A Bean Plant

By Taran

Uncovering Life Cycles

This flip book is the perfect follow-up to any life-cycle investigation. Ask students to recall what they've learned, and list their ideas on the chalkboard. Then have each student use the information to make a life-cycle flip book. To make a book illustrating a four-stage life cycle, a student folds a 12" x 18" sheet of drawing paper in half (to 6" x 18") and makes three equally spaced cuts in the top layer. Then she sequentially labels and illustrates the four resulting flaps with the stages of the life cycle being reviewed. Under each flap she writes a brief description of the stage. You can adapt the project to different life cycles by increasing or decreasing the number of flaps. What an easy way for students to show their newfound knowledge of a life cycle!

egg

baby

The young trout called a parr, develops black stripes on its body.

adult

Books For The Teacher

Life Cycles Of A Dozen Diverse Creatures
Written by Paul Fleisher
Includes photographs
The Millbrook Press, Inc.; 1996

An Extraordinary Life: The Story Of A Monarch Butterfly
Written by Laurence Pringle
Illustrated by Bob Marstall
Orchard Books, 1997

Cycles Of Life

Challenge your youngsters' life-cycle savvy with this activity. Duplicate student copies of the life-cycle cards on page 196. Instruct students to color and cut out one strip of cards at a time, stack the cards in sequential order beginning with the title card, and then staple the card stack to a 3" x 12" construction-paper strip as shown. Have students continue in this manner until each strip of cards has been sequenced and stapled to the construction-paper strip. Encourage students to use their completed projects to impress their family members with their knowledge of life cycles.

Frog

Life Cycles

Spider

Penguin

201

Patterns

Use with "What A Change!" on page 200.

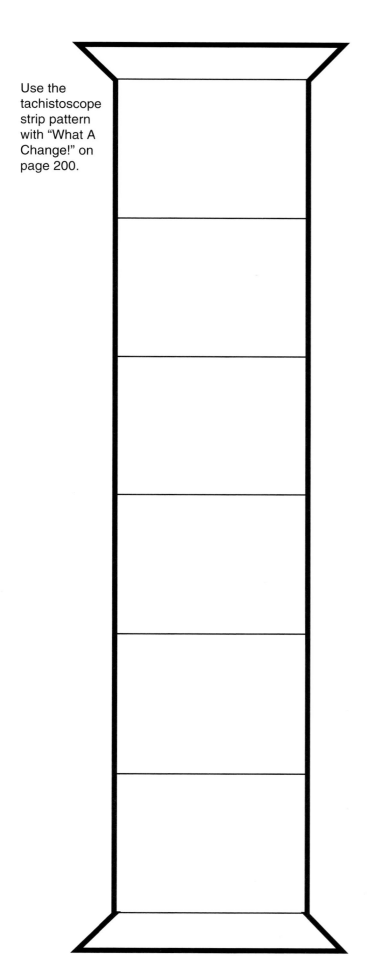

Use the tachistoscope strip pattern with "What A Change!" on page 200.

Use the alligator life-cycle cards with "From Egg To Alligator" on page 199.

Cities Under The Sea

Make a splash with this tropical collection of coral reef activities. It's an underwater investigation your students won't soon forget!

Discovering

ideas contributed by Susan Baldwin, Michele Converse Baerns, and Charles J. Wohl

Taking The Plunge

Dive into your study of coral reefs with this class graphing activity. Trim the top of a length of blue bulletin-board paper to resemble waves; then mount the paper on a bulletin board or wall. Label each of several sentence strips with the name of a unique coral reef animal: parrot fish, brain coral, octopus, clown fish, moray eel, crown-of-thorns starfish, etc. Next have each child write his name along the bottom edge of a three-inch square, then illustrate himself in the remaining space. Ask each student to study the animal names on display and determine which one sounds most interesting; then assist each child in taping or stapling his picture alongside his preferred creature. When each child's picture is displayed, use the resulting graph as a springboard for a variety of questions like "Which creature was preferred the most?", "How many more students chose the clown fish than the parrot fish?", "What do you think a brain coral is?", and so on. Then tell students that these intriguing creatures—and plenty more—live in undersea communities called coral reefs.

Leave the graph on display, and, if desired, cut out and label a large paper circle (bubble) for each animal posted. As students uncover facts about each creature, invite the students who were most interested in the creature to write the facts on the corresponding bubble.

Where In The World?

Coral reefs are often called the tropical rain forests of the sea because they are so colorful and full of life. In fact, more types of undersea creatures live in coral reefs than anywhere else in the ocean! Here's a fun way for students to brush up on their mapping skills as they discover where the coral reefs of the world lie. Give each child a copy of the world map on page 208 and a one-foot length of red yarn. Display a large world map for student reference and ask students to complete the following map-related tasks: label each of the continents, label each of the oceans, and complete the compass rose. Then have each student color his map by using the map key. Explain that the shaded areas on the map indicate coral reefs. When the maps are colored, instruct each child to glue his length of red yarn along the equator, trimming the yarn ends as needed.

Allow time for students to study the completed maps; then help them conclude that coral reefs lie near the equator in the world's tropical waters.

Revealing Reefs

Your students may be surprised to discover that coral reefs grow in three basic formations: *fringing reefs, barrier reefs,* and *atolls.* For a fun hands-on activity, have students shape the different types of reefs from clay. Each child will need a paper plate on which to work and a ball of modeling clay in each of the following colors: blue (water), yellow (land), and red (coral reef).

To shape a *fringing reef,* a student uses yellow clay to shape a section of land on his paper plate; then, along the land's shoreline, he attaches a red-clay coral reef. Explain that fringing reefs grow outward from the shoreline. To shape a *barrier reef,* the student begins with a section of land; then he attaches a blue-clay lagoon along the shoreline, followed by a red-clay coral reef. Explain that a barrier reef is separated from land by a lagoon. And to shape an *atoll,* a student shapes a circular blue-clay lagoon; then he adds a ring of coral around the lagoon and surrounds it with blue-clay water. Explain that an atoll is a ring of coral far out in the ocean that has a sunken island or volcano beneath it.

204

Coral Reefs

anemone

sea slug

parrot fish

Sing A Song Of Coral

After investigating coral polyps, the tiny animals that build the reefs, students will enjoy learning this catchy adaptation of "Sing A Song Of Sixpence." If desired have students begin in a squatting position and perform the provided movements for each song line.

Sing a song of coral,
Slowly stand up and extend arms upward.

Swaying in the sea.
Sway extended arms back and forth.

Feeding on the plankton,
Grasp air with hands as though capturing plankton.

To build a colony.
Move toward center of open area.

Watching out for fishes,
Cup hands around eyes and look around.

Who'd make a meal of me!
Press hands against cheeks, open mouth wide.

I'm just a little polyp,
Shrug holding arms at side with palms up.

And I'm happy to be free!
Extend and sway arms overhead.

Reef Residents

At first glance a coral reef looks like a beautiful garden. It is a splendid view! However, it is not plants that provide the dazzling colors, it is the reef's animal residents. A wide variety of invertebrates inhabit the reef, including corals, jellyfish, seahorses, sponges, sea anemones, worms, eels, crabs, and lobsters. The reef also teems with vertebrates—with the most abundant vertebrates being fish. A single coral reef can be home to more than 1,000 different fish species! Use the reproducible activity on page 209 to introduce students to ten different reef residents. Then, if desired, have the students use their completed activities to make colorful animal cards by following the directions in "Coral Reef Cards" below.

Coral Reef Cards

There is no doubt that youngsters will be intrigued by the unique creatures that reside in the reef. Encourage students to learn facts about a variety of residents by introducing coral reef cards. Make a supply of three-inch-square light blue construction-paper cards available to students. To make a set of ten cards, a student refers to photographs found in books and magazines to color the reef residents on his completed copy of page 209. Then he cuts out the boxes along the bold lines and glues each one to a different light blue card. Next he locates a fact about each reef resident and writes the fact on the back of the resident's card. Also instruct each student to label the backs of his cards with his initials or another personalized symbol. Then give each child a resealable plastic bag in which to store his card collection.

Encourage students to build their card collections by making cards for other reef residents. To create each additional card, a child illustrates and labels a coral reef resident on one side of a light blue card, then he writes a fact about the resident and his initials on the back of the card. For additional motivation, agree to laminate (or cover with clear Con-Tact® covering) any student's card collection that contains 20 or more completed cards. You can count on these card collections becoming the talk of the classroom!

The Night Shift

Night life on the coral reef is hopping! As the parrot fish and other colorful day creatures settle down for the night, the night shift comes on the scene. Moray eels and octopi emerge from their hiding spots, lobsters and shrimp crawl from their holes, and coral polyps extend their tentacles in search of food. There's plenty of action right up until morning, when the day shift takes over again. Use the project on page 210 to introduce your students to three *diurnal* (daytime) and three *nocturnal* (nighttime) coral reef animals.

Duplicate page 210 on white construction paper and have each youngster color a copy. To complete his project, a student cuts out patterns A and B on the bold lines. Then, on cutout A, he cuts along the dotted lines to create one large window and three small ones. (Provide assistance as needed.) Next the student places cutout A on top of cutout B, aligns the edges, and pokes a brad through the black dot, joining both cutouts. To view diurnal animals, the student positions the daytime sky in the large window. When the nighttime sky is featured, nocturnal animals are on display.

Colossal Parrot Fish

One of many spectacular fish on the coral reef is the parrot fish. In this group alone there are about 75 different species! Most parrot fish are brightly colored and have unusual front teeth that resemble a parrot's beak. Parrot fish are unique in that they use their strong teeth to bite or scrape coral off the reef and chew it up, eating the algae that live inside. The by-product of this process is a beautiful white or pink coral sand. One adult parrot fish can produce about one ton of sand each year!

Bring the colors of the coral reef into your classroom with this small-group project. Each group needs a pair of giant-size cutouts that can be used to create a three-dimensional parrot fish. (If desired, enlist the help of a parent volunteer to cut the shapes from white or pastel bulletin-board paper.) Challenge the members of each group to devise a plan for decorating their fish cutouts. A plan might involve using markers, crayons, colored chalk, and/or construction-paper scraps. Then provide the students with the needed supplies and let the decorating begin. To assemble the projects, provide assistance as each group lightly stuffs (with newspaper) and staples its project. Then suspend the resulting projects from your ceiling with monofilament line.

Check out pages 53 and 54 for art projects related to the coral reef!

Coral Crunchies

Here's a tasty snack that's fit for a parrot fish! But you can count on your youngsters loving it too! Serve each youngster a coral crunchy (see the recipe) and a desired beverage. The coral crunchies look like coral and crunch like coral, but only the parrot fish knows if they taste like coral!

Coral Crunchies
(makes about 30 servings)

Ingredients:
1 stick butter or margarine
16 oz. miniature marshmallows
food coloring
10–12 oz. chow mein noodles
2 cups shredded coconut

Directions:
Melt the butter in a large saucepan over medium heat. Add the marshmallows and stir until completely melted. Stir in a desired color of food coloring; then remove the mixture from the heat and stir in the chow mein noodles and coconut until they are completely coated. Drop by generous spoonfuls into individual cupcake liners.

Survival Savvy

The colors and patterns of coral reef residents are beautiful—and they are often necessary for survival. Some markings help animals blend into the colorful reef. Markings like stripes and spots (called *disruptive patterns*) make it difficult for an enemy to see the outline of an animal's body. And some bright colors actually keep enemies away by signaling that the animal is either poisonous or it tastes very bad!

Invite students to keep these survival techniques in mind as they create striking reef scenes. To create a reef scene, use a pencil to draw a simple coral reef setting on watercolor or heavy paper. Squeeze a trail of glue along your pencil lines; then sprinkle white art sand (available at craft stores) over the glue. Let the project dry overnight; then shake off the excess sand and paint the scene using watercolors. When the painting is dry, mount it on a slightly larger piece of construction paper. Before putting the paintings on display, ask each youngster to present her painting to the class and explain the survival technique that is pictured.

Save The Reefs!

Healthy coral reefs are an important part of our world. In addition to providing a safe place for a myriad of sea creatures, the reefs help reduce global warming by taking carbon dioxide out of the air. Unfortunately reefs are being threatened by pollution and by hunters who upset the balance of nature by illegally removing coral, shells, and tropical saltwater fish from reefs. Invite students to spread the word about coral reefs! Here are a few ways this can be done:

- Write a class letter to the Center For Marine Conservation (1725 DeSales Street NW, Suite 600, Washington, DC 20036) to request information on how to fight coral reef pollution and damage. When the information arrives, compose a class list of ten ways to preserve coral reefs. Post the list outside your classroom door.
- Provide assorted art supplies that can be used to create coral reef posters. Have each student create an informative poster. Post the completed projects around the school or in approved areas throughout the community.
- Have each student prepare a brief oral presentation that explains the importance of coral reefs and why the future of the reefs is being threatened. Then invite individual classes to visit your classroom. After a group of visitors has viewed the coral reef projects on display, have several students give their presentations.

Reading About The Reef

Enhance your study of the coral reef with these outstanding books. They're perfect for the primary classroom, and as an added bonus, several titles include breathtaking photographs of coral reefs and their residents.

Coral Reef: A City That Never Sleeps
Written by Mary M. Cerullo
Photographed by Jeffrey L. Rotman
Cobblehill Books, 1996

Life In The Coral Reef
Written by Bobbie Kalman and Niki
  Walker
Photographed by Tom Stack and
  Associates
Crabtree Publishing Company, 1997

A City Under The Sea: Life In A Coral Reef
Written by Norbert Wu
Includes photographs
Atheneum Books For Young Readers,
  1996

Webs Of Life Series: *Coral Reef*
Written by Paul Fleisher
Includes photographs
Benchmark Books, 1998

The Incredible Coral Reef: Another Active-Learning Book For Kids
Written by Toni Albert
Illustrated and designed by Ada Hanlon
Trickle Creek Books, 1996

Coral Reef Hideaway: The Story Of A Clown Anemonefish
Written by Doe Boyle
Illustrated by Steven James Petruccio
Soundprints, 1995

Undersea City: A Story Of A Caribbean Coral Reef
Written by Dana Meachen Rau
Illustrated by Katie Lee
Soundprints, 1997

Colors Of The Sea Series: *Coral Reef Survival*
Written by Eric Ethan and Marie
  Bearanger
Includes photographs
Gareth Stevens Publishing, 1997

Name

Where In The World?

Color the map.
Use the map key.

Map Key
land = yellow
coral reef = red
water = blue

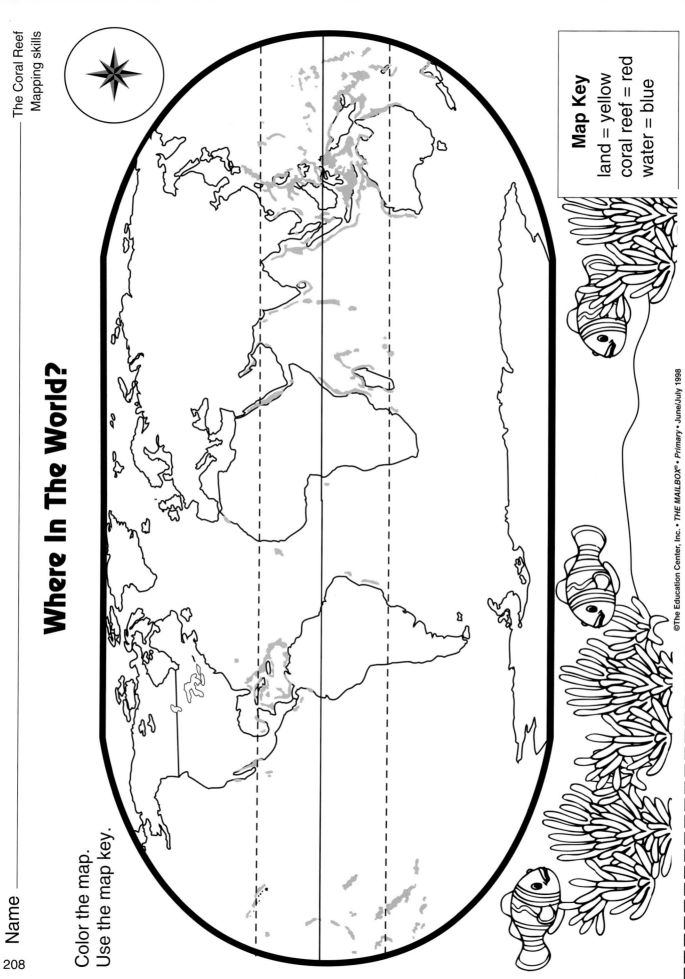

©The Education Center, Inc. • *THE MAILBOX® • Primary •* June/July 1998

Note To Teacher: Use with "Where In The World?" on page 204.

208

Who's Who On The Reef?

Write the name of each resident on the lines.
Use the Word Bank.

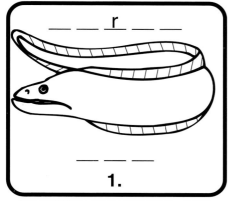

_ _ _ r _ _ _

_ _ _ _

1.

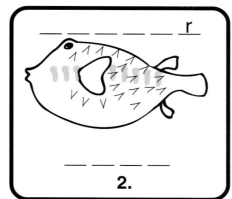

_ _ _ _ _ _ r

2.

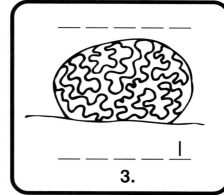

_ _ _ _

_ _ _ _ l

3.

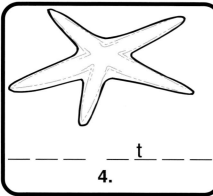

_ _ _ _ t _ _ _ _

4.

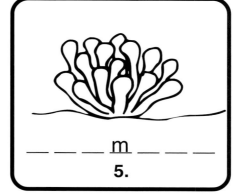

_ _ _ _ m _ _ _

5.

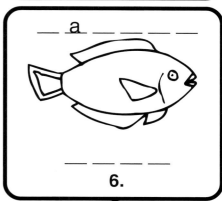

_ a _ _ _ _

_ _ _ _

6.

_ _ _ _ _ _ s

7.

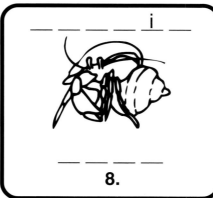

_ _ _ _ i _

_ _ _ _

8.

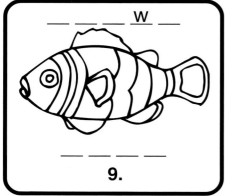

_ _ _ w _

_ _ _ _

9.

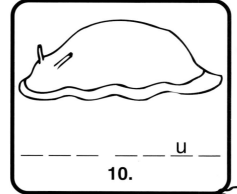

_ _ _ _ u _

10.

Word Bank
Puffer Fish
Parrot Fish
Clown Fish
Moray Eel
Sea Slug
Hermit Crab
Sea Star
Octopus
Anemone
Brain Coral

Bonus Box: Use a blue crayon to outline each box that shows an animal.

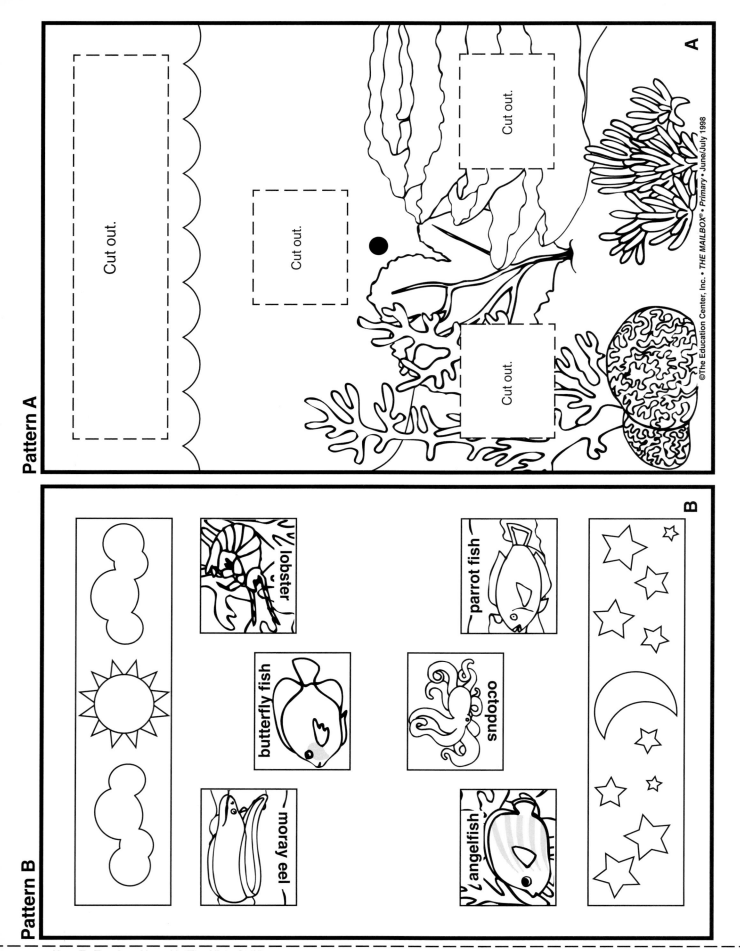

A

Cut out.

Cut out.

Cut out.

Cut out.

©The Education Center, Inc. • THE MAILBOX® • Primary • June/July 1998

Pattern B

B

lobster

butterfly fish

moray eel

parrot fish

octopus

angelfish

Note To Teacher: Use with "The Night Shift" on page 206.

Social Studies

ON-THE-SPOT COMMUNITY COVERAGE

Coming up next is On-The-Spot Community Coverage. Today's special segment features suggestions for using literature to enhance your community studies. Stay tuned for informative picture-book reviews and ready-to-use teaching ideas. For WMBX, this is Rita Mailbox reporting.

books reviewed by Anne Bustard

Making Popcorn Balls
One time my aunt, my mom, and I made pink popcorn balls for a school carnival. They were very sticky. My aunt got popcorn stuck in her hair. We laughed so hard we cried.

Who's Who In My Family?
Written & Illustrated by Loreen Leedy
Holiday House, Inc.; 1995
When the students in Ms. Fox's class embark on a family tree project, they learn how everyone's family is unique. Cartoony illustrations coupled with handwritten text give this book a friendly feel. As an added bonus, there's a list of family-related words with simple definitions on the last page.

By the conclusion of the book, students will be eager to talk about their own families. Reiterate that just as every community is unique and special, so are the families that form a community. Then have each child copy and complete the title "Who's Who In [student's name]'s Family?" near the top of a 12" x 18" sheet of drawing paper. Ask each child to illustrate and label the members of his immediate family (including himself!) on his paper. As the students share their completed projects with the class, reinforce family words like those listed at the end of the book. For an attractive Open House display, mount the students' projects on the foliage of a large, paper tree cutout. Title the display "Room _____'s Family Tree."

Dad   Juanita   Me   Zip
Steve

Family Pictures • Cuadros De Familia
Written & Illustrated by Carmen Lomas Garza
Children's Book Press, 1990
In this book of cherished memories, the author describes her experiences growing up in a small Texas town near Mexico's border. Brightly colored folk-art paintings bring her Hispanic community to life. The words on each page—written in both English and Spanish—are as vivid as the illustrations.

One family and its place in a community is the focus of this delightful book. Discuss the special times that the author shared with her family. Then give each child a construction-paper booklet that contains five sheets of story paper. Ask each child to describe and illustrate a favorite family memory on each booklet page. Encourage students to write descriptively and to complete detailed illustrations like the author of *Family Pictures* has done. When the booklet pages are complete, have each child write her name and the title "[student's name]'s Family Pictures" on the front cover, then add desired artwork. Invite each interested student to share a favorite family memory from her booklet before taking the booklet home to her family.

It Takes A Village
Written & Illustrated by Jane Cowen-Fletcher
Scholastic Inc., 1994
The African proverb "It takes a village to raise a child" springs to life in this satisfying story of collaboration. While her mother sells mangoes at the marketplace, Yemi cares for her younger brother Kokou all by herself—or so she thinks! Rich colored-pencil and watercolor illustrations add texture and depth to the people and sights of this caring Benin community.

Seeing how the members of this close-knit community willingly assist Yemi with her baby-sitting endeavor may prompt students to recall times when they've needed to enlist the help of others to achieve a goal. Ask students to explain the benefits of collaboration as you write their ideas on the chalkboard. Then challenge students to think of ways that they could collaborate and also help out their community. Ideas might include collecting grocery-store coupons to give to a local food bank, donating toys and books to a homeless shelter, and cleaning up a vacant lot. (*The Kid's Guide To Service Projects* by Barbara A. Lewis [Free Spirit Publishing Inc., 1995] describes more than 500 ways that youngsters can participate in successful community service.) If desired, each month have the class choose a different community-related goal on which to collaborate.

Starring First Grade
Written by Miriam Cohen & Illustrated by Lillian Hoban
Greenwillow Books, 1985
It's all for one and one for all by the end of this first-grade class's dramatic debut. A play based on The Three Billy Goats Gruff *is the latest production for this class of individuals. And thanks to teamwork among the cast members, the play is a grand success. Illustrated with whimsical, cherublike children, this story of life in a classroom community seems very true to life.*

Witnessing the antics of this first-grade class will help students realize the importance of cooperation within a community! Remind students that the troubles begin when Jim forgets the class goal and begins to pursue a personal one. Ask students what they learned from this story and how they intend to apply their new knowledge in and out of the classroom. Then, if you're up to the challenge, enlist your students' help in planning a simple class production for a neighboring classroom, your students' families, or a nearby senior center. You can count on plenty of cooperation as this community project unfolds.

213

Tikvah Means Hope

Written & Illustrated by Patricia Polacco
Bantam Doubleday Dell Books For Young Readers, 1994

Written in response to the hillside fires in Oakland, California, local resident Patricia Polacco tells a poignant story of community love in action. Unable to go home for two days while the fires burn, Mr. Roth and his neighbors wonder what will be left of their homes, their neighborhood, their community. As the friends help one another begin to recover from the disaster, small miracles bring them hope.

Polacco's moving account of the Oakland fires is packed with community-related references. Have students share the references they remember, like the community helpers who assisted during the disaster, the community spirit that was displayed, and the neighborhood and religious communities that were described.

There's a good chance that learning about the Oakland fires will pique your students' interest in the history of their community. Suggest that several students write or visit long-standing community residents in search of memorable community events. Other students can contact the Chamber Of Commerce, a public library, a local museum, and other appropriate places to learn about notable community events. Then enlist your students' help in compiling the gathered data on a community timeline. To do this, draw a line down the middle of a long strip of bulletin-board paper. Post the strip and the title "A Timeline Of [name of community]." Have each child write an important date and event on provided paper, then illustrate his work. Under your students' direction, display the illustrated events in chronological order along the timeline.

1868
Founded by Josiah Springfield.

1894
First horse auction.

Mrs. McKay's Flower Garden

Mrs. McKay has a beautiful flower garden. There are so many colors of flowers and no weeds! The garden always makes me feel happy.
—by Tasha

The Garden Of Happiness

Written by Erika Tamar & Illustrated by Barbara Lambase
Harcourt Brace & Company, 1996

With a lot of help from friends, a once ugly, vacant city lot is transformed into a glorious flower and vegetable garden. And even though all of the plots have been taken, Marisol finds room to plant a single seed. Thanks to her tender loving care, the plant brings joy to everyone on the block and provides inspiration for a group of young muralists.

All across America, people have joined together to turn forsaken vacant lots into beautiful neighborhood and community gardens. *The Garden Of Happiness* is a heartwarming tribute to the pride and hope found in multicultural neighborhoods all over New York City. For another colorful tribute to community gardens, read aloud *City Green* by Dyanne DiSalvo-Ryan (Morrow Junior Books, 1994). As a follow-up to these stories, ask each student to illustrate and write a short report about a well-cared-for place in his community. Encourage students to recognize in their reports the efforts that have been dedicated to the care of these places. After a student shares his illustrated report with the class, make arrangements for him to deliver it to the residents, owners, caretakers, or managers of the location he spotlighted. You'll be promoting community beautification and positive community relationships, too.

Around Town
Written & Illustrated by Chris K. Soentpiet
Lothrop, Lee & Shepard Books; 1994
Enjoy a fun-filled day in the city—whether it's your home or you're just visiting. Follow a young girl and her mother as they explore their community on a hot, shiny summer day. Feed the pigeons, cool off in the fire hydrant, and pause to watch some jugglers. It's a refreshing celebration of community within a city.

This joyful celebration of city life is likely to make students eager to take a trip around their town! Review the fun-filled experiences that this mother and child share; then ask your students to think of ways to spend a fun-filled Saturday afternoon in their community. List the students' ideas on the chalkboard. To make a class big book titled "Around Our Town," have each child copy a different idea from the chalkboard onto a 12" x 18" sheet of white construction paper. Then have each child illustrate his entire page using crayons or markers. While the students are working, ask each one in turn to sign a book page labeled "Authors and Illustrators." Laminate the pages for durability; then hole-punch and stack them, placing the autographed page on top. Next bind the project between two slightly larger pieces of poster board, title the front cover, and add desired cover artwork. For a fun book-sharing follow-up, make arrangements for different small groups of students to share the big book with other classes in your school.

Like Me And You
Written by Raffi & Illustrated by Lillian Hoban
Crown Publishers, Inc.; 1985
In this story, originally written as a children's song and now between the covers of a book, Raffi emphasizes that we are all members of the biggest community of all—the world. No matter where we live—Spain, India, Germany, Chile, or Japan—we are a lot alike. Cheery illustrations of children posting letters worldwide send a warm message.

Even though this simple book doesn't spell out the similarities that people around the world share, students are sure to have plenty of their own ideas. After discussing these similarities, invite students to talk about what they can do to help make our world community a peaceful, honest, and healthy place to live. To spread the word about what can be done, have each child create a poster that shares his idea(s) for improving our world. Post these posters around the school. Then, for a musical finale, use the score at the end of the book to teach your students this delightful song about our global community.

The Island Of Enchantment
Puerto Rico

There's no time like the present to visit the tropical paradise of Puerto Rico. With this first-class collection of activities, you'll have just what you need to acquaint your youngsters with the land, culture, history, and unique wildlife of the island. Pack your bags and begin your Puerto Rican adventure today!

ideas by Lisa Shulman

A Rich Port

Sail into your study of Puerto Rico by helping students locate on a world map the region known as the Caribbean or West Indies. Explain that these islands are actually the tips of undersea mountains, and are the result of volcanic activity deep in the earth. Next have students look closer to find the island of Puerto Rico (which means "rich port" in Spanish). Students will see that Puerto Rico is one of the largest islands in the Caribbean. A closer look at the map will reveal that many smaller islands are also part of Puerto Rico.

For an island that is about the size of Connecticut, Puerto Rico has an amazing variety of physical features. Sandy beaches, rugged mountains, dry deserts, and even an area of rain forest are all part of this unique country. Have students continue their investigation of Puerto Rico by completing the reproducible mapping activity on page 220.

Making Comparisons	Past	Present
homes	Not enough housing.	Lots of new and improved housing.
family life		
work	Almost everyone farmed.	Manufacturing and lots of jobs that help tourists.
schools		
food		
languages	Mostly Spanish.	English is being taught in the schools. Many more people speak Spanish and English.

That Was Then, This Is Now

Forty years ago Puerto Rico was an agricultural country. Today it is the most industrialized and urbanized nation in the Caribbean. As students learn about this ever changing country, record their observations on a chart like the one shown. Continually encourage students to compare and contrast Puerto Rico's present living conditions with those of the past. Find out what your students feel are the advantages and disadvantages of the changes that have taken place.

The Uncommon Commonwealth

Is Puerto Rico part of the United States? Yes. Is Puerto Rico a state? No. There's little doubt that this information will confuse and intrigue your students. Explain that the island of Puerto Rico is a United States *commonwealth.* This means that Puerto Rico has its own constitution, government, flag, and national anthem, but that the United States manages some of Puerto Rico's affairs. In fact the people of Puerto Rico are citizens of the United States!

Use this display to encourage students to uncover a wealth of interesting facts about Puerto Rico. Mount a large paper replica of Puerto Rico's flag and the title as shown. Nearby provide a supply of precut paper stars or the materials needed to make them. Invite students to share the facts they discover about Puerto Rico by writing each fact on a star cutout and attaching it to the display. To avoid duplications, caution students to always check the posted facts before adding one of their own. Periodically, during your study of Puerto Rico, take time to read the facts on the board. It's a great way to reinforce and introduce facts about this enchanting island.

Puerto Rico

Did You Know...

that 200 different kinds of birds spend the winter in Puerto Rico?

Christopher Columbus

Your students probably know that in 1492 Columbus sailed the ocean blue. But they may not know that in 1493 Columbus set sail again. And this time he landed on the island that we call Puerto Rico! When Columbus landed on the island, he named it San Juan Bautista. So how did the island come to be called Puerto Rico? Historians believe that on an early map the name of the island (San Juan Bautista) and the name of the island's first European settlement (Puerto Rico) were accidentally switched. And that's why today the island is called Puerto Rico and its capital is called San Juan!

On November 19, 1993, the United States issued a Christopher Columbus stamp commemorating the 500th anniversary of Columbus's landing on Puerto Rico. This year celebrate Discovery Of Puerto Rico Day (November 19) by asking students to design colorful 12" x 18" posters in Columbus's honor. Encourage students to show Columbus and his crew landing on or investigating the newfound island. If you'd like some really unique posters, inform students that Columbus and his crew had their first taste of pineapple while they were exploring the area!

| Around The Classroom ||
English Word	Spanish Word
book	el libro
chair	la silla
clock	el reloj
desk	el escritorio
door	la puerta
flag	la bandera
floor	el piso
map	el mapa
paper	el papel
pencil	el lápiz
wall	la pared
window	la ventana

wall
la pared

book
el libro

¡Hola!

That's "hello" in Spanish—the island's official language. In addition to learning the Spanish language, students attending school in Puerto Rico also learn English. During your study of Puerto Rico, incorporate a bit of Spanish into your daily activities. To do this, label individual 3" x 5" cards with both the English and Spanish terms for a variety of classroom items. (Refer to the provided table.) With your students' help, post the cards near these items. Each day make it a point to use the Spanish words in your daily classroom activities, and encourage students to do the same! "Please line up quietly at *la puerta.*"

Tropical Treats

Do you think you could interest students in eating a hog plum, genipap, or custard apple? Tropical fruits such as these are plentiful in Puerto Rico, as well as other more common fruits like pineapples, bananas, coconuts, and oranges. To give youngsters a taste of the island, arrange for a parent volunteer to prepare a batch of banana fritters using the provided recipe. Serve the fritters with freshly made lemonade, or make tropical smoothies using frozen bananas, pineapple juice, and orange juice. Delicious!

Banana Fritters
(makes 24 fritters)

4 large bananas
1/3 cup plus 2 tbsp. flour
1/2 tsp. baking powder
4 tbsp. sugar

2 eggs, beaten
dash of cinnamon
oil for frying

In a medium bowl, mash the bananas. Add the flour, baking powder, sugar, cinnamon, and eggs. Stir well. Carefully drop tablespoons of batter into 1/2 inch of hot oil and fry for about 1 minute per side (until golden brown). Remove the fritters from the oil with a slotted spoon and place on paper towels to drain.

(For a more health-conscious treat, fry the prepared batter as you would pancakes. The result is 24 small and tasty banana pancakes.)

Marvelous Masks

Puerto Rican art has been influenced by the island's mix of Spanish, African, and native Taino cultures. This is especially evident in traditional folk art such as mask making. Carved from wood or coconuts, some masks were originally used to scare people. Masks are still worn today in parts of Puerto Rico during festival times. Wild, colorful masks are a trademark of many Puerto Rican artists, and are popular among tourists.

Students won't be able to disguise their delight when you invite them to create wild, colorful masks! To make a mask, visualize a desired design; then sketch it onto a thin, white paper plate. Use crayons, markers, or tempera paints to "colorize" the design. To give your mask dimension, cut a pie-shaped wedge from the project; then overlap and staple together the cut edges. Since many Puerto Rican masks depict animals, students may wish to attach ears and other desired details cut from construction paper. Display the finished projects as a colorful reminder of Puerto Rico's diversity and folk art.

Colorful Birds

Hundreds of colorful birds make their homes in Puerto Rico. One such bird, the Puerto Rican parrot, lives only in Puerto Rico. To teach students more about this endangered bird, read aloud the background information provided on this page. Then give each student a copy of the parrot-related project on page 221. Each student will also need a 6" x 18" length of construction paper, crayons, scissors, and glue. Ask each child to fold her length of construction paper in half to 6" x 9", then follow the directions on page 221. To complete the project, a student glues her parrot cutout to the front of her folded paper and she glues the events (in order) inside the folded paper. She then writes her name and a desired title on the front of the project. Encourage students to use their completed projects to help them tell their family members about the plight of the Puerto Rican parrot.

Protecting The Puerto Rican Parrot

Long ago there were close to one million Puerto Rican parrots living in the lush forests of Puerto Rico. The parrots built their nests in dry tree cavities high above the ground. But as more people moved to the island, trees were cut down to make room for farms, towns, and cities. This left the birds with fewer places to build their nests, which resulted in few eggs being laid. The parrot population quickly dwindled. By 1975 there were only 13 parrots left on the island. Now efforts are being made to help the Puerto Rican parrots. Scientists have provided artificial nesting cavities in the El Yunque rain forest. They also watch over the parrots' nesting places (both artificial and natural) to make sure the parrot chicks born are safe and healthy. In addition, scientists have built large aviaries for the parrots to grow and raise their young in. Puerto Ricans hope that these efforts to save the Puerto Rican parrot will succeed.

Oh, Juan Bobo!

Juan Bobo is the folk hero of many Puerto Rican stories. Not unlike Amelia Bedelia, Juan Bobo manages to get himself into heaps of trouble due to an innocent lack of understanding. Quite often this lovable simpleton sidesteps disaster and teaches a few lessons to the wiser folks around him. Familiarize your students with some tales about Juan Bobo. (Three such books are reviewed to the right.) Discuss the silly mistakes that Juan Bobo makes in each story as he tries to accomplish the task at hand. Then challenge your students to write their own Juan Bobo stories. For the best results, have students brainstorm possible tasks that Juan's mother might give him like going to the market, cleaning the house, or planting a garden. Next have each child choose a situation and write and illustrate a short story about the foolish things Juan Bobo does. Bind the completed stories into a class book titled "Oh, Juan Bobo!" This volume of silly stories is sure to be a popular addition to your classroom library!

Juan Bobo: Four Folktales From Puerto Rico
Retold by Carmen T. Bernier-Grand
Illustrated by Ernesto Ramos Nieves
HarperCollins Publishers, 1994
This easy reader selection consists of four simple stories, perhaps the most common Bobo tales on the island. And as an added bonus, the complete tales are retold in Spanish at the end of the book. Lots of color, heaps of humor, and spirited, stylized characters complete the book.

Juan Bobo And The Pig
Retold by Felix Pitre & Illustrated by Christy Hale
Lodestar Books, 1993
Liberally seasoned with common Spanish phrases translated in context, this silly story teaches a lesson about pretension. Juan Bobo's mother has some airs about her, and Juan—without ever trying—makes her take a second look at herself.

Juan Bobo And The Horse Of Seven Colors: A Puerto Rican Legend
Retold by Jan Mike & Illustrated by Charles Reasoner
Troll Associates, 1995
The stories of Juan Bobo probably began with rural Puerto Ricans as a safe way to poke fun at the Spanish aristocrats on the island. This lively tale tells how Juan Bobo unwittingly goes from being a peasant to a palace resident through a lucky encounter with a magical, rainbow-colored horse.

books reviewed by Deborah Zink Roffino

Small And Large

The animals of Puerto Rico come in all sizes and shapes. One of the island's smallest animals is the *coquí*—a one- to two-inch tree frog whose croak "Ko-kee! Ko-kee!" sounds like a bird's song. The commonwealth's largest snake is the Puerto Rican boa. It can grow to be seven feet in length! The most dangerous animal on the island is a giant centipede that grows to be 15 inches or longer. It delivers a painful and poisonous bite!

Put your youngsters' measurement skills to the test with this small-group math activity. Each group will need a ten-foot length of adding-machine tape, scissors, rulers, pencils, and crayons. Challenge each group to measure and cut a seven-foot length, a two-inch length, and a 15-inch length from its tape, then illustrate each length to resemble the animal to which its length corresponds. Mount the resulting projects on a classroom wall or in the school hallway. Invite students to investigate other animals that live on the island, too. There are plenty more!

Play Ball!

Baseball is Puerto Rico's national sport. Puerto Ricans enjoy baseball all year long since their season begins just as the season in the United States mainland ends. You won't strike out using this baseball review as the culminating activity to your study of Puerto Rico! Divide the class into two teams (A and B) and have each team generate a list of review questions (with answers!) about Puerto Rico. Then set up four chairs in your classroom to represent first base, second base, third base, and home plate.

To play the game, assign a pitcher from team A or let the players on that team rotate the position. The first batter from team B steps up to home plate and the pitcher "pitches" the player a question. If the batter answers correctly, she moves to first base. An incorrect answer is an out. Play continues in this manner, with base runners progressing one base each time a batter provides a correct answer. The team's runs and outs are tallied. After three outs, team A steps up to bat and team B pitches their questions. At the end of game time, students will be batting a thousand with their knowledge of Puerto Rico!

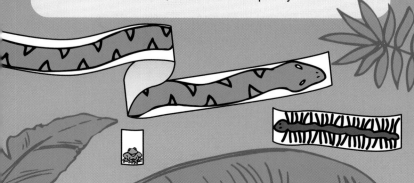

Mapping Out Puerto Rico

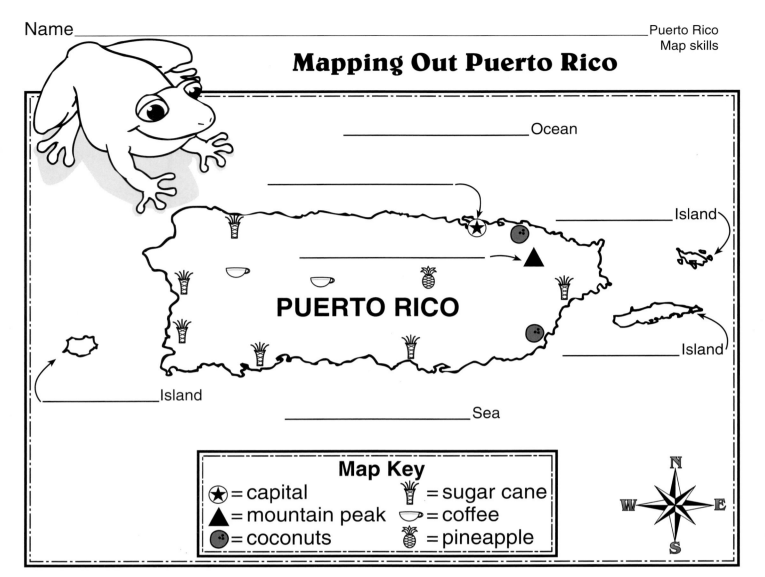

_____ Ocean

Island

PUERTO RICO

Island

_____ Island

_____ Sea

Map Key
★ = capital   🌴 = sugar cane
▲ = mountain peak   ☕ = coffee
● = coconuts   🍍 = pineapple

Use the clues to label the map.
1. The ocean to the north of Puerto Rico is the <u>Atlantic</u> Ocean.
2. The sea to the south of Puerto Rico is the <u>Caribbean</u> Sea.
3. The capital of Puerto Rico is <u>San Juan</u>.
4. Puerto Rico includes many islands. Label these three:
   • <u>Mona</u> Island is to the west of Puerto Rico.
   • <u>Culebra</u> Island is north of <u>Vieques</u> Island.
5. Puerto Rico's rain forest is on a mountain called <u>El Yunque</u>.

Use the map to answer these questions.
1. What two crops grow in the coastal areas of Puerto Rico?

_____ and _____

2. What two crops grow near the center of the island?

_____ and _____

Name _____

The Puerto Rican Parrot

Use the code to
color the parrot.
Cut on the dotted
lines.
Arrange the events
in order.

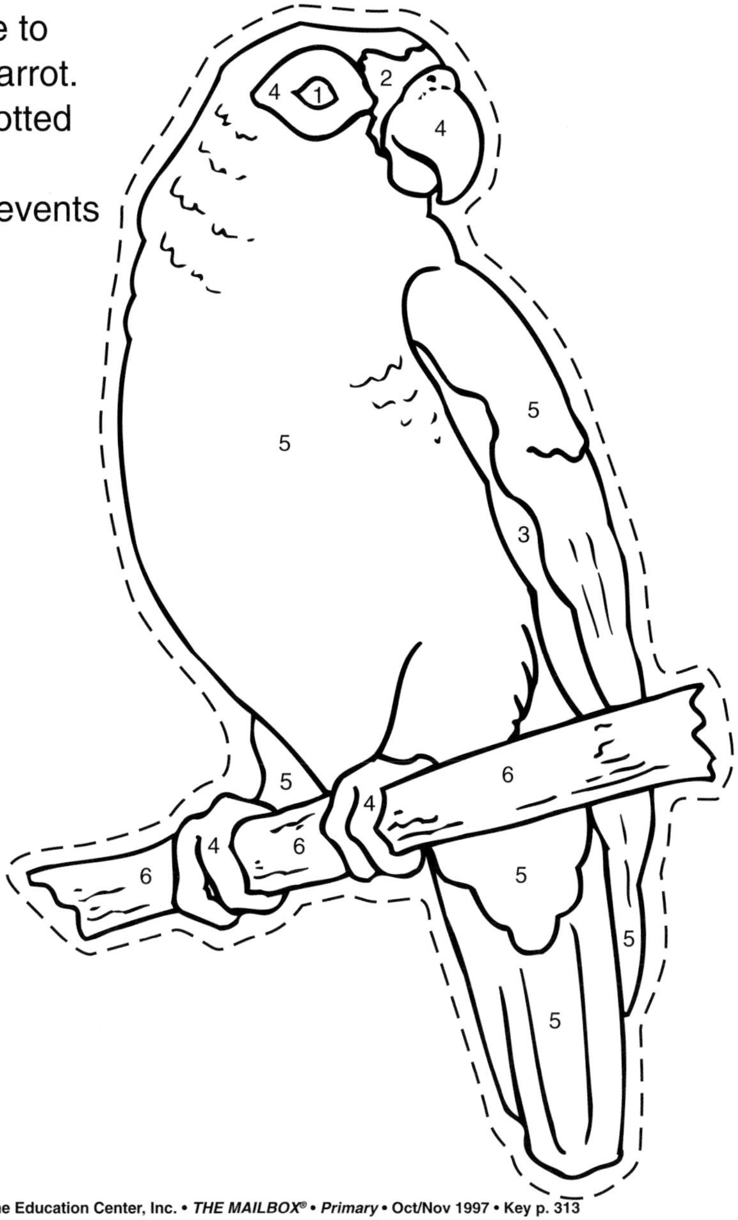

Color Code
black = 1
red = 2
blue = 3
white = 4
green = 5
brown = 6

The parrots could not find trees for their nests.

Long ago Puerto Rico had many trees and parrots.

The number of Puerto Rican parrots is growing!

Fewer eggs meant fewer baby parrots were born.

Scientists started building nests for the parrots.

Then many of the trees were cut down.

Without nests the parrots could not lay their eggs.

More eggs meant more baby parrots were born.

The parrots found nests and laid their eggs.

The number of Puerto Rican parrots began to shrink.

©The Education Center, Inc. • THE MAILBOX® • Primary • Oct/Nov 1997 • Key p. 313

Note To Teacher: Use with "Colorful Birds" and "Protecting The Puerto Rican Parrot" on page 218. Each child needs a 6" x 18" length of construction paper for the project.

The Land Of The Midnight Sun
SWEDEN

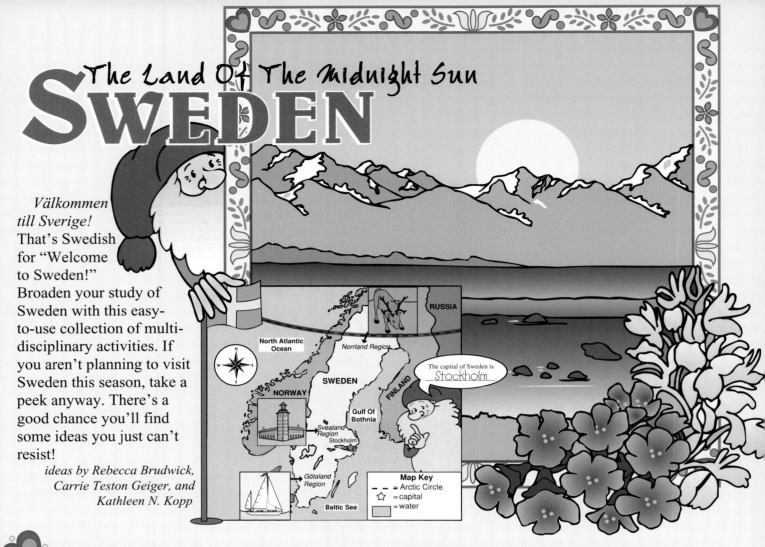

Välkommen till Sverige! That's Swedish for "Welcome to Sweden!" Broaden your study of Sweden with this easy-to-use collection of multi-disciplinary activities. If you aren't planning to visit Sweden this season, take a peek anyway. There's a good chance you'll find some ideas you just can't resist!

ideas by Rebecca Brudwick, Carrie Teston Geiger, and Kathleen N. Kopp

Taking A Look At Sweden

Sweden is the fourth largest country in Europe; yet it is just slightly larger than the state of California. Help students locate Sweden on a world map or globe. As a class, examine Sweden's coastline and note that the Arctic Circle intersects northern Sweden. Ask students what this information could tell them about the country. (Students may hypothesize that the country is cold and has a lot of ports. Some students may realize that being so close to the Arctic Circle will affect the length of the days and nights in Sweden.) Accept all answers, recording them on a length of bulletin-board paper labeled "Speculations About Sweden." Then have students continue their investigation of Sweden by completing the reproducible mapping activity on page 226.

Say It In Swedish!

Almost all Swedes speak Swedish, and many Swedes speak English too. In Sweden, when students enter third grade, they begin to read and write in English. No doubt your students will be thrilled to learn a bit of Swedish as they explore the country. Since some Swedish words are very similar to English words, students will experience success right away! Refer to (or photocopy) the chart on page 227 to introduce students to some Swedish words and sayings.

The Land Of The Midnight Sun

The midnight sun? Tell students that northern Sweden is called the Land Of The Midnight Sun and ask them what this phrase might mean. Lead students to understand that there are weeks during June and July when the sun does not set in northern Sweden. In other words, the sun can be seen at midnight! This also means that during winter, there are times when the sun *cannot* be seen.

Have students form small groups, and ask each group to brainstorm the advantages and disadvantages of summer nights when the sun never sets. List the groups' ideas on a chart like the one shown. Then have each group brainstorm the pros and cons of winter days without sunlight and record these ideas on the chart. As a large group, discuss the posted information; then take a class vote to find out how many students would (would not) enjoy living in northern Sweden.

Summer	Winter
Sun shines all day and night.	It's dark all day and night.
Advantages: More time to play! Nighttime wouldn't be scary. Gardens would grow fast.	**Advantages:** Get more sleep. You could see the stars all the time.
Disadvantages: It might be hard to sleep. Can't see the stars. Might not cool off.	**Disadvantages:** You would use more electricity.

Trolls And Such

Swedish folklore is filled with references to some pretty interesting beings! Funny-looking and mischievous creatures called *trolls* supposedly make their homes in the forests of Sweden. You need to beware of the trolls because some can be very mean! A little closer to home are *tomtar*. These little old men, who can be as small as a human hand, live in barns, under floors, and in chests. They love people who live neatly and do good work, and will bring these people good luck and small gifts.

For a bit of Swedish fun, inform students that you think you caught sight of a *tomte* in the classroom! Suggest that he came to visit because he heard a study of Sweden was in progress. Challenge students to keep their classroom and desks neat and organized. Remind students that the tomte will also be looking for neat and accurate work. To keep interest high, duplicate a supply of the notes found on page 227. Periodically—as you continue to study Sweden—tuck a clean-desk note and a piece of wrapped candy inside each neatly organized student desk. Also complete and staple a good-work note to each example of outstanding student work. Who knows? Maybe your tomte will stay all school year!

Nobel Prizes

Each year on December 10, the king of Sweden presents Nobel Prizes—the world's most prestigious awards—to outstanding individuals who contribute positively to the world. The prizes are a legacy of Alfred Nobel, a Swedish scientist. Prior to December 10, ask students how they contribute positively to the world. Write their ideas on the chalkboard. Next have each child write his name on the bottom of a thin, white six-inch paper plate, then turn the plate over and write in the center of his plate a positive contribution for which he would like to be recognized. Then have each child sponge-paint yellow tempera around the rim of his plate and sprinkle the wet paint with gold glitter.

Later, when the projects have dried, shake off the excess glitter, hole-punch the top of each plate, thread an 18-inch length of blue ribbon or yarn through the hole, and tie the ribbon ends. On December 10 present each child with his "Nobel Prize" during a special classroom celebration.

A Name A Day

Namnsdag, or names day, is a Swedish tradition your students are sure to enjoy! In Sweden each day of the year has been given a name. For example, the name for December 11 is Daniel, and on this *namnsdag,* people named Daniel may receive greeting cards and flowers from their friends and family members. Names day is not a birthday celebration; it's just another fun and special day!

To start this Swedish tradition in your classroom, randomly assign each student's name to a different school day. (Students who share first names will celebrate on the same day.) A student celebrating *namnsdag* is spotlighted throughout the day. This can be done by inviting the student to sit at a special desk or table, and by granting special names-day privileges. Be sure to present each celebrating student with a handcrafted card that has been signed by his classmates. A chorus of a familiar birthday tune renamed "Happy Names Day To You" might also be in order!

An Outstanding Recycler!

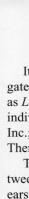

Reindeer Reports

It's the time of the year when students are most interested in reindeer, so why not investigate these migrating mammals and the people of northern Sweden, called *Sami* (also known as *Lapplanders*), who breed and herd them. Round up several reindeer references for use by individuals or small groups of students. (*Reindeer* by Emery Bernhard [Holiday House, Inc.; 1994] is an appealing picture book that introduces a wealth of factual information.) Then have each student make a booklet in which to record his reindeer-related discoveries.

To make a reindeer-shaped booklet, staple a supply of heart-shaped writing paper between two brown heart-shaped covers as shown. Cut out two smaller brown heart shapes for ears; then cut a set of antlers from dark paper. Glue these cutouts to the back booklet cover. On the front cover, glue paper or button eyes, a paper nose, and a tissue-paper topknot.

The Christmas Season

Officially the Christmas season begins December 13 on Santa Lucia Day—the Festival Of Light; however, the anticipation begins long before then! When Christmas Eve finally arrives, it is a festive time that includes Christmas dinner and the exchanging of gifts. Church services and family events fill Christmas Day. The holiday season may extend to Twelfth Night (January 6) or to St. Knut's Day on January 13. On St. Knut's Day, it is a Swedish custom that the Christmas tree be dismantled and tossed outside while a traditional song is being sung. Use the following activities to acquaint students with Advent calendars, St. Lucia Day festivities, and a popular Christmas tree decoration:

Advent Calendars

Swedish children love the Christmas season and can hardly wait to begin their holiday preparations. One way Swedish families mark December days is with Advent calendars. The calendars come in all shapes and sizes, the most popular ones having little numbered windows. Beginning with Advent Sunday, a child opens one window every morning to discover a tiny picture or toy inside. To make an Advent calendar, give each student a white construction-paper copy of page 228 and 24 one-inch construction-paper squares. Then assist students as they follow the provided directions.

Santa Lucia Day

Traditionally this occasion is observed by dressing the family's oldest daughter in a white robe, a crimson sash, and a leaf-covered crown of candles. Today most Swedish homes, offices, and schools choose a "Lucia." Boys also dress in white, but instead of candles they wear tall cone-shaped hats covered with stars. On the morning of December 13, the costumed children serve coffee and Swedish pastries.

Commemorate this Swedish celebration by having each student make either a leaf-covered crown of candles or a star-covered cone-shaped hat. (See page 44 for directions for making each project.) Then have the students wear their completed projects as they serve themselves pastries.

The Christmas Tree

Christmas trees are usually brought into Swedish homes one or two days before Christmas. Decorations may include candles, apples, heart-shaped baskets, Swedish flags, and straw ornaments.

These heart-shaped baskets (*julgranskorgar*) are easy to make and look pretty on any Christmas tree! Give each student two 4-inch paper circles, one red and one green, and a 1" x 9" strip of red or green paper. To make a basket, fold each circle in half. Hold the fold of a different circle in each hand and bring the pieces together. Insert one piece inside the other so that a point forms at the bottom and the sides flare out, making a heart shape. Glue the overlapping surfaces together and securely glue each end of the paper-strip handle inside the basket. If desired, give each student a few unshelled nuts or wrapped candies for his Swedish decoration.

A Scandinavian Sweetheart

A study of Sweden would not be complete without Pippi Longstocking—the carrot-topped heroine created by well-known Swedish author Astrid Lindgren. Plan to read at least one Pippi adventure during your Sweden study. Titles include *Pippi Longstocking, Pippi Goes On Board,* and *Pippi In The South Seas.* While your media specialist is tracking down books about Pippi, ask her to look for other books written by Astrid Lindgren and by other Swedish authors, like Sven Nordqvist, Gunilla Bergström, and Barbro Lindgren. Read on!

A Swedish Souvenir

A favorite souvenir to bring home from Sweden is a Dala horse. Dala horses are hand-carved, brightly painted wooden toys that have been made in the Dalarna province of Sweden for more than 150 years. The horses, usually little red ones, are a popular symbol of Sweden.

Have each student decorate a construction-paper Dala horse to carry home as a souvenir of your Sweden study. To begin, give each child a red construction-paper copy of the Dala horse pattern on page 229, and make available a large selection of brightly colored construction-paper scraps. Show students a picture or two of a Dala horse; then let the decorating begin! A student cuts out his horse shape. Next he cuts a mane, a bridle, and an assortment of shapes from colorful construction paper and glues them to his horse cutout. He then signs and dates the back of his work. Encourage students to share a few facts about the Dala horse and Sweden when they show off these souvenirs to their friends and family members.

Sumptuous Smorgasbord

Culminate your Sweden unit with what is perhaps the best known of Sweden's culinary traditions—the *smörgåsbord!* This traditional Swedish feast is a far cry from its literal translation of "bread and butter table," and it is also unlike the random offering of food that most Americans associate it with. A traditional Swedish *smörgåsbord* can be any size; however it must include classic herring dishes, Swedish meatballs, and a potato casserole named *Jansson's Temptation.* The traditional meal is also eaten in a prescribed order and requires several clean plates per person!

For your classroom smorgasbord, enlist the help of your students' parents in preparing a variety of kid-pleasing dishes. At the end of the eating extravaganza, have your students stand as a group and graciously recite the Swedish phrase *Tack for maten!* ("Thank you for the food!") to their generous hosts.

225

bers and friends.

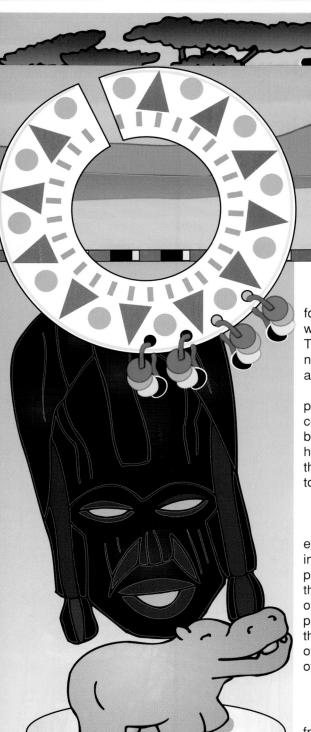

Nomads And Necklaces

About three percent of Kenya's people are nomads who raise livestock for a living. These people move from place to place in search of food and water for their animals. The best-known Kenyan nomads are the *Masai.* These tall, slender people are proud and strong. All Masai wear beautiful necklaces made of colorful beads. Your students will stand tall and proud as they make and wear these necklaces.

To make a necklace, cut through the rim of a nine-inch thin white paper plate; then cut away the center of the plate. Use crayons or markers to color a design around the collar. For added appeal, hole-punch the front bottom rim of the resulting necklace. Thread a length of yarn through each hole; then string a few dyed pasta pieces or beads (paper or wooden) onto the yarn length before securely tying the yarn ends. The necklace is ready to wear!

Wonderful Wood Carvings

Wood carving is a highly respected art form in Kenya. It was first discovered early in the 20th century when some African carvings were brought into European art galleries. There they drew the attention of many European artists, including a young Pablo Picasso. Let your budding artists try their hands at some simulated wood carvings. Each student needs a lump of brown modeling clay, a plastic knife, and a paper plate. Working atop the plate, a student molds his clay to resemble a piece of wood; then he uses the knife to carve out a desired shape. Urge students to carve the shapes of African animals or favorite relatives—both of which are popular subjects of Kenyan wood-carvers.

Kenyan Cuisine

Corn, or *maize,* as it is called in Kenya, is the country's basic food. It is frequently ground into a porridge and mixed with other vegetables and beef or fish to make a stew. Rice, sweet potatoes, bananas, potatoes, coconuts, and pineapples are also grown there. Use these recipes to give your students a taste of Kenya!

Akwadu: Coconut-Banana Bake
(makes 30 samples)

Ingredients:
5 large bananas (not overripe)
soft margarine
1/4 cup orange juice

1 tsp. lemon juice
3 tbsp. packed brown sugar
2/3 cup shredded sweetened coconut

Directions:
Peel each banana and cut it into thirds. Slice each piece of banana lengthwise. Arrange the pieces in a jelly-roll pan or a shallow casserole—flat side up. Dot each piece with margarine. Combine the juices; then, using a spoon, lightly drizzle the mixture over each banana piece. (Discard any leftover juice.) Sprinkle each banana with brown sugar, then with coconut. Bake at 375° until the coconut is golden—about 8 to 10 minutes. Serve immediately.

Sweet-Potato Bake
(makes about 30 small portions)

Ingredients:
6 large sweet potatoes
vegetable shortening

margarine or butter
brown sugar

Directions:
Wash and dry each sweet potato; then rub a thin layer of vegetable shortening into the skin. Place the sweet potatoes on a baking sheet. Bake at 325° for approximately 1 1/2 to 2 hours until well-done. Allow the sweet potatoes to cool slightly until they can be safely handled; then remove the skins. Place the sweet-potato flesh in a bowl, and use a fork to gently mash and stir; then spoon into small disposable cups. Dot each cup of sweet potato with margarine or butter, and sprinkle with brown sugar.

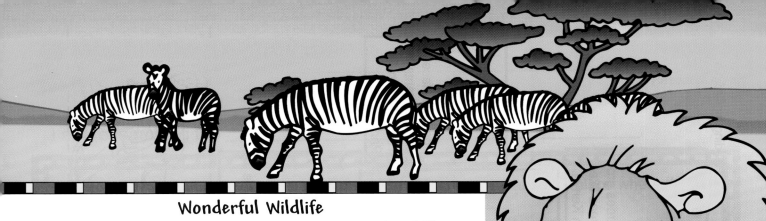

Wonderful Wildlife

Kenya is a treasure trove of wildlife! In an effort to protect its wildlife population from unwelcome hunters, Kenya has developed an extensive system of game reserves and national parks. Animals that stay within the borders of these areas are protected by park rangers. People from all over the world enjoy visiting these places to watch and photograph the fascinating animals that live there.

Display a list of animals that live in Kenya and gather assorted books in which these animals are featured. Then distribute student copies of the research form on page 235. Ask each student to choose an animal and write its name on the line, then research the animal by completing the form. Also make available construction paper and other art supplies for the Bonus Box activity. As students are working, prepare a simple safari backdrop on a bulletin board.

Set aside time for each student to share his findings with his classmates. Also ask each youngster to pin his animal rendering to the safari backdrop. Later enlist your youngsters' help in adding details to the bulletin board and rearranging the animals as needed to create a unique safari scene.

Problems With Poachers

Educate your students about a problem facing Africa's wildlife. Explain that many of Africa's animals are in danger because of *poachers,* people who hunt illegally. Poachers kill animals so they can sell the animals' horns, tusks, skins, and/or hides. Even though game wardens are heroic in their efforts to track down poachers, there is evidence that the threat remains. Lead your youngsters in a poster campaign that will educate them and others in your school about the dangers that Africa's animals face. Have each student illustrate a self-selected animal on a 12" x 18" sheet of construction paper, briefly explain why this animal is hunted, and include a message about boycotting items made from the mentioned material(s). Display these eye-catching posters in the cafeteria and other prominent locations around the school.

Some Animals In Kenya
antelope
baboons
buffaloes
cheetahs
crocodiles
eagles
elephants
flamingos
giraffes
hippopotamuses
hyenas
leopards
lions
monkeys
ostriches
pythons
rhinoceroses
zebras

Help Save This
AFRICAN ANIMAL!

- An elephant is a peaceful animal.
- It should not be killed for its ivory tusks!

Never **buy** ivory.
Don't **wear** it either.
Please help!

Native Americans Of The Southwest

For countless centuries the beautiful, yet harsh land of the Southwest has been home to many different groups of Native Americans. Use the following activities and literature suggestions to supplement your investigation of these remarkable desert dwellers.

ideas contributed by Stacie Stone Davis and Charles J. Wohl

Surveying The Southwest

The Southwest stretches throughout Arizona and New Mexico and into southern Utah and southwestern Colorado. With your students' help, locate this region on a U.S. map. As you and your students investigate the area, reveal that it is home to the vast Grand Canyon, the colorful Painted Desert, the rugged Sangre de Cristo Mountains, the red sandstone buttes and mesas of the Monument Valley, the saguaro-cactus forests of the Sonoran Desert, and much, much more. Show students photographs of the area from assorted resource books and ask them to speculate about the day-to-day struggles of living in this area long ago. Then challenge students to be alert for signs of how the environment of the Southwest influenced the lifestyles of the Native Americans who settled there.

A Meaningful Matrix

Native Americans have lived in the Southwest for thousands of years. Scientists have learned much about their complex and rich lives by studying both the past and the present. As students discover information about the past living conditions of specific Native American groups, record it on a matrix like the one shown. Use the gathered information to help students identify and better understand the similarities and differences among the Native American groups of the past.

Group	Home	Food	Art Forms	Other Facts
The Pueblo				
The Hopi	Adobe villages	Corn!	basket weaving pottery silver work kachina dolls	
The Pima	Permanent home called a sandwich home. It was rectangular. It was built with mud and cactus.	corn, squash, beans	basket making	
The Navajo	Permanent home called a hogan. It was made of wood.	corn, fruit	basket making weaving silver work	sheepherders
The				

Teaching Tips

As you prepare to teach about Native American peoples and their cultures, remember that good information, common sense, thoughtfulness, and sensitivity are your best guides. Always differentiate between the past and the present. Avoid activities that perpetuate stereotypes, such as role-playing or the choosing of "Indian" names. Constantly ask yourself how you are increasing your students' knowledge of these rich cultures and ways of life. And always respect the sacred nature of objects and practices associated with Native American cultures. If you are unsure if an activity is appropriate, the best thing you can do is consult a Native American for advice.

Stories In The Stone

Scattered throughout the Southwest are stone drawings called *petroglyphs*. Even though scientists are not sure what most of the drawings mean, they feel certain that the drawings were one way that native southwesterners communicated.

Draw a few simple characters like the ones shown on this page, and ask students to conclude what each may mean. Then let your students try their hand at creating and deciphering paper petroglyphs. To make his drawing, a child trims a 9" x 12" sheet of tan paper to create a large stone shape. On one side he secretly writes in English a message that a southwestern Native American of long ago may have wished to tell others. On the other side of his cutout, he draws a picture or a series of symbols to convey the message. When the projects are finished, have each child, in turn, show his drawing to his classmates and invite them to decode it. At the conclusion of this activity, students will have a much clearer understanding of why scientists often do not agree on the meanings of Native American petroglyphs!

More About Petroglyphs

Use this picture book to further investigate the stone drawings of the Southwest.

The Same Sun Was In The Sky
Written by Denise Webb & Illustrated by Walter Porter
Northland Publishing Company, 1994

A youngster and his grandfather examine the *petroglyphs* in a southwestern desert and theorize about the ancient people who etched them.

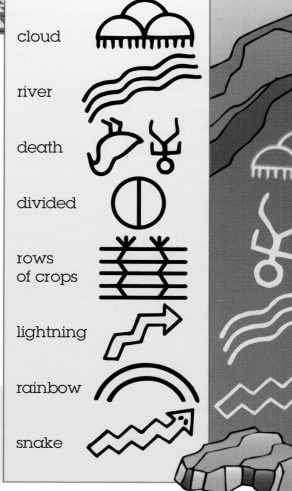

cloud
river
death
divided
rows of crops
lightning
rainbow
snake

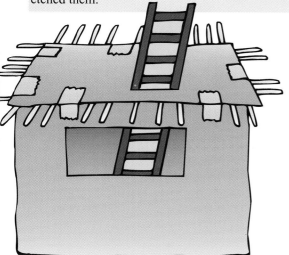

Southwestern Homes

Native southwesterners used materials from their environment to build their homes. Whether a home was permanent or temporary depended on the lifestyle of the builder. Because the Pai and the Apache moved frequently, their homes were easy to build. The Tohono O'odham and Pima peoples, who lived among the desert's saguaro cactus, built homes from mud and cactus ribs. Perhaps the most prevalent structure of the Southwest was the Pueblo home. Each flat-roofed dwelling was constructed from *adobe,* a mixture of clay and sand that covers much of the Southwest.

To construct a Pueblo village in your classroom, have each child create a Pueblo home from a brown paper lunch bag. To do this he cuts away the top six inches of the bag before he opens it. Then he uses scissors, paper scraps, toothpicks, glue or tape, and crayons or markers to craft a roof, a window, an entry hatch, a ladder(s), and other desired details. Arrange the student-made dwellings on a paper-covered table so that you create a village with a central plaza. For added fun, provide modeling clay and invite students to sculpt beehive ovens, native peoples, and other authentic elements for the display.

Did You Know?
- A typical Pueblo adobe home was about 12 feet by 20 feet.
- An adobe home was entered through a hatch in the roof or through a window.
- A family slept on rugs or animal skins. There was no bed.
- There were no tables or chairs.
- Every home had a trough for grinding corn.
- Pueblo houses were generally built by the women.

A Southwestern Affair

People from the world over come to the Southwest to purchase the unrivaled Native American art that is crafted there. One of the largest art-and-craft fairs held each year is the Santa Fe Indian Market. Because art is a fun and educational way to learn about the culture and lifestyles of the first southwesterners, four craft-type projects follow. Boost your youngsters' self-esteem by designating an area of your classroom where students can proudly showcase the Native American art that they create. As an added bonus, the resulting southwestern display is just what you need for an impressive culminating activity (see "It's A Southwestern Celebration!" on page 241).

Pueblo Pottery

Making fine pottery has always been important to the Pueblo. The clay pots made by Pueblo ancestors were used for cooking, serving, and storing food. Today Pueblo artists still hand-form their clay pots. Because Pueblo pottery is prized by collectors from around the world, it is an excellent source of income for many Pueblo Native Americans.

Each student can create her own Pueblo-style pottery using a ball of Crayola® Model Magic®, a paintbrush, and tempera or acrylic paints. Invite each student to shape her ball of modeling compound into a pot or a small turtle (a shape that many Pueblo children make when they are just beginning to learn about pottery). After the student's pottery piece has dried overnight, have her use the paints and paintbrush to embellish it as desired.

Pam Crane

Stunning Navajo Silver Work

One of the best-known Native American crafts today is the beautiful turquoise-and-silver jewelry made by the Navajo. Surprisingly enough the Navajo only began making the jewelry in the mid-1800s—not all that long ago! Show students photographs (or actual samples) of Navajo jewelry. Explain that the jewelry holds special meaning to the Navajo people because in their culture turquoise represents harmony and beauty.

Students will enjoy making stunning pendants that resemble this Navajo art form. To make a pendant, cover a three-inch tagboard circle with aluminum foil. Use craft glue to attach pieces of turquoise-colored Play-Doh® to the foil. When the glue has dried, use a toothpick to carefully etch details into the foil. Securely tape the center of a three-foot length of string or cord to the back of the project. For added appeal crumple small pieces of foil around the string to create shiny silver beads as shown. Tightly tie the string's ends so that the stunning silver work will be easy to slip on and off for wearing. Interested students can also craft bracelets and belts from similar supplies.

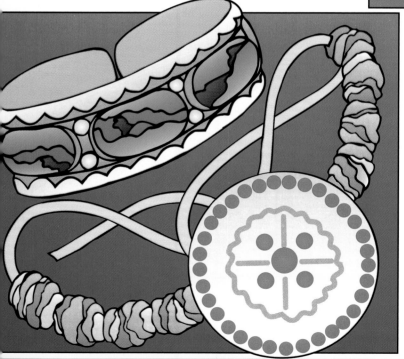

Hopi Dolls That Teach

Perhaps the most distinctive of all Hopi creations are the *kachina dolls*. Each doll is carefully carved from the root of a cottonwood tree and painted to resemble a Hopi spirit or *kachina*. Because there are more than 250 different kachinas in the Hopi culture, Hopi children are often given the dolls as a way to teach them about the spirits. A kachina doll is a very valued possession and is never handled as a toy. Over time the kachina dolls have become very detailed and fanciful, and are now also purchased by non-Hopi collectors from around the world for their artistic beauty.

These colorful, student-created doll booklets are the perfect place to record information about the Hopi. To make his booklet, a student traces a doll-shaped template (like the one shown) onto a cereal-box panel and cuts along the resulting outline. Then he uses colorful paper, glue, markers or crayons, craft feathers, yarn, and other available materials to decorate the cutout to his liking. Assist each student in stapling a stack of blank paper rectangles to the front of the cutout. Next instruct each child to write "Facts About The Hopi" and his name on the top rectangle, then write and illustrate a fact about the Hopi Indians on each remaining rectangle. Encourage students to use their completed booklets to *teach* their family and friends about the Hopi.

Facts About The Hopi

by Mara Floyd

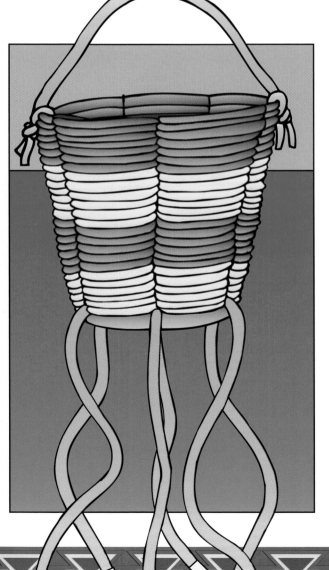

Apache Baskets

Traditionally the Apache were hunters and gatherers who frequently moved from place to place in search of food. Breakable clay pots were impractical for this lifestyle, so the Apache used yucca, beargrass, and other plants to weave light baskets in which to store and carry food and water. Today the Apache make beautiful baskets for use in ceremonies and to sell to collectors. The following basket-weaving project is sure to please your students. For the best results, complete Steps 1 and 2 for each student in advance.

Lightweight Basket

Materials Needed For One Basket:

9-ounce clear plastic cup	clear tape
natural twine: four 1-foot lengths	scissors
raffia: two or more different colors	hole puncher
masking or colored electric tape	ruler

Directions:

1. In the cup make an odd number of vertical cuts that are about one inch apart and stop at the base.
2. Punch two holes in the cup rim opposite each other.
3. To prevent raveling, tape each end of each twine length with the masking tape.
4. Holding the center portion of one twine length taut, slide the twine to the base of the container through two opposite slits.
5. Repeat Step 4 two more times, varying the placement of each twine length.
6. Tie and knot one end of a length of raffia around one plastic strip—making sure the raffia is pushed to the base of the cup and the knot is to the inside.
7. Weave the entire length of raffia in and out of the plastic strips, making sure the exposed end is inside the cup.
8. Varying the color of the raffia used as desired, repeat Steps 6 and 7—starting where the last length of raffia ended—until the cup is covered.
9. Use the clear tape to secure any loose ends of raffia inside the cup.
10. To make a basket handle, thread and tie each end of the remaining twine length through a different hole in the cup rim.

A Taste Of The Southwest

One of the main crops of the first Native Americans living in the Southwest was corn. In time other crops like pumpkins, squash, and beans were cultivated. Add to the flavor of your southwestern study by preparing a corn dish. It could be as simple as popping corn for the class or baking corn muffins. If you're a bit more adventurous, try one of the following recipes.

Navajo Faux Fry Bread
(makes about 25 small servings)

Ingredients:
2 cups self-rising cornmeal
1 1/2 cups buttermilk

2 eggs
2 tablespoons sugar

Directions:
Mix the ingredients together. Using an electric fry pan or a skillet and a hot plate, prepare spoonfuls of the batter as you would pancakes.

Pueblo Corn Pudding
(makes about 25 small servings)

Ingredients:
3 cups milk
1/2 cup molasses or
   dark corn syrup
1/3 cup cornmeal
2 eggs, slightly beaten

2 tablespoons melted butter
1 1/2 tsp. pumpkin pie spice
1/8 tsp. salt

Directions:
In a large saucepan, stir together the milk and molasses. Cook over medium heat until hot—but not boiling. Slowly stir in the cornmeal. Continue cooking and stirring. When the mixture thickens, remove it from the heat, and stir in the eggs and butter. Next add the pumpkin pie spice and the salt. Stir until well blended. Spray the bottom and sides of a square baking pan with nonstick cooking spray, and pour the mixture into the pan. Bake at 325° for about 1 hour and 15 minutes. Let the pudding cool; then cut it into squares to serve. Top each serving with a dab of whipped cream if desired.

A Southwestern Trickster

Coyote is a trickster celebrated in folklore the world over. But he is arguably the most famous in the American Southwest. Coyote is both a trickster and a wise teacher. He survives against impossible odds; however, no matter how tricky he is, he is usually the brunt of his own joke or trick. Read aloud a sampling of Coyote trickster tales from the Southwest. A story worth considering is *Coyote And The Magic Words* written by Phyllis Root and illustrated by Sandra Speidel (Lothrop, Lee & Shepard Books; 1993). Then invite each child to write and illustrate an original story featuring this southwestern trickster. Mount each child's work on colorful paper, and exhibit it on a bulletin board titled "Coyote Tales."

Outstanding Teacher Resources

Desert Dwellers: Native People Of The American Southwest
Written & Photographed by Scott S. Warren
Chronicle Books, 1997

Pueblo Indian
Written by Steven Cory & Illustrated by Richard Erickson
Lerner Publications Company, 1996

The Navajos: People Of The Southwest
Written by Nancy Bonvillain & Includes Photographs
The Millbrook Press, Inc.; 1995

Keeping The Culture Alive

It is important that students understand that Native American culture is an important part of our country's past *and* its future. Use the following literature selections to introduce students to some present-day Native American children who are proudly carrying on the heritage of their southwestern ancestors. Students will enjoy discovering the similarities and the differences between their lives and the lives of the children they learn about.

books reviewed by Deborah Zink Roffino

Dancing Rainbows: A Pueblo Boy's Story
Written & Photographed by Evelyn Clarke Mott
Cobblehill Books, 1996

A young Tewa boy and his grandfather invite readers to join them as they prepare for their tribe's annual Feast Day celebration. Vivid photographs capture the preparations and provide a detailed look at colorful costumes and dances that are an important part of this traditional event.

Earth Daughter: Alicia Of Ácoma Pueblo
Written & Photographed by George Ancona
Simon & Schuster Books For Young Readers, 1995

Family and culture are celebrated in this inviting look at a Pueblo people and their time-honored art of pottery making. Full-color close-ups bring the pottery-making process to life—from searching for just the right clay to selling the completed pieces at a festive Pueblo craft fair.

Pueblo Boy: Growing Up In Two Worlds
Written & Photographed by Marcia Keegan
Puffin Books, 1991

This slim paperback is a beautifully executed photo-essay of the day-to-day life of Timmy Roybal, a ten-year-old Native American growing up at the San Ildefonso Pueblo in New Mexico.

Apache Rodeo
Written by Diane Hoyt-Goldsmith
Photographed by Lawrence Migdale
Holiday House, Inc.; 1995

Ten-year-old Felecita provides the narration for this superbly photographed visit to the Fort Apache Reservation in Whiteriver, Arizona. Her enthusiasm for traditional Apache events like the annual rodeo is contagious. And her descriptions of everyday events and activities will lead students to see the similarities between their lives and life on the reservation.

My Navajo Sister
Written & Illustrated by Eleanor Schick
Simon & Schuster Books For Young Readers, 1996

A young girl fondly remembers a summer spent living on a ranch near a Navajo reservation. Wispy pastels capture the memories, Navajo culture, and Arizona landscape.

A Rainbow At Night: The World In Words And Pictures By Navajo Children
Written by Bruce Hucko
Chronicle Books, 1996

Through this lively collection of paintings and drawings, youngsters will learn about special traditions of Navajo life and the kinship that all children—regardless of their backgrounds—share. Each piece of artwork is accompanied by a photo of and a quote from the artist, a brief paragraph of explanation and/or insight, and a suggested follow-up activity from the children's "art coach."

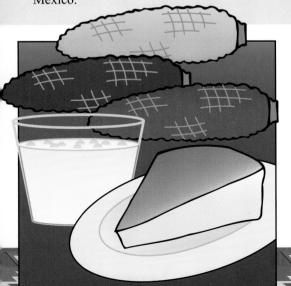

It's A Southwestern Celebration!

Conclude your study of southwestern Native Americans with a festival of learning! Encourage students to invite their families to this special celebration. The guests of honor can stroll through the classroom area where student projects are on display (see "A Southwestern Affair" on page 238), check out the student-created Pueblo village (see "Southwestern Homes" on page 237), and read the Coyote tales on exhibit (see "A Southwestern Trickster" on page 240). Plan for students to serve their guests a southwestern snack that includes a sample of fry bread or corn pudding (recipes on page 240). Then invite interested youngsters to share what they have learned about Native Americans of the Southwest and to field questions from their visitors on the topic. Conclude the festivities with an oral reading of one or more student-selected Native American picture books: fiction, nonfiction, or both!

BUILDING CHARACTER

Compassion. Helpfulness. Perseverance. Respect. Responsibility. The list of key character-building qualities goes on and on—and so does the challenge of teaching these virtues to young children. Use the following character-building activities from our subscribers to help your students learn to care for themselves and others.

HELPFULNESS

COMPASSION

Caring For Others

Nurture compassion in your students with monthly community service projects. Ideas include collecting wish-list items for a local animal shelter, making get-well bags for hospital patients, creating holiday cards or ornaments for a retirement home, collecting needed items for a local shelter, and helping older neighbors with light yard work. Students will experience the joy of giving of themselves and come to realize the benefits of compassion—by both the giver and the receiver.

Diane Benner—Gr. 2, Dover Elementary, Dover, PA

Respect Day

Designate a day for your classroom, grade level, or entire school to refine their skills of respect. Start Respect Day with a class meeting or an assembly. Discuss the meaning of respect, have volunteers role-play respectful behavior, and answer students' questions. Then challenge students and staff members to spend the entire day displaying their most respectful behavior. This large-scale, concrete example of respect will encourage students to carry this positive behavior beyond the school walls. You may find that more value days—like Courtesy Day, Cooperation Day, and Kindness Day—are in order!

Debbie Green—Gr. 3, Northwest Heights Elementary School
Durant, OK

COOPERATION

Terrific Tales

Reinforce a variety of character-building traits with a Terrific Tales board. Title a sheet of poster board "Terrific Tales About _____" and laminate the resulting poster for durability. Display the poster in an easily accessible location. Near the poster, place a pad of self-adhesive notes and a container of pencils. At the start of each week use a wipe-off marker to program the poster with a desired character trait like "Honesty," "Fairness," or "Helpfulness."

After confirming that students understand the meaning of the spotlighted trait, invite them to be on the lookout for examples of it. When a youngster realizes that a classmate has exhibited the featured behavior toward him, he goes to the poster, describes the incident on a self-adhesive note, and signs and attaches the note to the poster. During the week read some of the posted notes aloud. Then, at the end of the week, read each note aloud and present it to the student who demonstrated the featured behavior. To reprogram the poster, wipe off and replace the featured trait. Your students' self-esteems are sure to soar!

Valerie Masin—Grs. K–3
District 504
Burwell, NE

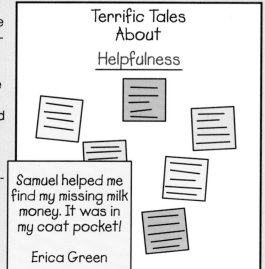

Terrific Tales
About

Helpfulness

Samuel helped me find my missing milk money. It was in my coat pocket!

Erica Green

COURAGE

HONESTY

FAIRNESS

COURTESY

Distinguished Descriptions

Inspire students to display praiseworthy behavior with this simple strategy. When selecting student volunteers or announcing classroom helpers, refrain from immediately naming each student. First share several positive statements about a student and if desired, invite class members to identify the student who is being described. Consider statements like "This week's plant waterer is a great team player, both on the soccer field and in the classroom," and "The student who will assist me with this science experiment is always willing to help his classmates with their spelling." You'll be reinforcing a variety of positive behaviors and boosting the self-esteem of your youngsters, too!

Kelly Pflederer—Gr. 2
Academy of the Sacred Heart
St. Louis, MO

It Takes Teamwork!

Bolster cooperation skills with this unique approach to teamwork. Begin each team-based activity (curriculum-related or recreational) by asking the members of each team to meet and respond to several predetermined questions like "What is the team's goal?" and "What can the team do to meet its goal?" Then, during the team-based activity, encourage team members to follow directions, display positive attitudes, and support each other. As a follow-up to the activity, have the team members meet again. Ask each student on the team to name one positive way that he contributed to the activity. Also invite team members to identify teammates who complimented them during the activity. Implement this approach and you'll see increased self-esteem, confidence, and cooperation in your classroom in no time!

Janice Yocum and Judy Boutz
Independence, MO

Words Of Value

Honesty. Courtesy. Perseverance. This easy-to-implement writing activity can reinforce these and other character traits. Program individual index cards with character-related words; then store the cards in a decorated container. At the beginning of each week, ask a student volunteer to draw a card from the container, read the word on the card aloud, and show it to the class. Invite students to explain the meaning of the chosen word. When you feel that the meaning of the word is well understood, display the word card on a classroom wall. Then instruct each student to write a sentence containing the featured word (or a form of it) on a provided paper strip. Near the end of the day, have each student read her sentence aloud; then post the students' sentences on the wall with the featured word. Challenge students to practice the featured character trait all week long—and suggest that they refer to the posted sentences for added inspiration.

Jeannette Freeman—Substitute Teacher Grs. 1–2
Antilles Elementary School
Fort Buchanan, Puerto Rico

Honesty

Joey was honest and returned the money he found.

I am an honest person.

I like my friends to be honest with me.

243

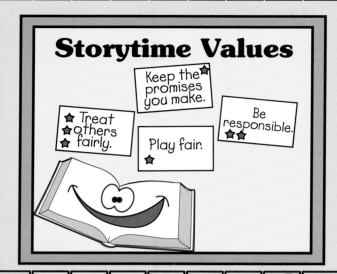

Storytime Values

★ Treat ★ others ★ fairly.

Keep the promises you make. ★

Play fair. ★

Be responsible. ★★

Characters With Character

Children's literature is an excellent place to find examples of positive character traits. Follow up an oral reading of a favorite picture book or beginning chapter book by asking students to identify the positive values of the main character(s). To create an on-going display, write the student responses on individual cards or cutouts and post them on a bulletin board titled "Storytime Values." Repeat the activity each time you finish an oral reading of a children's book. Periodically review the character traits on display and add a star to each card that features a value that your students feel they consistently portray.

Jackie Hostetler—Gr. 1
Tri-County R-VII Elementary School, Jamesport, MO

CONFIDENCE

Positive Response

Promote student dignity and heighten self-esteem with this positive response strategy. When a student responds incorrectly to a question, instead of pointing out that his answer is wrong, state the question to which the student's answer corresponds. Then provide the correct answer to the original question. For example, if the question asked is "What is the sum of 6 + 7?", and a student replies "14"—respond as follows: "14 is the sum of 7 + 7. That means the sum of 6 + 7 is 13." Since words like "no" and "wrong" are avoided, a student's dignity is preserved and the feeling of being wrong is minimized. This approach is sure to increase student participation. And since students learn by example, you can look forward to hearing your youngsters stating positive responses for incorrect answers, too!

Pat Boswell—Gr. 3, Bonn Elementary School, Germany

DIGNITY

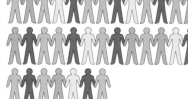

Roll Call For Respect

Encourage respect among your students with this two-fold tip. When you observe a student showing respect for herself, for others, or for her school or community, award the student with a respect coupon. When a child earns three coupons, invite the student and a special guest to eat their lunches at a designated "Table Of Respect." When a fourth coupon is earned, allow the student to place a personalized cutout on a classroom display titled "Roll Call For Respect." This visual reminder of respectful behavior makes it easy for students and visitors to see that respect is a valued trait in your classroom.

Debbie Green—Gr. 3
Northwest Heights Elementary School
Durant, OK

Roll Call For Respect

RESPECT

The Wall Of Fame

Here's an ideal way to recognize your students' good deeds. Title an area of a classroom wall "The Wall Of Fame" and duplicate a supply of the induction form on page 254. When a student observes a classmate performing a good deed like being kind, compassionate, or helpful, he completes and submits to you a copy of the induction form. Post the completed forms, along with snapshots of the inductees, on The Wall Of Fame. As students earn recognition, they will be encouraged to continue their kind behavior.

Adriana Paciocco—Gr. 2
Eagle Elementary School
West Bloomfield, MI

I, _Joey Gomez_, induct _Matthew Taylor_ into The Wall Of Fame because _he asked me to play with him at recess._

I, _Lizzy Leon_, induct _Breyanna Lynne_ into the Wall Of Fame becaus_e_ _said she was s___ _I didn't feel we___

RESPONSIBILITY

Rob Mayworth

LOYALTY

Hug Day

Hugs, hugs, hugs! What a great way to show someone you care! Have students describe how they feel when they are hugged and when they give hugs. Lead students to understand that hugging is one way to show someone that you care. Then find out other ways your students show their friends and family members that they care about them. To encourage students to show their compassion for others, designate one day a month as Hug Day (or Show You Care Day). On Hug Day display a sign on the classroom door that invites all who enter the room to demonstrate their caring spirit throughout the day. If desired, post a list of appropriate caring gestures like hugs, handshakes, and pats on the back. At the end of the day, invite students to talk about how showing and receiving compassion made them feel. Just imagine the good things you'll hear!

Nancy Kaczrowski
Luverne, MN

PERSEVERANCE

Wiggling With Character

Keep a visible reminder of classroom character goals with this year-round display. You will need a large construction-paper circle for each month of the school year, plus one more. For each month choose one value on which to focus; then write the selected values near the tops of the individual circles. Decorate the remaining cutout to resemble the face of a caterpillar. Mount the circles in sequential order on a classroom wall. Be sure the resulting character caterpillar is easily accessible. Each month introduce the selected value, and discuss with your students what the value means and different ways that it can be demonstrated. Label the corresponding caterpillar segment accordingly. Then challenge students to display the featured character trait throughout the month. To reinforce your students' efforts, place a Gummy caterpillar (worm) in a clear container on your desk each time you observe a student displaying the featured value. When you have a class supply, distribute the candies to the students; then start another collection. Throughout the year periodically review the character goals of past months. You can count on plenty of positive growth when you use this approach to character education!

Kristi Gullett—Gr. 2
Peoria Christian School
Peoria, IL

Respect Honesty Fairness

BUILDING CHARACTER
WITH...CARING!

Who cares? Your students do—and you do, too! Use these character-building activities to strengthen your students' understanding of the virtues of caring and kindness. Watch youngsters exhibit considerate behaviors as they learn about caring for themselves and others!

ideas by Darcy A. Brown

CARING

A Chain Of Caring

This classroom caring chain reminds students to always care for one another! Ask students to brainstorm ways that they exhibit kindness and list their ideas on chart paper. Provide each student with a strip of pastel construction paper. Have each student choose an idea from the list and write a sentence about it on her paper strip. Collect the programmed strips and use them to make a paper chain like the one shown. Display the completed chain on a wall or bulletin board with the title "We Care!" Throughout the year encourage students to program paper strips for the classroom chain as they observe additional acts of kindness.

CARING

"We Care!" Basket

For those times when you'd like to shower a student or his family with caring thoughts (due to a serious illness, hospitalization, a death in the family, etc.), involve your youngsters in creating this one-of-a-kind gift. Begin by sharing your favorite version of the children's book *Stone Soup*. Discuss how the characters in the story helped one another make a delicious soup. Next display a basket for the class. Explain to your students that they will be working together to create a special gift basket. Ask each student to bring to school a small piece of fruit. When the gifts of fruit have been collected, have students write personal messages of caring on fruit-shaped cutouts. Arrange the messages and fruit in the basket. Wrap the entire basket in colorful plastic wrap and secure the top with a bow and a personalized gift tag. Then present or deliver the "We Care!" basket. Continue this thoughtful practice throughout the year. Youngsters will experience the joys of kindness, caring, and generosity with every special gift!

Patty Young—Grs. K–4
Linton Hall School , Bristow, VA

246

Lending A Caring Hand!

Encourage students to lend a caring hand as they create this adorable booklet! As a prewriting activity, read aloud a favorite children's book that depicts caring behavior. (One excellent choice is *The Child's World Of Caring* by Jane Belk Moncure [The Child's World, Inc.; 1997]. The book's simple text and colorful pictures portray a wide variety of caring behavior.) Next invite students to brainstorm ways that they can show how much they care. Give each student a large construction-paper hand cutout. On the chalkboard list an assortment of sentence starters—such as "I care for myself when I...," "I care for others when I...," and "I care for the Earth when I...." Have each student copy, complete, and illustrate one sentence on her cutout. Collect the students' completed work and assemble it into a booklet. Hole-punch the resulting booklet pages and two hand-shaped booklet covers; then use yarn to bind the pages between the covers. Add the title "Lending A Caring Hand," a class byline, and desired decorations to the front booklet cover. Then place the class caring booklet at a center or in your classroom library for everyone to enjoy!

Recipes For A Caring Student

Create a stir as youngsters write recipes for a caring student! Don a chef's hat as you read aloud a few recipes with your class. Review the different words that are used when writing a recipe (cup, teaspoon, stir, mix, etc.); then have students brainstorm qualities that make a caring student. Write the students' ideas on chart paper. Provide each student with a preprogrammed copy of a large recipe card. Instruct each child to refer to the chart as he lists the necessary ingredients for a caring student. Next have him write directions for mixing these ingredients. Mount the completed recipes on a bulletin board for an eye-catching display. For added fun, place the chef's hat near the display for students to wear as they read each other's recipes!

The Caring Crown

Motivate caring students with this noble idea! Make a child-size crown similar to the one shown and laminate it for durability. Embellish the crown with glitter pens, stickers, or plastic jewels. Each day spotlight a different student who continually exhibits caring behaviors. Crown the student king or queen of the day and take a picture of the royal youngster with an instant camera. Use a permanent marker to write a personal message on the bottom of the photo. Send the picture home with the child to share with her family. Your kings and queens will wear the caring crown with pride!

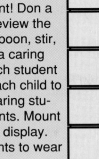

Missy

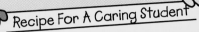
Recipe For A Caring Student

Ingredients:
1 cup of kindness
2 teaspoons of helping others
2 cups of love
1 cup of niceness
3 teaspoons of sharing

Directions:
Dump the kindness, love, and niceness into a bowl. Mix. Sprinkle with sharing and helping others. Mix again. Give to one student to eat. Now you have a caring student!

CARING

A Rainbow Of A Room!

Reinforce the value of sharing and kindness with this unique activity. Draw a large fish on poster board, cut it out, and laminate it for durability. On the fish, tape one plastic jewel for every student. Display the colorful creation on a classroom wall or bulletin board and invite students to share their comments about it. After a few days, suggest to students how nice the room would look if additional jeweled fish were displayed. Then read aloud Marcus Pfister's book *The Rainbow Fish* (North-South Books, 1992). Discuss how happy the Rainbow Fish became when he learned to share with others. Have students describe additional ways they can share. Next provide each student with a small construction-paper fish cutout. Have him decorate his fish shape and embellish it with a jewel from the larger fish. Mount the student-decorated fish on the walls for a rainbow of a room!

Pam Wilson—Gr. 3, Ebenezer School, Statesville, NC

Books Worth Caring About!

Enlist the help of your school librarian or media specialist in locating additional children's books to enhance your values unit. Some good choices are:

Chester's Way
Written & Illustrated by Kevin Henkes
Greenwillow Books, 1988

Gramma's Walk
Written & Illustrated by Anna Grossnickle Hines
Greenwillow Books, 1993

Grandaddy's Place
Written by Helen V. Griffith
Illustrated by James Stevenson
Greenwillow Books, 1987

Snow White And Rose Red
Written by Jacob and Wilhelm Grimm
Retold & Illustrated by Bernadette Watts
North-South Books, Inc.; 1988

The Ugly Duckling
Written by Hans Christian Andersen
Retold by Adrian Mitchell
Illustrated by Jonathan Heale
Dorling Kindersley Publishers, Inc.; 1994

BUILDING CHARACTER
WITH...HONESTY!

Instill the virtue of integrity by teaching the importance of honesty. Use these activities to encourage youngsters to make conscientious and trustworthy decisions.

ideas by Darcy Brown

WHAT WOULD YOU DO?

Inspire your youngsters to make honest and truthful decisions with this notable idea! In advance write a number of decision-making situations on index cards. Place the cards in an empty container. To begin the lesson, have students talk about times they have been in situations that tested their honesty. Then have a child draw a card from the container and read it aloud. Ask youngsters to describe what they would do in this situation and explain why. Encourage discussion among the students. When appropriate have another child draw a card. Repeat the process until all of the cards have been discussed. For added fun invite small groups of students to act out some of the situations.

Your friend asks you to do his homework for him.

You cheat on a test.

HONESTY

HONESTY ACROSTIC POEMS

Help youngsters further investigate honesty when they create these awesome acrostic poems. As your students brainstorm ideas about the importance of being honest, list their ideas on chart paper. Next have each child use capital letters to write the word "honesty" down the left side of a sheet of drawing paper. Instruct students to refer to the chart as they write a descriptive word or phrase that begins with each letter of the word. Allow time for students to decorate their work. If desired mount the completed poems on larger sheets of construction paper. Then spread the word about honesty by displaying the projects around the room.

Honorable
Others trust you
Never lie
Everyone is fair
Say nice things
Tell the truth
You are honest

Jocelyn

AS HONEST AS GEORGE WASHINGTON!

Use the famous legend of George Washington and the cherry tree to talk about the importance of telling the truth. Conclude the discussion with this "cherry-ful" activity that reinforces the values of honesty and truthfulness. Provide each student with a white construction-paper copy of the patterns on page 255, a six-inch green pipe cleaner, and a six-inch square of writing paper. Students will also need pencils, scissors, crayons, and access to clear tape and a stapler.

To make a cherry project like the one pictured, a child colors and cuts out her patterns. Next she traces the cherry cutout onto her writing paper. Inside the resulting outline, she completes the sentence starter. Then she cuts out the shape, aligns her colored cherry atop the resulting cutout, and staples the shapes together near the top left edge. To complete her project, the student tapes her leaf cutout near one end of her pipe cleaner and then tapes the resulting stem to the back of her project. Mount the completed cherries on a large paper tree with the title "As Honest As George Washington!"

You should always tell the truth because...

...one's... Not telling the truth could make him cry.

248

FANTASTIC FABLES

Fables are a great way to reinforce students' understanding of good character! Each day read aloud a fable, and discuss the lesson or moral of the story. After youngsters have heard a number of fables, challenge them to write and illustrate original fables that reinforce the importance of honesty. Remind students that the character(s) in their stories should learn a lesson about truthfulness. If desired ask each student to write a moral at the end of his fable that relates to the honesty lesson that he described. Invite students to share their creations with the rest of the class. Then collect the students' fables and staple them between two construction-paper covers. Add a title such as "Fantastic Fables," a class byline, and desired decorations to the front cover.

Kimberly Hofstetter—Substitute Teacher
Oakland County School District
Bloomfield Hills, MI

A PLEDGE TO BE HONEST

As a culminating activity, have youngsters make a pledge of honesty. Give students copies of the honesty pledge on page 255. Sing the pledge (to the tune of "Sailing, Sailing") or read it aloud as your class follows along. Talk with students about what the pledge means; then ask each child to sign his name and write the date on the lines. If desired have students mount their pledges on slightly larger sheets of construction paper. Challenge youngsters to memorize the pledge, then sing or recite it to others. No doubt your youngsters will perform the pledge with pride!

PLENTIFUL POTS

Use this literature connection to help your youngsters recognize the importance of telling the truth. In the story *The Empty Pot* by Demi (Henry Holt And Company, Inc.; 1990), Ping learns a valuable lesson about honesty and perseverance. After sharing the story with your class, invite students to talk about how Ping's courage and honesty helped him become the emperor of China. Then have your youngsters create these unique reminders to commemorate Ping's accomplishment. Provide each student with a small Styrofoam® cup (with drainage holes punched in the bottom), soil, water, and a choice of flower seeds. Have youngsters use the materials to plant seeds in honor of Ping. Put the seed cups on a tray or cookie sheet and place them in a sunny location in your classroom. Memories of Ping's courage will live on as students care for their seeds.

TRULY TRUTHFUL TALES!

Bolster honest behaviors with these one-of-a-kind stories:

To Tell The Truth
Written by Patti Farmer & Illustrated by Stephen Taylor
Stoddart Kids, 1997

Honest Tulio
Written & Illustrated by John Himmelman
BridgeWater Books, 1997

Believing Sophie
Written by Hazel Hutchins
Illustrated by Dorothy Donohue
Albert Whitman & Company, 1995

Mary Marony And The Chocolate Surprise
Written by Suzy Kline
Illustrated by Blanche Sims
G. P. Putnam's Sons, 1995

Zack's Tall Tale
Adapted by Shelagh Canning
Illustrated by Davis Henry
Aladdin Paperbacks, 1996

King Bob's New Clothes
Written by Dom DeLuise
Illustrated by Christopher Santoro
Simon & Schuster Books For Young Readers, 1996

BUILDING CHARACTER
WITH...RESPONSIBILITY!

Understanding responsibility is the first step towards practicing it! Use these creative character-building activities to give students a clear picture of responsibility. Then stand back and watch them put their new knowledge into practice!

ideas by Darcy Brown

R E S P O N S I B I L I T Y

"Egg-ceptionally" Responsible!

Provide an excellent example of responsible behavior by reading aloud *Horton Hatches The Egg* by Dr. Seuss (Random House, Inc.; 1968). In this delightful tale, Horton the elephant takes over Mayzie bird's job of sitting on an egg while she flies south for a vacation. At the conclusion of the story, ask students to describe Horton's responsible behaviors. Then put your youngsters' responsible behaviors to the test with this egg-sitting project. To make a nest for his egg, a student paints an eight-ounce Styrofoam® cup brown. When the paint has dried, he fills the cup halfway with Spanish moss (available at craft stores). Next he decorates a hard-boiled egg with permanent markers, gives his egg a name, and places it into the nest. Each student should immediately begin to care for his egg. Then, at the end of the day, have each youngster take his egg home overnight, along with a note to his parent that explains the egg-sitting project.

The following day, ask students to share their caretaking experiences. Then, on a lined egg cutout, have each youngster describe the responsible behaviors he exhibited as he cared for his egg. Mount these cutouts on a bulletin board similar to the one shown and collect the hard-boiled eggs for disposal. No doubt your youngsters will have a memorable "egg-sperience" with responsibility!

Colleen Duggan-Neubert and Pat Horgan
Plantation Park Elementary, Plantation, FL

We've Been "Egg-ceptionally" Responsible!

Homework Helper

Looking for a fun way to promote responsible homework behaviors? Then try this idea! Write "R E S P O N S I B L E" on a chalkboard or chart. Discuss the meaning of the word and have youngsters brainstorm responsible behaviors like completing homework assignments and getting to school on time. Then challenge students to take responsibility for their homework assignments. Explain that each time the entire class completes a homework assignment on time, you will circle a different letter in "R E S P O N S I B L E." When every letter has been circled, reward the class for its responsible behavior with a special privilege, such as extra recess time, extra free-time reading, or individual homework passes. Repeat this activity as often as desired. What a great way to foster responsibility!

RESPONSIBLE

Graphing Responsibilities

Enlist your students' help in creating a responsibilities graph! On a large sheet of bulletin-board paper, draw a bar-graph outline. Ask youngsters to name responsibilities that they have at home. Label each column of the graph with a different responsibility; then add a title and other needed programming. To complete the graph, each student attaches a personalized sticky note in every column that names a responsibility that he has. Evaluate the resulting graph with the class. To encourage students to become more responsible at home, leave a pad of sticky notes near the graph. Invite students to update the graph as they increase their responsibilities. Then, as a class, periodically reevaluate the graph and note any increase in responsible behaviors.

Responsibilities At Home

How Many Kids?

Responsible Pet Care

National Pet Week (annually the first full week of May) is a perfect time for students to review the responsibilities of owning a pet. Share a pet-related story, like *Arthur's New Puppy* by Marc Brown (Little, Brown And Company; 1993), with your class. Invite youngsters to recall the pet-care responsibilities described in the story, and to state other pet-related responsibilities that they have experienced. Then have each youngster make a poster of pet-care pointers to commemorate National Pet Week. To do this a student designs a colorful poster that depicts responsible ways to take care of pets. After each child shares his poster with his classmates, spread the word about responsibility by displaying the students' work around the school.

Take Care Of Your Pets
feed them every day
play with them
pet them a lot
be patient
National Pet Week
May 3–9, 1998

Community Cleanup

Bolster responsible behaviors when you involve youngsters in a school cleanup project! Brainstorm responsibilities that community members have in maintaining a community that is clean and safe. Then challenge students to become responsible members of their school community by participating in a school cleanup project. As a class outline a project that is practical for your situation. For example you might adopt a small area outside your classroom to keep clean for the remainder of the school year. Or you may plan to clean up a different area of the school grounds each week. For each cleanup mission, have students don orange paper vests and plastic gloves, and carry individual trash bags. Enlist assistance from parent volunteers if desired. In no time at all, your youngsters will be bursting with responsibility!

Shannon Criss—Life Skills Program
Ephrata School
Ephrata, WA

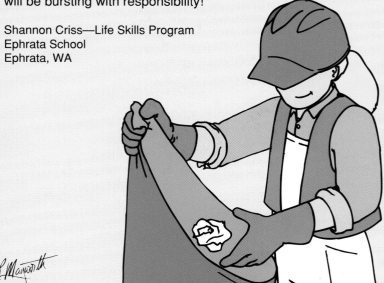

Praiseworthy Pennants

As a culminating activity, have youngsters create these one-of-a-kind responsibility pennants! Begin by having students brainstorm responsible behaviors. List the students' responses on the chalkboard. To create a pennant, a student writes her name and the title "Responsibility is…" on a large pennant cutout; then she illustrates examples of responsible behaviors on her pennant by referring to the class list. Have youngsters share their pennants with their classmates. Display the completed projects around your room for personal reminders of responsibility!

Responsibility is...
Susan K.

Books About Responsibility

Encourage your students to be more responsible when you share these additional titles:

Annie Shows Off: Responsibility
Adapted by Shelagh Canning
Illustrated by Davis Henry
Aladdin Paperbacks, 1996

Clean Your Room, Harvey Moon!
Written & Illustrated by Pat Cummings
Aladdin Paperbacks, 1994

Keep The Lights Burning, Abbie
Written by Peter and Connie Roop
Illustrated by Peter E. Hanson
Carolrhoda Books, Inc.; 1985

Tick-Tock
Written by Eileen Browne
Illustrated by David Parkins
Candlewick Press, 1994

RESPONSIBILITY

BUILDING CHARACTER
WITH...CITIZENSHIP

Opportunities for being a good citizen are everywhere—in the classroom, on the playground, at home, and in the community. Use these character-building activities to foster an understanding of citizenship and to promote its importance in our country and in our world.

ideas contributed by Darcy Brown

CITIZENSHIP

Who's A Citizen?

Begin your study of citizenship by informing students that a *citizen* is a member of a special community or group of people. Explain that a person can be a citizen of a very large community like the United States Of America and a person can also be a citizen of much smaller communities like a classroom, a neighborhood, and a city. Inform students that to become a citizen, special requirements must be fulfilled. For example, a classroom citizen must be enrolled in school, attend class regularly, and follow the established rules. Emphasize that being a citizen is a privilege and responsibilities come with this privilege. Then ask students to name the responsibilities that they have as classroom citizens. Wrap up the discussion by giving each student a signed and dated copy of the Classroom Citizen Certificate on page 256. Invite each child to color his certificate; then, if desired, tape each child's certificate to his desktop as a visual reminder of his important classroom role.

Hooray For You!

You Are A Valued Citizen In Our Classroom!

Ms. James
Teacher's Signature
6/12/98
Date

Citizenship Journals

Heighten your students' awareness of classroom citizenship with this daily writing activity. Each child needs a blank writing journal like the one shown. Ask each student to describe in his journal examples of admirable classroom citizenship or citizen behavior. Clarify that students may write about behaviors they observe in other classroom citizens or describe their own acts of good citizenship. After several days of journal writing, divide students into small groups and ask each group member to take a turn reading aloud his favorite journal entry to date. Repeat the group activity as often as desired, varying the groups each time. What a great way to promote citizenship!

My Citizenship Journal
Jasmine

Mrs. Weiss
I never litter, I obey the traffic laws, and my family donates gifts to the senior center.

In The Community

Expand your students' understanding of citizens and citizenship in the community by reading aloud Jane Cowen-Fletcher's book *It Takes A Village* (Scholastic Inc., 1994). In this book the members of a close-knit village assist a young girl with her baby-sitting duties. At the conclusion of the story, ask students to recall how different community members help the young girl, and have them speculate why the citizens respond as they do. Remind students that in addition to being classroom citizens, they are also citizens of their local community. Lead students to understand that good citizenship in the local community is fostered in the same manner that it is in the classroom—by being responsible, helpful, compassionate, and so on.

Create a colorful display of community citizenship with this homework activity. Send each child home with a one-foot length of colorful bulletin-board paper. In a parent letter, ask that the child and family members and/or friends trace the shapes of their hands on the paper. Ask that each person cut out and sign his shape, then program it with examples of how he contributes to the well-being of the local community. When the hand cutouts are returned, use them to create a colorful border for a bulletin board titled "Look How We Lend A Hand In Our Community!" To complete the display, have each child illustrate how he or his family lend a hand; then mount the illustrations on the display.

Proud To Be An American

Students may be surprised to discover that not everyone in the United States becomes a citizen in the same way. Many people are born as U.S. citizens, but those who are not must apply and qualify for citizenship. Give students a rare look into the latter process by reading aloud *A Very Important Day* by Maggie Rugg Herold (Morrow Junior Books, 1995). This beautifully illustrated picture book briefly chronicles 12 different families—each from a different country—that make their way to downtown New York City (in a snowstorm) to be sworn in as citizens of the United States. The nervous excitement that is generated by this very special occasion is contagious. As an added bonus, the author has included background information about the citizenship process.

For a fun follow-up, enlist your students' help in locating on a world map each of the 12 countries represented in the book. Then invite students to discuss the things that make them proudest to be U.S. citizens.

A Celebration Of Citizenship

Culminate your study of citizenship with a celebration! Encourage students to invite their parents to your classroom festivities. The guests can view the students' star-spangled projects, read excerpts from their children's citizenship journals, and marvel over the helping-hands display to which they contributed. Plan to serve a healthy and patriotic snack of blueberries, sliced strawberries, and banana wheels. Then conclude the affair with a presentation of citizenship awards. To make an award for each student, program, decorate, and cut out a construction-paper copy of the ribbon pattern on page 256. Students will feel especially honored to be recognized for their citizenship efforts in the presence of their guests. And they'll no doubt be motivated to carry on the good-citizen habits that they have formed during your study.

Karen Smith—Gr. 1
Pine Lane Elementary Homeschool
Pace, FL

Super Citizen

Michele

Student Name

is recognized for

being an exellent listener, a helpful friend , and a great sport.

CITIZENSHIP

Star-Spangled Citizens

Get to the heart of citizenship with this patriotic project. To begin, each student uses templates to trace a seven-inch heart shape onto both blank and lined white paper, a nine-inch heart onto blue paper, and eight or more star shapes onto red paper. Then he cuts out the shapes. On the lined white heart the student describes why he is proud to be a citizen. On the blank white heart he illustrates himself and writes his name. He programs each red star with a good-citizen behavior that he practices. To assemble his project, he glues each smaller heart to a different side of the blue heart. Then he glues the stars around the outer edges of his project in a desired fashion. To prepare the project for hanging, the student hole-punches the top of the project, threads a length of monofilament line through the hole, and securely ties the ends of the line.

Continuous Five-Star Citizenship

Continue encouraging good-citizen behaviors with this weekly activity! Use a permanent marker to personalize a resealable plastic bag for every student. Then, each Monday, place five star cutouts in every bag and distribute the bags among the students. Make sure that no student receives his own bag or a bag that he has already received. Then, during the week, ask each student to quietly observe the student whose bag he has and on each star cutout to write a brief note of praise for a different good-citizen behavior that he observes. For a star-studded end-of-the-week finale, have each student return the bag of citizenship compliments to its owner. Ask the students to remove the stars from their bags, read them, and carry them home to share with their families. Then collect the plastic bags for use the following week.

253

Pattern

Use the shield pattern with "The Kenyan Flag" on page 230.

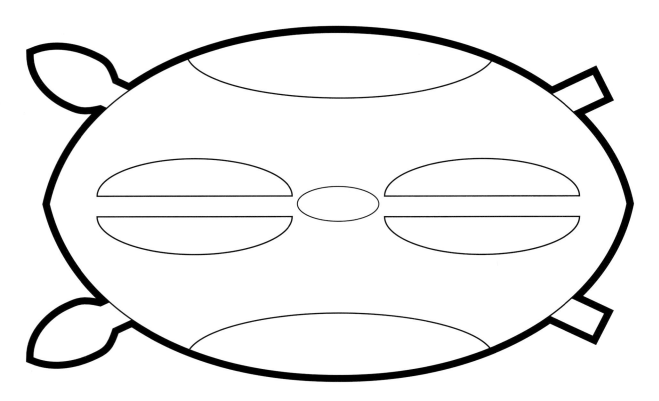

Use the form with "The Wall Of Fame" on page 245.

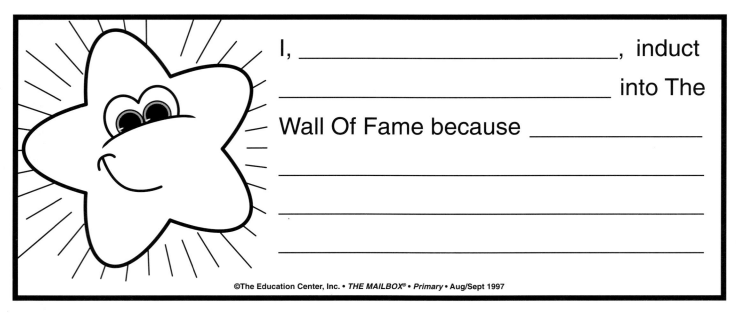

I, _____, induct

_____ into The

Wall Of Fame because _____

_____

_____

_____

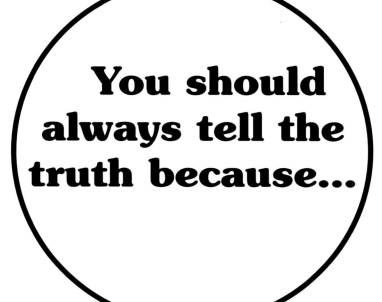

You should always tell the truth because...

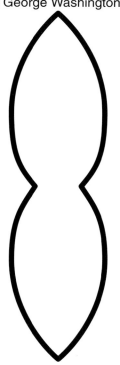

Use the pledge with "A Pledge To Be Honest" on page 249.

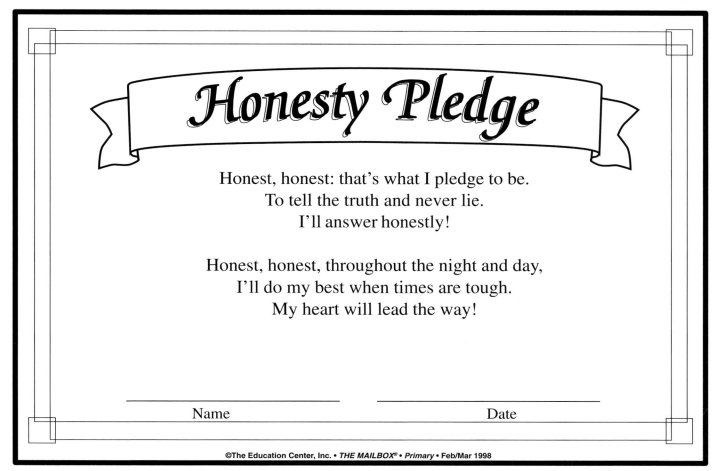

Honesty Pledge

Honest, honest: that's what I pledge to be.
To tell the truth and never lie.
I'll answer honestly!

Honest, honest, throughout the night and day,
I'll do my best when times are tough.
My heart will lead the way!

_____   _____
Name   Date

Pattern And Certificate

Use the certificate with "Who's A Citizen?" on page 252.

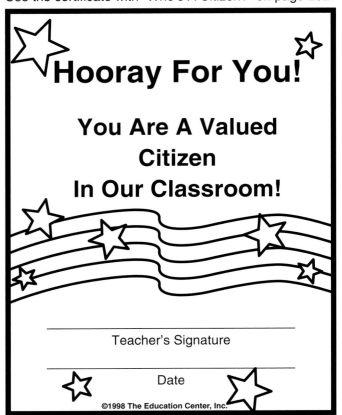

Hooray For You!

You Are A Valued
Citizen
In Our Classroom!

_____
Teacher's Signature

_____
Date

©1998 The Education Center, Inc.

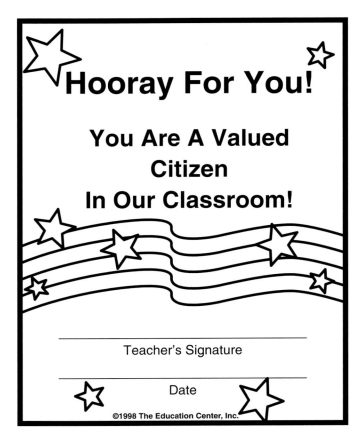

Hooray For You!

You Are A Valued
Citizen
In Our Classroom!

_____
Teacher's Signature

_____
Date

©1998 The Education Center, Inc.

Use the ribbon pattern with "A Celebration Of Citizenship" on page 253.

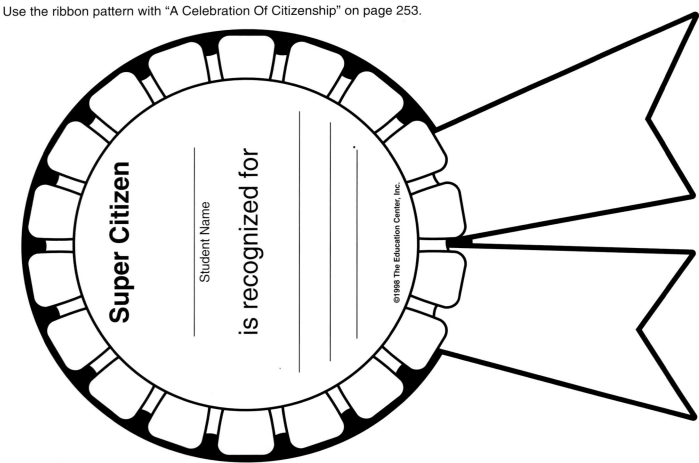

Super Citizen

Student Name

is recognized for

©1998 The Education Center, Inc.

SEASONAL UNITS

Hurrah For Grandparents!

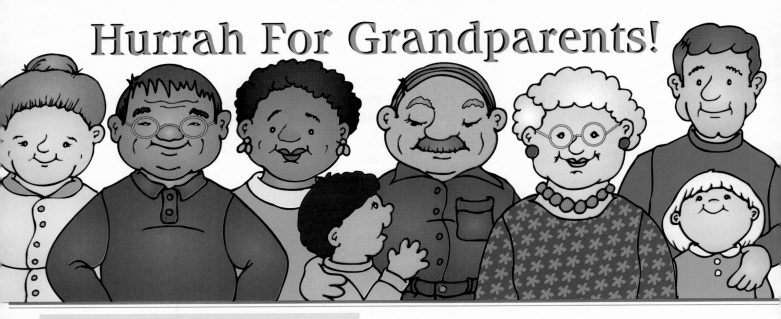

Aren't grandparents just grand! Since National Grandparents Day is just around the corner—the first Sunday following Labor Day—why not incorporate some grandparent-related activities into your teaching plans? This collection of ideas features activities that can be completed anytime of the school year (pages 258–259) and tips and activities especially for a classroom grandparent celebration (pages 260–262). Remember that any time is ideal for recognizing grandparents and other older adults, so choose a time during the school year that works best for you!

ideas by Rebecca Brudwick and Lisa A. Kelly

What Special Names!

Mopsy and Popsy, Grandma and Grandpa, Nana and Gramps. Grandparents answer to assorted names that often hold very special meanings. Invite students to share their special names for their grandparents and tell how they think these names originated. For added fun, use the provided table to introduce students to words from other countries that mean Grandmother and Grandfather. If desired, copy the words for each country on an index card. Then under your students' guidance, attach each card to its corresponding country on a world map or globe.

Country	Grandmother	Grandfather
France	Grand-mère	Grand-père
Germany	Grossmutter	Grossvater
Spain	Abuela, Abuelita	Abuelo
Italy	Nonna	Nonno
Russia	Babushka	Dyedushka
China	Zu-mu	Yeye, Zufu
Africa (Swahili)	Nyanya	Babu

A Grand Quilt

Spotlight the special qualities and talents of your youngsters' grandparents with a quilt-making project. To introduce the activity, read aloud *The Patchwork Quilt* by Valerie Flournoy (Dial Books For Young Readers, 1985). In this delightful book, a young girl helps her grandmother make a quilt by using scraps cut from her family's old clothing. Follow up the story by inviting students to talk about the special qualities and talents of their grandparents. Then give each child a six-inch square of white drawing paper. Ask each student to copy, complete, and illustrate the sentence "My _____ is special because…" on his paper square. Also have each child write his name in the top right-hand corner of his paper and glue his completed work in the center of a seven-inch construction-paper square. To assemble the quilt, glue the student-made quilt blocks on a length of bulletin-board paper; then use a marker to draw stitches around the projects. Display the resulting labor of love for all to see.

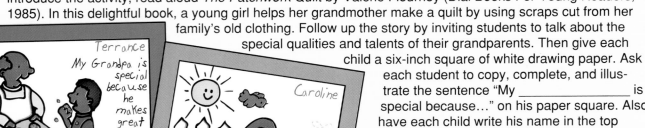

It's In The Mail

This writing activity could be the beginning of grandparent pen pals! In a parent note, request that each child bring to school a stamped envelope labeled with the child's return address and a grandparent's mailing address. When the envelopes have been collected, read aloud *Grandaddy's Stars* by Helen Griffith (Greenwillow Books, 1995). In this short chapter book, a young girl makes a list of all the important things she plans on showing her grandaddy when he comes to visit. At the conclusion of the story have each youngster write a list of things that she would like to tell the grandparent to whom she will be writing. Then have each child refer to her list as she pens a letter to her grandparent. Suggest that each student also include in her letter questions for her grandparent to answer and an invitation to write back!

Grandparent Look-Alikes

These adorable grandparent look-alikes are sure to steal the hearts of the loved ones after whom they have been designed!

How to make a grandparent look-alike:

1. Fold a 12" x 18" sheet of colored construction paper in half along the width; then keeping the paper folded, fold the paper into thirds.
2. Unfold the paper. Using the fold lines as guides, cut away the lower left and right rectangles as shown. Save one of these rectangles for later use.

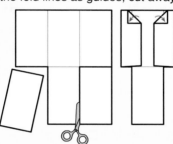

3. To make a shirt/blouse and a jacket, glue a 6 1/2" x 8 1/2" piece of construction paper to the center top of the project. Next fold over the paper on each side of the shirt to make a jacket. Make lapels for the jacket by folding diagonally as shown.
4. For sleeves, fold in half the rectangle from step 2 and cut along the fold line. Glue one end of each resulting sleeve to the back of the jacket.
5. To make pants, cut the lower rectangle in half lengthwise.
6. To make a skirt, trim the lower rectangle to a desired length and attach two construction-paper legs.
7. Cut out a head, hands, and shoes from construction paper; then glue the cutouts in place. Glue construction paper, yarn, or cotton to the head to resemble hair.
8. Use crayons and/or construction-paper scraps to add facial features and other desired details.

The Grandparent Gazette

What could be more fun than writing a hot-off-the-press news story about a grandparent! Have students brainstorm some of the extraordinary, memorable, and just-plain-fun things that their grandparents have done. Next distribute student copies of a newspaper form like the one shown, and have each student write and illustrate her story on the provided paper. If desired, invite interested students to write more than one story—each one spotlighting a different grandparent or older adult.

To create a class-written newspaper, decorate the front page of an actual newspaper to show the title "The Grandparent Gazette," the date, and a class byline. Mount your students' completed projects on the newspaper pages. Laminate the pages for durability; then place the newspaper in your class library for all to read.

An Event To Remember

Turn the spotlight on your students' grandparents and other older friends by planning a classroom celebration in their honor. Follow these simple steps to create an occasion that will be cherished and remembered by all!

Grand Invitations

Be sure to give plenty of notice to your anticipated guests of honor. As a class, discuss the important elements of an invitation; then create an invitation for your grandparent celebration. Duplicate the invitation and assist students as they fill out their personal copies. Or have students carefully copy and complete their invitations. Be sure to make special arrangements for students whose grandparents are unable to attend. These students may wish to invite other older relatives or friends.

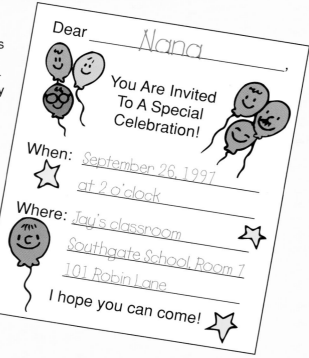

Dear _____ Nana ,

You Are Invited To A Special Celebration!

When: September 26, 1991 at 2 o'clock

Where: Jay's classroom
Southgate School, Room 7
101 Robin Lane

I hope you can come!

Papa Joe

A Warm Welcome

In preparation for your grandparent celebration, have each child craft a nametag for his special visitor. Then on the day of the event, have each child welcome his guest and present him with the personalized nametag. As students show their guests around the classroom, encourage them to spotlight the projects and decorations that were completed in their grandparent's honor.

Marvelous Memories

For a fun icebreaker, distribute student copies of page 262 and have each youngster use the questions on the page to interview her guest. Each child and her guest may work together to record the guest's responses on the lines. Once the interviews are complete, ask each child to introduce her guest to the rest of the class. Suggest that a child state her guest's full name and share one or two facts about her guest that she learned during the interview. If desired, follow up each introduction by asking the guest to attach a sticky dot to a world map to show his or her place of birth. After the introductions have been completed, take time to talk about the different birth places shown on the map.

I'd like to introduce my gramma, Gracie Foster.

Perfect Partners

Keep the atmosphere of your celebration upbeat and relaxed by planning several partner activities for students and their guests to complete. If desired, briefly introduce each center activity; then assign each pair to a center. After the pairs have worked at their assigned centers for about 15 to 20 minutes, use a predetermined signal to rotate the pairs clockwise to the next center. Continue in this manner until each pair has visited every center. Suggestions for centers include:

- **Game Center:** A few days before the event, ask students to bring games from home for this center. Suggest games that can be played by partners or foursomes like checkers, dominoes, card games, and easy-to-play board games.

- **Puzzle Center:** Feature one large or several small jigsaw puzzles at this center for students and their guests to assemble.

- **Mystery Word Center:** For this center, place construction-paper squares labeled with the letters needed to spell "grandparent" in each of several resealable plastic bags. Also place at the center copies of a reproducible like the one shown. Each child and his guest work together to create as many words as possible using the letters in one resealable bag. Set aside time later in the celebration for the pairs to share the words they created.

- **Reading Center:** At this center, place a large basket of your students' favorite books. Each child chooses a story to read to or with his guest.

- **Writing Station:** Stock this center with story paper, pencils, and crayons. Each twosome thinks about some of the special times that they've shared. Then the twosome chooses one special time to describe and illustrate on a sheet of story paper. Provide a place at the center for the pairs to leave their completed work. After everyone has completed the center, compile the papers into a class book.

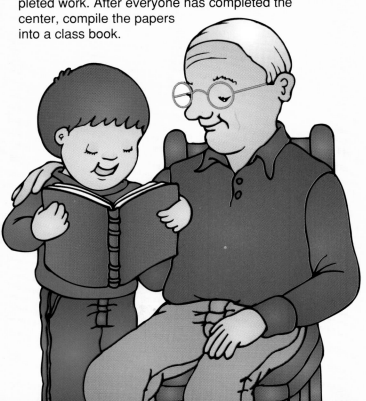

Names _____

Mystery Word Center
List the words you make! Use the back of this paper if you need more room!

Two-Letter Words	Three-Letter Words	Four-Letter Words
_____	_____	_____
_____	_____	_____
_____	_____	_____
_____	_____	_____
_____	_____	_____
_____	_____	_____
_____	_____	_____
_____	_____	_____

Five Or More Letters

_____ _____
_____ _____
_____ _____
_____ _____

Mystery Word: _____
(uses all the letters!)

A Grand Finale

As a culmination to the day, enlist your students' help in serving their guests a tasty snack of cookies and milk. While everyone is enjoying the snack, ask your guests to reminisce about their school days of long ago. No doubt your students will have a few questions for the guests as well. This would also be a good time for the pairs to share the words they made at the Mystery Word Center (see the description above). Then, last but not least, invite your guests to return to the classroom. Whether a grandparent is listening to students read, helping students practice math facts, or joining a young friend for lunch, these special visits will be looked forward to by all. And your students will be taking advantage of one of society's most valuable resources.

Marvelous Memories

Ask your guest the following questions.
Write his or her answers on the lines.

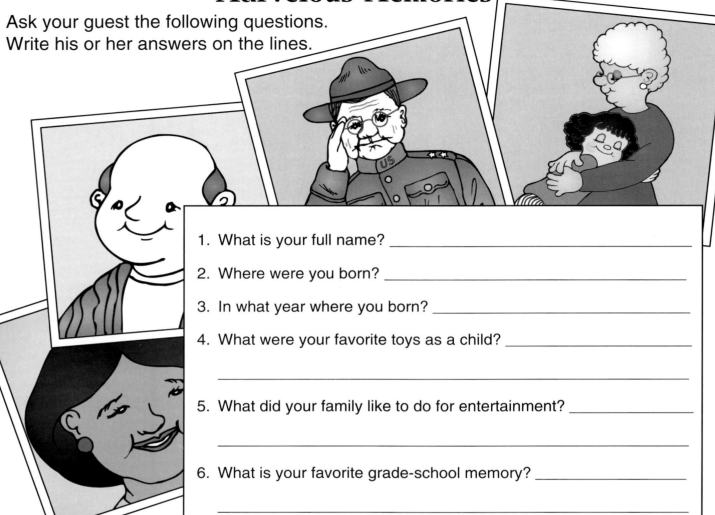

1. What is your full name? _____

2. Where were you born? _____

3. In what year where you born? _____

4. What were your favorite toys as a child? _____

_____

5. What did your family like to do for entertainment? _____

_____

6. What is your favorite grade-school memory? _____

_____

7. What do you enjoy doing now? _____

_____

8. What is your favorite place in the whole world? _____

_____

9. What inventions have changed the way you live? _____

_____

10. What one thing do you wish had not changed over the years?

_____

_____

©The Education Center, Inc. • *THE MAILBOX®* • *Primary* • Aug/Sept 1997

262   **Note To Teacher:** Use with "Marvelous Memories" on page 260.

The Wonderful World Of Watermelon!

Welcome your students with this fresh-off-the-vine assortment of back-to-school ideas. You'll find that these watermelon-related activities are the perfect remedy for those "wish-it-were-still-summer" blues!

ideas by Susan Baldwin and Kathleen Kopp

The Wonder Box

Set the stage for this juicy unit with a wonder box. You will need a watermelon and a lidded box large enough to hold the melon. Use gift wrap or bulletin-board paper to wrap the lid and the box. Place the melon inside the box, secure the lid, and attach a construction-paper sign labeled "The Wonder Box." Then display the box for all to see. Eventually invite students to ask questions to determine the box's contents. Explain to students that they may only ask questions that can be answered with a "yes" or a "no." Once students have identified the box's contents, remove the melon from the box for everyone to view. Not only will students enjoy the excitement of the activity, but they'll be working on their questioning skills too!

Sandra Heid—Gr. 2
Hettinger Elementary School
Hettinger, ND

The Wonder Box

What-A-Melon!

Whet your students' appetites for watermelon-related fun with this listening activity. On white construction paper, duplicate student copies of the watermelon pattern on page 269. Have each student color and cut out her watermelon pattern, and attach a craft-stick handle. Read a watermelon statement from the provided list. If a student thinks the statement is true, she holds up her watermelon. If she thinks the statement is false, she does nothing. Continue in this manner until all of the statements have been read. Next reveal that all the statements are true. Then reread each statement to the class. Students can't help but be amazed at this remarkable patch of facts!

- Watermelons probably first grew in Africa.
- Watermelons are about 93 percent water.
- The flesh (inside) of a watermelon can be white, greenish white, yellow, orange, pink, or red.
- Most watermelons weigh between 5 and 40 pounds.
- Watermelons grow on vines.
- Watermelons are vegetables.
- According to *The Guinness Book Of Records 1996*, the largest watermelon grown to date weighed 262 pounds.

- As many as 15 watermelons may grow on one watermelon vine.
- Thomas Jefferson grew watermelons at his home.
- Every part of the watermelon can be eaten.
- The average American in the United States eats about 16 pounds of watermelon each year.
- The watermelon is a cousin to the cucumber.
- In some places watermelon juice is used to make syrup.
- In some places watermelons are fed to farm animals.

Watermelon Nametags

These fashionable nametags are sure to receive rave student reviews. You will need one watermelon-decorated paper plate for every two students. Cut the plates in half; then punch two holes in each plate half as shown. A student uses a white or green paint marker to personalize his watermelon half. He then threads a length of yarn through the holes in his nametag, ties the yarn ends, and wears the nametag around his neck. Not only will your students enjoy this activity, but it will save you plenty of time too!

Renee Myers—Gr. 1
Snowville Elementary
Hiwassee, VA

A Patch Of Special Students!

Here's a picture-perfect booklet project that reminds students how special they are! For the best results, set aside time on each of three different days to work on the project. To begin, photograph each student. Then have each child write a story about herself that describes her hobbies, family, and other interests. Collect and edit these stories.

On the second day, give each child a paper-plate half, a supply of precut booklet paper (see the illustration), and her edited story. Have each student personalize the back of her plate half, then use a green crayon to color the plate's rim. While the students are quietly copying their stories onto the booklet paper, have small groups visit a painting center. At the center, have each student use thinned tempera paint to paint the rim of her plate green and the center of her plate red.

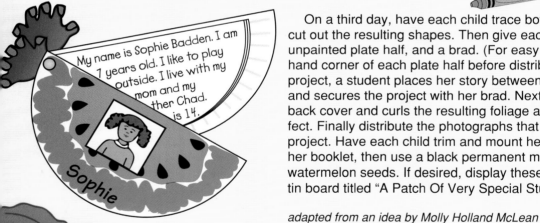

My name is Sophie Badden. I am 7 years old. I like to play outside. I live with my mom and my ...ther Chad. ...is 14.

Sophie

On a third day, have each child trace both of her hands on green paper and cut out the resulting shapes. Then give each child her painted plate half, an unpainted plate half, and a brad. (For easy management, hole-punch the left-hand corner of each plate half before distribution.) To assemble her booklet project, a student places her story between her paper-plate booklet covers and secures the project with her brad. Next she glues her hand cutouts to the back cover and curls the resulting foliage around her pencil for a desired effect. Finally distribute the photographs that you took on the first day of the project. Have each child trim and mount her photograph on the front cover of her booklet, then use a black permanent marker to write her name and draw watermelon seeds. If desired, display these one-of-a-kind booklets on a bulletin board titled "A Patch Of Very Special Students."

adapted from an idea by Molly Holland McLean
Laurinburg, NC

A Talking Watermelon?

Any way you slice it, your youngsters are sure to find this writing activity irresistible. Remind students that historians believe that the watermelon originated in Africa. Then share with your students the West African trickster tale *Anansi And The Talking Melon* retold by Eric A. Kimmel (Holiday House, Inc.; 1994). After discussing the story, challenge each child to write and illustrate his own trickster tale titled "Anansi And The Talking Watermelon." Have each student describe a trick—involving a watermelon—that Anansi plays on another animal. To make a class book, compile the students' completed stories between two decorated tagboard covers. Place the resulting book in your classroom library for all to enjoy!

The Pick Of The Crop

A watermelon grows much like many other plants. Its roots grow underground and its vine acts as a stem. The sweet flesh of the watermelon is protected by a thick rind. So how does one determine if a watermelon is ripe? Ask students to brainstorm a variety of methods; then record their responses on chart paper. Next have students ask their parents how *they* determine a watermelon's ripeness. To record his parent's response, provide each student with a copy of the reply form on page 269. The next day invite students to share their findings with the class. If desired, have students try their parents' suggestions on the watermelon from "The Wonder Box" (on page 263). Most experts agree that a watermelon is ripe when it has a yellow underside and it gives a hollow or muffled sound when thumped. But don't be surprised if you find a few other ways to tell when this juicy vegetable is ripe!

Fruit or Vegetable	Outside				Inside		
	Color	Shape	Texture	Firmness	Color	Seeds	Smell
watermelon	green	oblong	smooth	hard	pink	yes	sweet
cantaloupe							
honeydew							
cucumber							
squash							
pumpkin							

A Fruity Vegetable

Because watermelons grow on vines and must be replanted annually, they are considered to be vegetables. Watermelons belong to the gourd family that includes cucumbers, squash, and pumpkins. Put your students' observation skills to the test with this comparison activity. Post a chart like the one shown, and display a watermelon and an assortment of other produce. Under your students' direction, list the displayed produce. To complete the chart, record your students' observations about each listed fruit and vegetable, cutting open the produce as needed. Then use the chart to discuss the similarities and differences between the fruits and vegetables. Culminate the activity by cutting the fruits and vegetables into bite-size pieces for student sampling.

Similar Slices

Forming cooperative groups is a cinch with these colorful watermelon cutouts. Make a class set of red-and-green watermelon cutouts. Choose a standard number of cooperative groups and determine the number of students per group. Then label a set of cutouts for each group. Each set of cutouts must have a different construction-paper seed pattern. Laminate the cutouts for durability. When it's time to group the students, simply distribute the cutouts and have students who are holding matching cutouts work together. Collect the cutouts so that you can use them again and again. Students will be all smiles at the thought of working with different classmates each time cooperative groups are formed.

Darcy Gruber
Delavan, WI

How Does Your Watermelon Grow?

Watermelons grow best in hot climates and prefer sandy, irrigated soil. Florida, Georgia, California, Texas, Arizona, Indiana, North Carolina, South Carolina, Missouri, and Oklahoma lead the United States in watermelon harvest. For a fun cooperative-group activity, have students work together to create unique posters that advertise the watermelons from these states. Assign each of ten student groups a different state. Instruct each group to design a colorful poster that advertises the watermelons grown in its assigned state. Remind each group that its poster should persuade consumers to purchase its state's watermelons over those grown in other states. Provide the groups with white poster board or tagboard, construction paper, markers, and other poster-making supplies. Set aside time for each group to present its completed poster to the class; then display the mouthwatering projects in the school hallway or cafeteria for others to view.

Eat
North
Carolina

WATERMELON

• sweetest
• juiciest
• farm-grown
• seedless
• hand-picked
• low-fat

265

Melon Math

If you're looking for some appetizing math practice, this game for four players is the perfect choice. To make the game, duplicate four copies of the watermelon pattern on page 269. Program the seeds on each pattern with the numerals from one to ten; then color the resulting gameboards. Next label about 50 construction-paper cards with different math problems that have answers from one to ten. Program the backs of the cards for self-checking. Also program five or six blank cards with different player instructions like "Cover any answer on your gameboard," and "Overripe melon. Lose your turn." You will also need 40 one-inch black construction-paper squares. Laminate, cut out, and store the game components in a resealable plastic bag.

To play the game, each player needs a watermelon gameboard and ten black construction-paper squares. One player shuffles the game cards and places them faceup on the playing area. Each player in turn draws the top card and provides an answer; then he flips the card to check his answer. If the player is correct, he covers the corresponding seed on his gameboard. If he is incorrect, his turn is over. If a player gives a correct answer but that answer on his gameboard is already covered, his turn is over. The first player to cover all the answers on his gameboard wins.

The Watermelon Patch

Writing a story about watermelon facts is twice as much fun when a magic school bus is involved. Read aloud your favorite book in Joanna Cole's The Magic School Bus™ series. Then enlist your students' help in creating a book that features yourself, your students, a magic school bus, and plenty of watermelon facts. To begin, challenge students to brainstorm ideas for explaining each fact from page 263. Record your students' ideas on the chalkboard; then use these ideas as you compose a class story titled "A Magic School Bus At The Watermelon Patch." To make a big book, copy the resulting text onto a series of large story pages. As a class, determine a color scheme for the book; then have students work together to illustrate the story pages. Bind the completed pages between poster-board covers.

Melon-Patch Ponderings

Sweeten your students' problem-solving skills with this daily activity. Each morning read aloud or post a watermelon problem (see the sample problems shown) for students to ponder. Challenge students to create solutions for the problem before the end of the school day. If desired, have students record their solutions on copies of page 270. Then, at the end of the day, set aside time for the students to share their solutions with their classmates. As an added challenge, invite students to submit watermelon-related problems for their classmates to ponder.

Darcy Gruber
Delavan, WI

You have invited three friends to your house to enjoy a large slice of watermelon, but you can't find any knives to slice the melon. Use words or pictures to show three ways you could cut or break open the watermelon.

There was so much cooling rain and hot sun this summer that all the watermelon patches grew more watermelons than usual. Now your town has too many watermelons, and the townspeople are tired of eating them. Use words and pictures to name five other uses for all the extra watermelons.

What if the United States decided to use watermelons for money instead of coins and bills? What would be two advantages of this system? What would be two disadvantages?

Farmer Frank has a watermelon in his patch that weighs over 200 pounds! It is your job to move the melon from the patch to the county fair five miles away. Use words and pictures to show three ways you could move that huge melon!

Roasted Watermelon Seeds

Roasted watermelon seeds—a delicacy? They are in some countries! Invite your students to help you prepare this crunchy, exotic treat. To begin, serve a watermelon slice to each student. As students eat their melon slices, have them set aside their seeds. Collect the seeds, wash them thoroughly, and place them in a bowl. For every cup of seeds, add one tablespoon of cooking oil; then gently toss the seeds and oil. Evenly spread the seeds on a cookie sheet and bake them at 350°F for 10 to 12 minutes. Allow the seeds to cool and salt them to taste, and they're ready to serve. Now that's a unique snack!

Watermelon Cups

Watermelons have three distinct layers: the green outer rind, the white inner rind, and the flesh. This cool and tasty treat reinforces a watermelon's three layers, and it's a great way to top off your mouthwatering watermelon unit! Because the recipe involves several steps, we suggest that you either make the treat in advance or ask a parent volunteer to prepare it for your class.

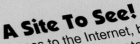

Watermelon Cups
(Makes 24 servings.)

Ingredients:
2 six-oz. packages of lime gelatin
2 six-oz. packages of watermelon gelatin
16-oz. container of nondairy whipped topping

raisins (6 to 8 per student)
24 nine-oz. plastic cups

Directions:
1. Prepare and soft set the lime gelatin; then spoon three tablespoons of gelatin into each cup. Refrigerate the cups until the gelatin sets.
2. Spread a thin layer of whipped topping in each cup. Return the cups to the refrigerator for about one hour.
3. Prepare and soft set the watermelon gelatin; then add 1/2 cup of gelatin to each cup. Return the cups to the refrigerator for about 30 minutes.
4. Add raisins (for seeds) to each cup. Refrigerate the watermelon cups until serving time.

A Site To See!

If you have access to the Internet, be sure to visit All About Watermelons—a watermelon website posted by the National Watermelon Promotion Board (http://www.watermelon.org/welcome.html). This site features information for the teacher, such as the history, nutritional value, production, and consumption of watermelon, and watermelon handling tips. The site also includes questions, a word scramble, recipes, and a coloring contest for kids. This site is a fun way to incorporate the computer into your watermelon activities.

Pick-Of-The-Patch Literature

Incorporate these mouthwatering books and activities into your watermelon studies.

Down By The Bay

Written by Raffi
Illustrated by Nadine Bernard Westcott
Crown Books For Young Readers, 1988
Savor the rhythm and rhymes in this delightful picture-book interpretation of one of Raffi's most popular songs. Two young friends—who live down by the bay—try to one-up each other with a series of hilarious rhymes.

Did you ever see an ape eating a grape, down by the sea?

After several oral readings (and singings!) of this irresistible story, invite students to create their own hilarious rhyming questions. Then have each child publish his favorite rhyme in a self-made watermelon pop-up card.

To make a watermelon pop-up card:

1. Fold in half a 9" x 12" sheet of white construction paper and round the corners at the end opposite the fold.
2. Cut two 2-inch slits in the center of the fold about 1 1/2 inches apart. Open the card and copy the chosen rhyme near the bottom of the card.
3. Illustrate the subject of the rhyme on a three-inch square of white construction paper. Cut out the illustration.
4. Pull the narrow strip in the center of the opened card forward and crease it in the opposite direction from the fold. Glue the cutout to the lower half of the strip; then illustrate the inside of the card as desired.
5. Close the card, making sure the strip stays inside.
6. Fold in half a 7" x 10" piece of red construction paper and round the corners at the end opposite the fold.
7. Partially unfold the red paper and slide the folded card inside. Glue the red paper to the white paper.
8. To complete the project, color the outer rim of the card green and draw several watermelon seeds.

Kristin McLaughlin—Gr. 1, Daniel Boone Area School District, Boyertown, PA

A reading of *Chestnut Cove* is the perfect springboard for a discussion about classroom cooperation. Ask students how they can foster cooperation in the classroom. Suggestions might include listening to everyone's ideas, taking turns, and sharing materials. Record the students' responses on a large watermelon cutout. When the cutout is filled with students' ideas, display it and the title "[teacher's name]'s Cove—A Classroom Of Cooperation" on a classroom wall.

Chestnut Cove

Written & Illustrated by Tim Egan
Houghton Mifflin Company, 1995
Cooperation was a way of life in the friendly town of Chestnut Cove. But when King Milford offers his entire kingdom to whosoever grows the largest, juiciest watermelon, the atmosphere of the small town slowly begins to change. Will greed and watermelons be the downfall of Chestnut Cove?

Watermelon Day

Written by Kathi Appelt
Illustrated by Dale Gottlieb
Henry Holt And Company, Inc.; 1996
Young Jesse must endure waiting all summer for her watermelon to grow. Her pappy agrees that her watermelon will be a big one, just right for a Watermelon Day. But will that day ever come? This sweet story of anticipation is one that all your students can relate to.

After hearing this story, there's little doubt that your youngsters will want to grow their own watermelons. Although watermelon seeds will not produce melons when grown indoors, they will yield attractive vines. Have each child label a clear plastic cup with his name, partially fill the cup with potting soil, and plant a watermelon seed in the soil. Next have each child water his seed and place his cup in a window or another sunny location. Discuss the feelings of anticipation that Jesse experienced in the story and invite students to talk about times when they have had similar feelings. Then, during the following weeks, have students water their seeds and measure the growth of their watermelon vines. If desired have students record their measurements, observations, and feelings of anticipation in watermelon-shaped journals.

Name_____

Getting The Scoop On Watermelons

I asked _____ how to tell if a watermelon

is ripe. Here is what I found out! _____

_____

_____

_____

_____

_____

_____

©The Education Center, Inc. • *THE MAILBOX® • Primary •* **Aug/Sept 1997**

©The Education Center, Inc. • *THE MAILBOX® • Primary •* **Aug/Sept 1997**

Note To Teacher: Use the reply form with "The Pick Of The Crop" on page 265. Use the pattern with " 'What-A-Melon '!" on page 263 and "Melon Math" on page 266.

Note To Teacher: Use this open page with "Melon-Patch Ponderings" on page 266. For a creative-writing activity, program this page with the title "Once Upon A Watermelon..." and have students write watermelon-related fairy tales. The page can also be used for parent communications. Or it can be programmed with math problems to solve, a watermelon-related spelling lesson, or other desired student activities.

270

Spotlight On Fire Safety

Spotlight fire safety during National Fire Prevention Week (annually the week including October 9). Approximately 2 1/2 million fires are reported each year in the United States. This makes fire safety one of the most important topics you can share with your students. Use the following information and red-hot activities to help youngsters learn how to be fire-safe and fire-smart!

by Sharon Murphy

Fire Hazards
- a hot iron
- a stove burner left on
- matches
- an overloaded electrical outlet

Fire-Prevention Tips
- Never play with matches.
- Always turn off electrical appliances when not in use.
- Never use the stove or oven unless an adult is near.
- Be sure to have an escape plan.

It Was The Cow's Fault

The Great Chicago Fire of 1871 was one of America's greatest disasters due to fire. It killed at least 300 people and left 90,000 people homeless. Legend has it that the fire was started by Mrs. O'Leary's cow. The cow's hoof knocked over a lit kerosene lantern, touching off a tragic fire that destroyed the city.

After sharing this legend with your class, ask students to think of other ways fires can start. Use their ideas to create a list of fire hazards. Next enlist your students' help in creating a list of fire-prevention tips. Display the resulting lists in a prominent classroom location.

Stop, Drop, And Roll

Despite precautions, fires do occur. This activity teaches children what to do if their clothing were to catch on fire. Tell students that fire needs air to burn. To demonstrate this concept, light a small candle; then cover its flame with an inverted glass jar and have students watch as the flame goes out. Explain to students that if their clothing catches on fire, they must keep air away from the flame. Point out that running only provides a fire with more air. So instead of running, students should *stop, drop* to the ground, and then *roll* back and forth to put the fire out. Help students conclude that rolling keeps air away from the flame—no air, no fire!

Try It Out!

Demonstrate the stop, drop, and roll technique; then engage students in the following activity so they can practice the movements themselves. You will need an open area and a method of playing marching music. Arrange students in a large circle. Explain to the students that when the music begins, they should begin marching around the circle in a clockwise direction. When the music stops, the students must *stop, drop* to the ground, and *roll* back and forth. Then, when the music begins again, they get up and continue marching. Plan to stop the music at varied intervals. What a great way to get students in step with a very important fire-safety technique!

Marcy Travers—Gr. 1
Blue Mountain School
Wells River, VT

A Safe Escape

Efforts to reduce the toll of fire can begin by teaching students how to safely exit a burning building. Post an approved list of suggested exiting procedures and carefully review the list with your students. Then, throughout your fire-safety unit, give each child an opportunity to demonstrate for his classmates how to safely exit a burning building. To prepare, place a real telephone (disconnected) outside your classroom door. Also inform your principal and co-workers about this activity so that no one will become alarmed if they hear a child within your room yell "Fire!" When it is a child's turn to demonstrate the procedure, he performs the posted steps. First the student yells "Fire!", then pulls a pretend fire alarm. Next the student crouches low to the ground and pretends to cover his mouth with a damp cloth. If your room has two exits, have the child maneuver to the alternate exit, feel the closed door, and pretend that it is hot. The child then maneuvers to the intended exit, touches the closed door, and then opens the door and exits through it. After closing the door behind him, the student dials 911 on the provided phone and states his address. (If desired, post a classmate near the phone to verify that the child concludes the drill correctly.) At the end of each child's turn, use a safety pin to attach a completed fire-safety badge (pattern on page 274) to the child's clothing.

Blake Tyler Harris
is fire-safety smart!
Ms. Marsh
Teacher
11/5/97
Date

How To Safely Exit A Burning Building

- As soon as you detect fire, yell "Fire!" to warn other people.
- If there is a fire-alarm box nearby, use it.
- Crawl low if the room becomes smoky. The air here will be clearer and easier to breathe.
- Cover your mouth and nose with a moist towel, T-shirt, or anything within reach, to keep dangerous fumes from entering your lungs.
- Always touch a door before opening it. If a door is hot, there might be a fire on the other side. Use another exit.
- Close the door behind you when you leave a room. It will help keep the fire from spreading.
- Once outside, if no adult is available, call 911 to report the fire.
- Never go back into a burning building for any reason. Get out and stay out!

Making Plans

Devising a classroom escape plan shows students the importance of being prepared for fire. Draw a floor plan of your classroom that can be duplicated for student use. Post an enlarged version of the map in the classroom, or create a transparency and project the map for all to see. Under your direction, have the students indicate each window and door on their copies of the map. Then have each student use a dotted line to identify two exit routes (if possible) from the classroom. Next enlist your students' help in determining a safe meeting place outdoors. To culminate the activity, review the primary plan for exiting the classroom during a fire drill. Then stage a mock fire drill and have the students quickly exit the classroom in an orderly fashion and proceed to the designated meeting place outdoors.

Upon your return to the classroom, emphasize the importance of a home escape plan. Then distribute student copies of the fire-safety checklist on page 274. Ask each child to complete and check off each item on the list with the help of an adult family member. Challenge students to return their signed checklists to school by a designated date. To encourage participation, recognize those students who meet the challenge with a predetermined reward or special privilege.

Red-Hot Safety Posters

Put your youngsters' fire-safety knowledge to the test with this cooperative-group activity. Give each small group a sheet of poster board that you've preprogrammed with a fire-safety prompt like "In the event of a fire you should," "To prepare for a fire you should," or "If your clothing catches on fire, you should." Then have each group create an eye-catching poster that provides accurate information. Display the completed posters around the school for everyone to see—they may just save a life!

Sherry Fretz—Gr. 3, Churubusco Elementary School
Churubusco, IN

If your clothing catches on fire, you should:
Stop!   Drop!   Roll!

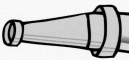

Red-Hot Literature

Spark reading interest with these red-hot fire-safety selections!

Fire! Fire!

Written & Illustrated by Gail Gibbons
HarperCollins Children's Books, 1987

This informative picture book explains how firefighters battle fires in the city, in the country, in the forest, and on the waterfront. The last three pages in the book feature a picture dictionary of additional fire-fighting equipment, a list of ways to prevent fires, and the steps to follow in case of fire.

After reading the book aloud, have students make booklets that show how fires are fought in different places. To make a booklet, stack three 8 1/2" x 11" sheets of white paper and hold the pages vertically in front of you. Slide the top sheet upward approximately one inch; then repeat the process for the second sheet. Next fold the paper thicknesses forward to create six graduated layers or pages (see the illustration). Staple close to the fold. Have each student write the title "Fighting Fires" and her name on the cover, then label the bottoms of the booklet pages as shown. Next have each student write and illustrate how fires are fought in each location. On the last page of the booklet, have the student describe and illustrate additional fire-fighting equipment. Students will be flipping over fire safety!

Fire Trucks

Written by Hope Irvin Marstown; includes photographs
Dutton Children's Books, 1996

Take a close-up look at various kinds of fire trucks and fireboats—and learn about a special airplane that's used in putting out forest fires! The pages of this slim volume are packed with vivid and informative photographs that are sure to capture the interest of all youngsters.

At the conclusion of this enlightening book, enlist your youngsters' help in making a class book titled "The ABCs Of Fire Fighting." List the letters of the alphabet on the chalkboard; then challenge students to brainstorm a fire-related term for each letter. Record the students' responses. Next have each child choose a different letter of the alphabet, and copy and illustrate its accompanying term on provided paper. To assemble the book, alphabetically sequence the pages and bind them between construction-paper covers. Place the completed book in your classroom library for students to enjoy. For added fun, send a photocopy of the class book to your local fire station along with a note thanking the firefighters for helping to keep the community safe.

In the city firefighters use aerial ladders, fire hydrants, and pumper trucks to fight fires.

In The City
In The Country
In The Forest
On The Waterfront
More Fire-Fighting Equipment

Fighting Fires

Written & Photographed by Susan Kuklin
Bradbury Press, 1993

Vivid color photographs and fact-filled text provide a fascinating inside look at the vehicles, equipment, and procedures used by firefighters.

Make arrangements for a firefighter to visit your classroom dressed in full fire-fighting gear. Before the firefighter arrives, prepare your students by reading aloud this enlightening picture book. Also prepare a list of student-generated questions for a question-and-answer period. Be sure to ask your guest to explain the importance of each article of protective clothing and gear that he wears during a fire. Also ask the firefighter to speak and breathe through the mouthpiece of his oxygen tank. (Youngsters can be frightened by the sight and sounds of a firefighter in full gear.) No doubt your students will be talking about this experience for days to come!

Kim Whitchurch—Gr. 1, Oakland School, Lafayette, IN

Ladder

Mask

Badges And Checklist

Use the badges with "A Safe Escape" on page 272.

is fire-safety smart!

_____
Teacher

_____
Date

©1997 The Education Center, Inc.

is fire-safety smart!

_____
Teacher

_____
Date

©1997 The Education Center, Inc.

Use the checklist with "Making Plans" on page 272.

Name _____

Fire-Safety Checklist

Complete and check off each item on the list with an adult.

____ My family has a home escape plan.

____ I know two ways to exit every room in my home. The two exits from my

bedroom are _____ and _____.

____ In case of a fire, my family's meeting place is _____

_____.

____ In my home we have _____ smoke detector(s).

____ Each smoke detector in my home is working.

____ I know the local emergency telephone number. It is _____.

I verify that each item on this checklist has been completed.

_____
Parent signature

Light Up The Season
With Holiday Literature!

Share the joys of the holiday season with this collection of children's literature and the accompanying activities. You're sure to receive a glowing response from your students!

by Rebecca Brudwick, Carrie Teston Geiger, Susie Kapaun, Sue Majors, and Cheryl Sergi

The Magic Dreidels: A Hanukkah Story
Written by Eric A. Kimmel & Illustrated by Katya Krenina
Holiday House, Inc.; 1996

When young Jacob accidentally drops his new brass dreidel into a well, the resident goblin gives the boy a magic dreidel to replace the one he lost. But when Jacob tries out his dreidel at home, it has no magic. A second trip to the well yields similar results. This trip—like the first trip—includes a visit with the neighborhood busybody on Jacob's way home. Determined to have magic dreidels for his family's Hanukkah celebration, Jacob returns to the well, and with the help of his goblin friend, he knows just what he must do!

Send your youngsters into a spin with this festive follow-up activity! First have each student copy and complete the following sentences on a sheet of personalized writing paper: "My magic dreidel spins out…," and "I plan to use my dreidel to…" Then have each student decorate a paper dreidel cutout using crayons, markers, glitter pens, sequins, glue, and other desired materials. Mount each child's projects on a bulletin board titled "Our Magic Dreidels."

Stephen

My magic dreidel spins out hot latkes, Hanukkah gelt, and Air Jordan basketball shoes! I plan to use my dreidel to have a party for my friends!

The Chanukkah Guest
Written by Eric A. Kimmel & Illustrated by Giora Carmi
Holiday House, Inc.; 1988

Bubba Brayna may not be able to see or hear very well, but one thing is certain—she makes the most delicious potato latkes in the village! So it comes as no surprise that Bubba is expecting a visit from the rabbi on this first night of Chanukkah. And even though her "guest" arrives a little early, Bubba's evening goes as planned—until the real rabbi knocks on her door!

If preparing potato latkes is out of the question, consider serving your youngsters jelly-filled doughnuts or another sweet treat that has been fried in oil. It's a Hanukkah celebration that is sure to be enjoyed by all. Then follow up by asking students to write and illustrate second-night-of-Chanukkah stories that feature Bubba Brayna, the rabbi, and another surprise guest!

The Trees Of The Dancing Goats
Written & Illustrated by Patricia Polacco
Simon & Schuster Books For Young Readers, 1996
When an epidemic of scarlet fever strikes a Michigan farming community in the midst of the holiday season, a Jewish family feels fortunate to have been spared. However, as the family members embark on their Hanukkah celebration, their thoughts turn to their Christian neighbors who are bedridden with the fever. What follows is an unforgettable example of unselfish friendship, present-day miracles, and the joy of sharing and recognizing the customs and beliefs of others.

Knowing that this story is based on a cherished childhood memory of the author's makes it even more poignant. Invite students to talk about the story and about the different ways that their families celebrate the holiday season. Guide students to understand that by bringing joy into the lives of their Christian friends, the Jewish family experienced joy themselves. Then invite students to talk or write about times when they have given and felt joy, too!

C
Clowns
catch
caramel
candies.
c

D
Dancing
dogs
dodge
drums.
d

AlphaZoo Christmas
Written & Illustrated by Susan Harrison
Ideals Children's Books, 1993
It is a zoo! Whimsical animals, from caroling crocodiles to skating swine, celebrate the holiday in style—alliterated style, that is!

At the conclusion of this festive romp, make plans to create another alliterated holiday adventure. This time focus on a student-chosen topic like the circus, the rain forest, or favorite book characters. Enlist your students' help in brainstorming writing subjects for each alphabet letter before randomly assigning the letters and asking each student to pen an alliterated sentence. Edit these sentences; then have each child copy her sentence and write the upper- and lower-case forms of her alphabet letter on a 4 1/2" x 7" piece of white paper. Finally have each youngster illustrate her work on a 4 1/2" x 7" piece of white paper. To complete the project, mount the students' work in sequential order on 9" x 12" sheets of colorful construction paper as shown. Laminate the pages and a desired booklet cover for durability; then hole-punch the project, bind it with metal or plastic rings, and display it for all to enjoy.

Merry Christmas, Old Armadillo
Written by Larry Dane Brimner & Illustrated by Dominic Catalano
Boyds Mills Press, Inc.; 1995
Old Armadillo drifts off to sleep with a heavy heart, for he believes his friends have forgotten him this holiday season. However, unbeknownst to the snoring senior, the joy of Christmas is close at hand.

This heartwarming story is the perfect prelude to organizing a class holiday project for a nearby nursing or retirement home. For a large-group project, have students use construction-paper strips, colorful markers, glitter, and glue to create the links for a sparkling paper chain that is sure to bring smiles to its senior recipients. Holiday cards and ornaments can be crafted from similar supplies. If students can't be present when their holiday gifts are delivered, plan to photograph or videotape the event. Plenty of hearts—both young and old—will be gladdened by this gift-giving experience.

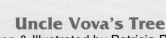

Uncle Vova's Tree
Written & Illustrated by Patricia Polacco
Philomel Books, 1989

Each year family traditions abound at Uncle Vova's farmhouse, where children, grandparents, and aunts and uncles gather to celebrate Christmas in Russian tradition. Uncle Vova hopes that his family can carry on his joyful traditions even when he is gone—which they do, with a little help from Uncle Vova's extended family.

Continue one of Uncle Vova's traditions with this paper-star project. For each student, securely tape two lengths of curling ribbon to the eraser end of an unsharpened pencil (see the illustration); then carefully curl the ribbon ends. To make his paper star, a student cuts out two identical star shapes from tagboard and decorates each one using markers or crayons. Next he glues or tapes together the edges of the stars, leaving an opening at the bottom of his project to insert the ribbon-clad pencil that you have prepared for him.
Happy holidays!

Night Tree
Written by Eve Bunting & Illustrated by Ted Rand
Harcourt Brace & Company, 1991

The true spirit of the season is poignantly portrayed as a family engages in its yearly Christmas tradition. It is an unpretentious reminder to remember all creatures—both great and small—during the holiday season.

Let this be the first year of an annual classroom tradition in which students decorate an outdoor tree with food for nearby wildlife. If there isn't a suitable tree on your school grounds, request that a live Christmas tree be planted for this purpose. Then reread the story for your students, and note the different edible decorations that the family prepared. List these ideas on the chalkboard along with additional decorating ideas your students may have. In a note to parents, explain the class project and request needed supplies. When the decorations have been made, plan a pilgrimage to the class tree. On the day of the event, have several parent volunteers on hand to assist students as they decorate the tree. Then top off the event with steaming hot cocoa and a Christmas carol or two!

Santa's Book Of Names
Written & Illustrated by David McPhail
Little, Brown And Company; 1993

What do you do when you discover that Santa has dropped his important Book Of Names *beside your fireplace? If you're Edward—who is a whiz with numbers but struggles to read—you race outside, stamp a large* B *in the snow, and hope that Santa figures out your clue! What do you do if you're riding with Santa in his sleigh, Santa loses his reading glasses, and he needs you to read aloud the names in his important* Book Of Names*? If you're Edward—you panic!*

When Edward comes to Santa's rescue, he discovers something about himself too. He can read! Invite students to talk about times when they felt certain they would fail and instead they succeeded. Follow up this discussion by asking students to brainstorm words and phrases of encouragement for times like these. Write the title "Remember Edward!" on a length of bulletin-board paper, and write the students' ideas beneath the title. Display the resulting poster of encouraging words and phrases in a prominent classroom location. Suggest that students refer to the poster for personal encouragement and when they wish to encourage others.

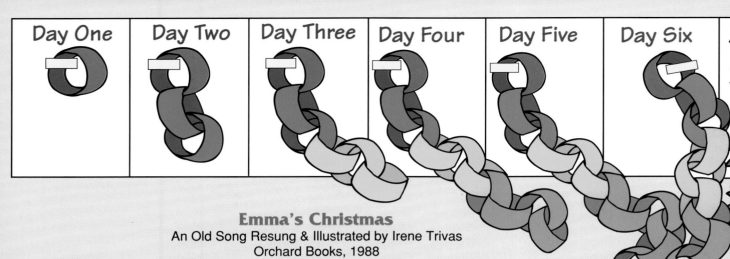

Day One	Day Two	Day Three	Day Four	Day Five	Day Six

Emma's Christmas
An Old Song Resung & Illustrated by Irene Trivas
Orchard Books, 1988

This fun-filled version of The Twelve Days Of Christmas *describes the courtship of Emma, a spunky farmer's daughter, by a young local prince. The prince is convinced that Emma is his own true love—now if he can only convince Emma!*

No doubt you'll want to explore a few more retellings of *The Twelve Days Of Christmas.* Jan Brett and Linnea Aspling Riley have each published a beautifully illustrated version. *The Twelve Days Of Christmas* by John O'Brien is unique in that it tells of a female suitor sending gifts to a man! Then, with your students' help, sum up your investigation of this 12-day celebration with some colorful math! Post a strip of bulletin-board paper that you have visually divided into twelfths and labeled as shown. Also precut a supply of colorful paper strips that can be used to make links for paper chains. For each of the 12 days of Christmas, have a different student or small group of students make a paper chain. Each chain should have the number of links that equals the number of gifts delivered on that day. For example, on the first day the chain would have just one link. On the second day, the chain would have three links (2 + 1), and so on. Tape one end of each chain to the appropriate section of the posted strip (see the illustration). Now that's an activity that really adds up!

The Christmas Blizzard
Written by Helen Ketteman
Illustrated by James Warhola
Scholastic Inc., 1995

Hang on to your candy canes! This Christmas tale is a king-size whopper! From sunbathing elves to frozen clouds and scattered cows, old-timer Maynard Jenkins spins a tale about the year 1922 when Christmas almost went on without Santa. But in the end, the holiday was saved by an ever-so-clever young lad who just happened to be Maynard himself!

After experiencing this hilarious escapade, there's little doubt that your youngsters will be eager to hone their own exaggeration skills. Begin by demonstrating for students how to stretch a simple fact like "The wind blew very hard," into an outlandish statement like "The wind blew so hard that the fur off my dog's back ended up in the next state where it became a rug in a museum." Then, on the chalkboard, write several simple sentences—like "It snowed for days," "It was a very cold Christmas," and "I ate too many Christmas cookies"—for each student to rewrite in exaggerated forms. Finally invite each youngster to write and illustrate a far-fetched tale about a favorite holiday experience. You can count on plenty of laughs when these colossal Christmas stories are shared!

The Christmas Box

Written by Eve Merriam & Illustrated by David Small
William Morrow And Company, Inc.; 1985

An entire family rushes downstairs on Christmas morning expecting to find a tree laden with gifts. Instead they find only one very long and very thin box. Christmas is a time for surprises, as this dazed family quickly discovers!

Put your youngsters' prediction skills to the test with this cleverly disguised problem-solving activity! Select a class Christmas gift—such as a new board game, children's book, or piece of science equipment—and gift wrap it in a box that also contains a class supply of wrapped candies. Then place the box inside another box of a slightly different shape and gift wrap the second box. Continue this procedure, gift wrapping a third and a fourth box; then display the resulting class gift for all to see. An hour or two later, ask students to predict the contents of the box. Write their predictions on chart paper, and ask two students to unwrap the box and remove its contents. When students see the size of the next gift-wrapped box, ask them to revisit their predictions, deleting those that now seem inappropriate and adding new ones. Continue in this manner until the class gift is at last revealed. Wow! Problem solving has never been so fun!

One Christmas Dawn

Written by Candice F. Ransom & Illustrated by Peter Fiore
BridgeWater Books, 1996

In the icy mountains of wintry Appalachia, a young girl fears that her daddy won't be able to make it home for Christmas. The year is 1917, and the weather is so bitterly cold that the twice-daily train has ceased to run. It seems as though only a miracle could deliver Daddy home by Christmas dawn.

So what is Old Granny Gobble? To find out, read the author's note at the end of the story; then let your youngsters try their hands (and feet and heads!) at playing this wintertime game. As the students are resting, ask them to contemplate how they might spend their long winter evenings if they did not have electricity to operate TVs, CD players, computers, and other similar items. List their ideas on chart paper, and challenge students to spend one or more evenings during the holiday season without the comforts of electronic entertainment. Invite students to share their experiences with their classmates.

Christmas Tree Memories

Written & Illustrated by Aliki
HarperCollins Publishers, Inc.; 1991

Sweet memories abound on Christmas Eve when a family gathers before its Christmas tree. As each ornament on the tree is mentioned, a precious memory is recalled. This timeless book is a celebration of family, friends, and traditions.

At the conclusion of the story, invite students to talk about holiday ornaments they have that evoke special memories. Then provide a supply of writing paper on which you have duplicated a large ornament shape. Ask each student to describe a special holiday memory on the special paper. When a student finishes writing, he cuts out his ornament shape(s) and sets the resulting page(s) aside. Next he uses an ornament-shaped template to trace two large ornament shapes on construction paper. Then he cuts out the two shapes and staples his story between the resulting covers. Finally the student decorates his booklet's front cover to his liking before he takes the project home to share with his family members.

Thank You, Santa
Written by Margaret Wild & Illustrated by Kerry Argent
Scholastic Inc., 1991

Rarely does Santa receive letters from children after *Christmas, so he is thrilled when he receives a thank-you note from Samantha, a young girl living in Australia. The two become instant pen pals; and by the time the next Christmas rolls around, Samantha has learned a whole lot about Santa and the spirit of giving.*

A letter-writing activity is the perfect follow-up to this delightful book of letters! In advance, make arrangements for your youngsters to write to students in another classroom, grade, or school—making sure that each youngster's letter will be answered. As a prewriting activity, review the friendly-letter format, and then reread a sampling of the letters found in the book. Discuss what each writer writes about, if the writer asks and/or answers questions, etc. Then let the writing begin! This activity could prove to be the beginning of a wonderful friendship for each of your students!

Mother Hubbard's Christmas
Written & Illustrated by John O'Brien
Boyds Mills Press, Inc.; 1996

Old Mother Hubbard is determined to have a merry Christmas, even though her cupboard is bare. And her faithful canine companion is right by her side—causing mischief at every turn.

This hilarious holiday twist on a favorite Mother Goose story will have your youngsters eager to add a holiday theme to their favorite nursery rhymes. Brainstorm story ideas with your students that include Jack and Jill fetching a Christmas gift and Jack Be Nimble jumping over a menorah. List the ideas on the chalkboard; then let the writing begin! When the holiday versions are written and illustrated, invite students to share their work with their classmates. A jolly time will be had by all!

The Story Of Kwanzaa
Written by Donna L. Washington & Illustrated by Stephen Taylor
HarperCollins Publishers, Inc.; 1996

The traditions and customs of Kwanzaa are described in this appealing book for young readers. As the author ushers the reader through a brief history of the holiday, an explanation of the seven days of Kwanzaa, and preparation and celebration tips, colorful illustrations help clarify the information that is presented.

Like many other holidays, Kwanzaa includes gift giving. Children give handmade gifts, or *zawadi,* to their parents, and parents usually present their children with educational gifts. These student-made Kwanzaa cards are sure to dazzle your youngsters' family members! On a 7" x 10" piece of white art paper, sponge-paint a candleholder holding three red candles on the left, one black candle in the center, and three green candles on the right. (For the best results, use sponges that have been cut into narrow rectangles.) When the paint is dry, fold in half a 12" x 18" sheet of colorful construction paper and glue the painting to the front cover. Glue a torn tissue-paper flame to the top of each candle. Inside the card write and personalize a Kwanzaa greeting and a brief message. *Harambee!*

If you're looking for additional Kwanzaa-related crafts and activities, check out these great books:

- ***Kwanzaa Fun: Great Things To Make And Do***
  Written by Linda Robertson & Illustrated by Julia Pearson
  Kingfisher, 1996

- ***Crafts For Kwanzaa***
  Written by Kathy Ross & Illustrated by Sharon Lane Holm
  The Millbrook Press, Inc.; 1994

WRITE ON!

Write On!

Thanksgiving Day

Thanksgiving Day
Turkey, turkey, turkey
Thanksgiving Day
Food, food, food
Thanksgiving Day
Yum, yum, yum
Thanksgiving Day
Family, family, family
Thanksgiving Day
Love, love, love

Anytime Poetry

Youngsters will be writing poetry for every occasion once you introduce this easy-to-follow format. To demonstrate the format, enlist your students' help in choosing a poem topic. Write the topic on chart paper as the poem's title; then write the topic again as the poem's first line. To create the second line of the poem, have a student choose a word that relates to the poem's topic, and write this word three times. Continue adding lines to the poem by alternating the poem's topic with student-selected words. If desired, alternate the colors of the lines so that the poem's topic is always written in the same color. Post the resulting poem in a prominent location and invite students to use the displayed format to pen original poetry. This simple format will encourage youngsters to write and read plenty of poems!

Phoebe C. Sharp—Grs. K–1 Special Education, Gillette School, Gillette, NJ

Superlative Sentences

Inspire students to write out-of-the-ordinary sentences with this unique activity! On the chalkboard list five or six simple sentences like "A castle appeared" and "A lion roared." Ask each student to illustrate one of the displayed sentences on a 12" x 18" sheet of paper. Encourage students to create detailed scenes. After a given amount of time, ask each child to write a sentence on a one-inch paper strip that tells about her illustration. Next challenge students to add more details to their sentences. To do this a child writes the words she wishes to add to her sentence on a second one-inch paper strip. She cuts these words apart, then she cuts her original sentence apart so that she can insert the additional words. Invite students to repeat this editing process until they are satisfied with their sentences. Then have each child glue her sentence to her illustration. Be sure to set aside time for students to share their superlative work!

Geraldine Gutowski, Sombra del Monte School, Albuquerque, NM

big fat lion roared loudly when a black and white zebra stepped on its fuzzy tail.

Georgia

Sandwich Day Celebration

Whether or not you plan to celebrate Sandwich Day (November 3), students are sure to sink their teeth into this writing project! If desired, set the mood for the activity by reading aloud a sandwich-related poem like Shel Silverstein's "Recipe For A Hippopotamus Sandwich" (from *Where The Sidewalk Ends,* HarperCollins Children's Books, 1974). Then give each child a sandwich-shaped booklet containing six or more blank cutouts. A student writes the title "My Sandwich" and his name on the top cutout. Then, on each of the following cutouts, he copies, completes, and illustrates the sentence "I put _____ on my sandwich." Encourage students to describe traditional and nontraditional sandwich stuffers. When his booklet pages are complete, the student adds desired decorations to the front and back of his booklet. Now that's a tasty writing project!

Jean Hoff—Gr. 1, Rahn Elementary, Mt. Morris, IL

My Sandwich by Kenny B.

I put two purple pickles on my sandwich!

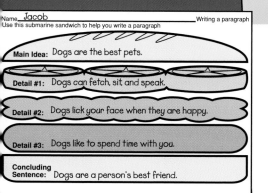

Name: Jacob   Writing a paragraph
Use this submarine sandwich to help you write a paragraph

Main Idea: Dogs are the best pets.

Detail #1: Dogs can fetch, sit, and speak.

Detail #2: Dogs lick your face when they are happy.

Detail #3: Dogs like to spend time with you.

Concluding Sentence: Dogs are a person's best friend.

Write On!

Ideas And Tips For Teaching Students To Write

A "Sub-stantial" Organizer

Watch your students sink their teeth into writing with this "sub-stantial" paragraph organizer! On a piece of poster board or chart paper, create a submarine sandwich similar to the one shown. Refer to the sandwich chart as you teach your students how to organize and write a paragraph. Next provide a copy of page 286 for each child. Direct students to write a paragraph on a given topic by completing their sheets and then transferring the ideas to another piece of paper. Encourage students to organize a paragraph in the same manner every time they are given a new topic. Youngsters' appetites for writing are sure to grow with every new paragraph!

adapted from an idea by Maureen M. Casazza, Honesdale, PA

The best holiday season I remember is the year we went to Disneyland. I saw Mickey Mouse. He looked like Santa. His dog Pluto looked like a reindeer. It was fun!

"Holly-day" Happenings

Create an adorable "holly-day" display with this writing idea! Draw a large holly leaf on white paper, add writing lines, and duplicate one holly leaf for every student. Provide an assortment of story starters, like "My favorite thing about December is..." and "The best holiday season I remember is...." Have each child select a story starter and write a story on his leaf. Then have the student cut out his holly leaf, glue it onto a slightly larger piece of green construction paper, and trim the green paper to create an eye-catching border. Arrange the completed cutouts on a wall or bulletin board in the shape of a giant wreath. Add a few red paper berries and a big, red paper bow for a colorful "holly-day" display!

Loretta W. Lombardi—Gr. 3, Mercer Christian Academy, Trenton, NJ

My family is great! My mom is a famous movie star. She gets to fly to California every day! My dad is a cowboy. He rides horses and lassos cows. My little brother can fly! He has wings and he can't even walk yet. My sister and I are twins. We do everything together!

Darcy

Family Exaggerations

Teach your students how to write in an exaggerated fashion with this fun idea! Before you begin, explain to your students that an *exaggeration* is a way to stretch the truth. Exaggerations allow writers to share amusing viewpoints—not to be hurtful or to lie to others. If possible share Diane Stanley's hilarious book, *The Good-Luck Pencil* (Four Winds Press, 1986). Although this book is out of print, check your local library for a copy. In the story, Mary Ann's good-luck pencil helps her write exaggerated stories about her family that come true! Invite each child to use his good-luck pencil to write an exaggerated tale about his own family or an imaginary one. Encourage students to be creative and funny. Allow time for students to share their exaggerated tales. Parents will chuckle when they read these amusing stories!

Candy Whelan—Gr. 3, Garlough Elementary, West St. Paul, MN

Write On!

Ideas And Tips For Teaching Students To Write

Personalized Poems

Inspire your budding poets to cite their likes, dislikes, and loves in personalized poems. To begin ask each child to list 20 different things that he *likes.* Urge students to consider a variety of topics, such as food, toys, animals, sports, places, and the weather. Next ask each child to list five things that he *does not like.* And finally ask each child to list five things that he *loves.* Then distribute student copies of the format shown for students to complete and illustrate, or display the format and have students copy, complete, and illustrate the sentences on writing paper. Encourage students to refer to their lists as they create poems that are accurate portrayals of themselves. Set aside time for students to share their poetry; then bind the illustrated works into a class book.

Pamela Pauley, Alice Street Elementary School, Truro, Nova Scotia, Canada

Once-Upon-A-Time Stories

For a timely creative-writing project that's loads of fun, try this! Ask each child to select a main story character from a list of animals. (For the best results, limit your list to animals that are easy to portray on paper-plate covers like the one shown: frog, mouse, bear, pig, bunny, dog, cat, etc.) To make his cover, a student traces a flattened paper plate onto an appropriate color of construction paper, then cuts out the circle and glues it to the plate. Next he uses colorful paper, markers or crayons, a brad, precut hour and minute hands, glue, and scissors to create an animated clock face that resembles the main character of his story.

Using his cover for inspiration, a student writes a once-upon-a-time tale on provided writing paper. Encourage students to give their main characters names and to include several time-related references in their stories. When a student's story is complete, he flips over his cover and staples his story, in sequential order, to the back of the cover. As each child takes a turn reading his story aloud for his classmates, have him manipulate the clock hands on the cover to coincide with the story events. Wow, time *does* fly when you're having fun!

Mary Ann Lewis, Tallahassee, FL

Colorful Comparisons

This tasty approach to writing similes assures sweet success! On the chalkboard tape one circle cutout in each of the following colors: brown, blue, orange, red, green, yellow. Also give each child a handful of M&M's® candies. As the students munch on their candies, ask them to brainstorm similes for each color of circle. Then have each student write her favorite simile for each color in a step booklet like the one shown. To make her booklet, a student draws a line that is 2 1/2 inches from one end of her brown rectangle (see the paper list below); then she folds the paper on the line. Next she slides the remaining rectangles into her booklet cover to create graduated layers, and staples the resulting booklet near the fold. On each booklet page, a student writes one or more similes that correspond to its color; then she personalizes the booklet cover as desired.

Construction Paper Needed For Each Booklet		
All colors are 4 1/2" wide.		
brown: 9 1/2" long	**orange:** 4" long	**green:** 5 1/2" long
blue: 3 1/4" long	**red:** 4 3/4" long	**yellow:** 6 1/4" long

Candy Whelan—Gr. 3, Garlough Elementary, West St. Paul, MN

Write On!

Ideas And Tips For Teaching Students To Write

Tropical Greetings!

With summer approaching, your students will welcome this tropical writing project! Begin by asking each child to imagine himself vacationing in a warm and sunny location and to consider what he'd like to tell his classmates about his tropical trip. Then have each child write a postcard-like message to his classmates on one side of a lined 5" x 7" index card. Next have each student mount his message on a 9" x 12" sheet of light blue construction paper and use crayons or markers to create a tropical scene around it. Encourage students to include themselves in their illustrations. If you have extra student photographs on hand, have students cut their faces and/or bodies from the snapshots and incorporate the cutouts into their artwork. Compile the completed projects into a class book titled "Hello From The Tropics!"

Jennifer Hayes—Grs. 3–4, St. Stephen's School, Halifax, Nova Scotia, Canada

Flamboyant Fish

Reel in some great descriptive writing with this splashy activity! Give each student a fish cutout to decorate. To promote creativity, provide a variety of decorating supplies like crayons, markers, glitter, sequins, paint pens, and scraps of wallpaper and fabric. Next ask each student to write a descriptive paragraph about his flamboyant fish. Collect the paragraphs and the fish; then display the fish in a prominent classroom location. Read each paragraph aloud and invite students to determine which fish from the display is being described. Students will quickly realize the importance of descriptive details and may be anxious to try this activity again. Perhaps creating, and then describing, striking seashells would be in order?

Diane Vogel—Gr. 3, W. B. Redding School, Lizella, GA

Whodunit?

Turn your students into supersleuths with this writing activity. To set the mood, read aloud a favorite mystery story. At the conclusion of the story, write a mystery title like "The Case Of The Missing Candy Bar" or a writing prompt like "It was a warm spring day when our teacher mysteriously disappeared during math class" on the chalkboard. Then divide the class into small groups and give each group a clear plastic bag that contains three unrelated objects, such as a paper clip, a nickel, and a plastic comb. Challenge each group to determine how each of the three objects in its bag could be used to help solve the mystery at hand. Then have each student write and illustrate his version of the story on story paper, or have the students alternate writing sentences for a group story. Be sure to set aside time for the students to share their work with their classmates. No doubt this activity will have everyone asking, "Whodunit"!

Carol Ann Perks—Grs. K–5 Gifted, Comstock Elementary, Miami, FL

285

289

Compute This!

Maximize computer technology in your classroom with these great tips.

Time Solution
Do you wish you could provide your students with more time to work individually at the computer? Try this!

A Site To See!
Having trouble keeping up with the latest computer terminology? Then maranGraphics Inc.'s *Computer Dictionary* is just the reference you need. This Internet site features an easy-to-follow directory that includes hundreds of com...

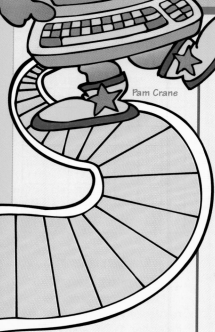

Compute This!

Maximize computer technology in your classroom with these great tips.

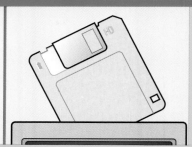

Computerized Lesson Plans
Why spend precious time rewriting your lesson plans week after week? On your computer, create a lesson plan template for each day of the week. Enter subject names, times, and other items that rarely change; then save the information. When it's time to write your lesson plans, open the related documents, add desired lessons and comments, and print. The resulting weekly plan will be easy to read and a snap to update if necessary. Did you ever think writing lesson plans could be so easy?

Janice Barger
Moon Lake Elementary
  School
New Port Richey, FL

A Site To See!
You won't need a sleigh to track down Santa at this fun stop. Let your modem carry you to The-North-Pole found at *http://www.the-north-pole.com*. While at this web site, students will enjoy sending E-mail to Santa, singing along to dozens of Christmas songs, and looking at photographs from the North Pole. An extensive list of Christmas traditions from around the globe adds to this site's versatility. Be sure to put this stop on your web wish list!

Another Holiday Hit!
For an enriching look at several spectacular celebrations, visit Holidays On The Net located at *http://www. holidays.net*. Choose from a year's worth of holiday information, including celebrations such as Hanukkah, Christmas, and Dr. Martin Luther King, Jr. Day. From spinning dreidels to the text of Dr. King's famous "I Have A Dream" speech, this site will prove its worth long after the winter holidays have passed.

Electronic Portfolios
Looking for a new way to manage student writing portfolios? Here's an approach that will spark kids' interest and save you time. Have students complete writing assignments using the classroom computer; then save the documents to personalized computer folders. For easy grading, you can access students' work at the click of a mouse, and add helpful comments right on their documents. The saved files can then be used to complete a variety of projects that require student writing samples. For example, have each child print out his favorite story and illustrate it; then bind the collection to make a class book for your library. Another beneficial project is to pair students for on-screen editing sessions. Have the students help each other find and correct writing errors in their work. After the editing is complete, have them each print copies of both stories to keep.

Diane Burshear
Computer Lab Director
St. Jude The Apostle School
Baton Rouge, LA

Internet Introduction
Even if your students don't already have Internet access at home or school, there's little doubt that the use of this technology is not far off. For kid-friendly descriptions of a *modem,* a *chat room, E-mail,* and more, share *My First Book About The Internet* by Sharon Cromwell (Troll Communications L.L.C., 1997) with your students. This valuable instructional tool also emphasizes important Internet safety tips. It's a must-read for anyone suiting up to surf the World Wide Web!

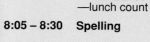

Mrs. Barger Weekly lesson plan
Room 221

Monday
December 15, 1997

AM
8:00 – 8:05   Introduction
  —pledge
  —attendance
  —lunch count

8:05 – 8:30   Spelling

8:30 – 9:00   Music

9:00 – 10:00   Reading

10:00 – 11:00   Writing

290

Compute This!

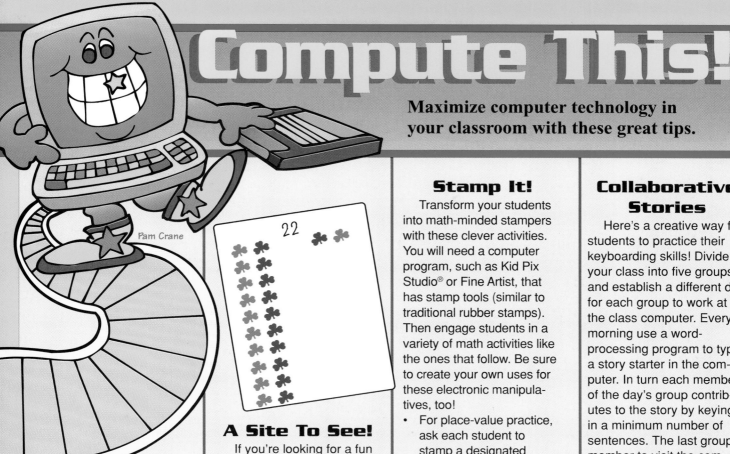

Pam Crane

Simon Says Assessment

Assess a student's basic computer knowledge with a game of Simon Says. To play a child sits at the computer. Say a series of commands such as, "Simon says, 'Point to the keyboard,' " and "Simon says, 'Find the mouse.' " You'll soon have an understanding of each child's computer knowledge. This nonthreatening approach is especially beneficial when new students enroll in your class.

Elizabeth Spohn—Computer
   Teacher
Butler Catholic School
Butler, PA

A Site To See!

If you're looking for a fun and educational web stop for your students, this site really delivers. Direct your students to Send A Message™ *http://www.usps.gov/ kids/welcome.htm*, a web site posted by the United States Postal Service (USPS). Your youngsters will have plenty of first-class fun playing interactive games as well as coloring a provided stamp outline and designing stamps of their own. This web site also provides information about stamp collecting and has links to other services of the USPS. Don't delay; connect today!

Stamp It!

Transform your students into math-minded stampers with these clever activities. You will need a computer program, such as Kid Pix Studio® or Fine Artist, that has stamp tools (similar to traditional rubber stamps). Then engage students in a variety of math activities like the ones that follow. Be sure to create your own uses for these electronic manipulatives, too!

- For place-value practice, ask each student to stamp a designated number. For example, 100 would be stamped as ten rows of ten stamps each, and 22 would be stamp-ed as two sets of ten stamps each plus two single stamps.
- For addition practice ask each student to use a different stamp to represent each of two or more provided addends. The total stamps shown equal the sum.
- For subtraction practice ask each student to stamp the first number of a provided equation, then use an eraser tool to wipe out—or subtract—the second number in the equation. The difference equals the remaining stamps shown.

Alyssa Weller—Gr. 1
South School, Glencoe, IL

Collaborative Stories

Here's a creative way for students to practice their keyboarding skills! Divide your class into five groups and establish a different day for each group to work at the class computer. Every morning use a word-processing program to type a story starter in the computer. In turn each member of the day's group contributes to the story by keying in a minimum number of sentences. The last group member to visit the computer concludes the story. Print a copy of the story for each group member and one to post in the classroom. At the end of each month, bind the posted stories into a book for your classroom library.

Janet Moody—Gr. 3
J. W. Faulk Elementary
Lafayette, LA

The Magic Key
Marvin saw the rusty key under a park bench. He just thought it was an old door key. But boy was he wrong!

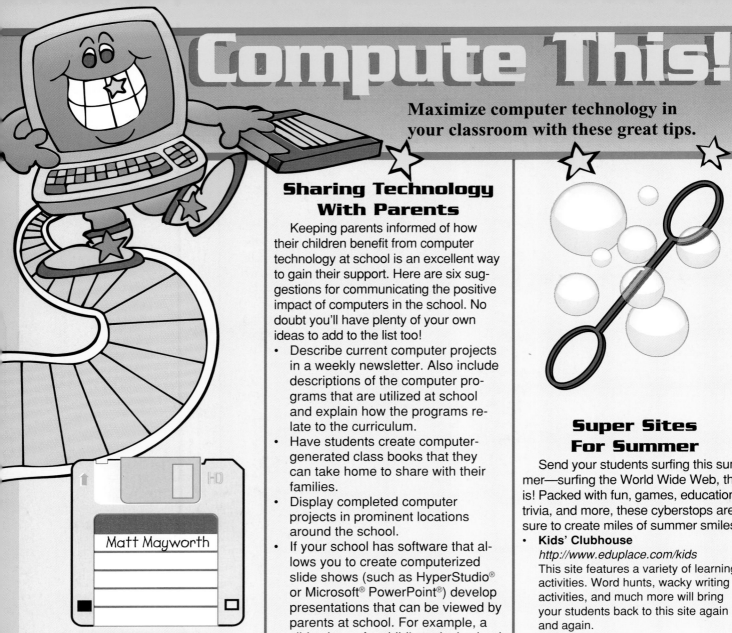

Compute This!

Maximize computer technology in your classroom with these great tips.

Disk Switch

You can count on students requesting this computer-related activity again and again! To begin, collect each child's labeled computer disk; then redistribute the disks, making sure that no one receives his own. Next have each child create a computer-generated mystery message (and illustration) for the classmate whose disk he has. Suggest that each student include in his message a few clues about his identity before he saves his final work to the disk. Then collect the disks and return them to their owners. There will be plenty of excitement as each child tries to identify which classmate wrote the mystery message on his disk!

Margie Siegel—Gr. 2
Wren Hollow Elementary School
Ballwin, MO

292

Sharing Technology With Parents

Keeping parents informed of how their children benefit from computer technology at school is an excellent way to gain their support. Here are six suggestions for communicating the positive impact of computers in the school. No doubt you'll have plenty of your own ideas to add to the list too!

- Describe current computer projects in a weekly newsletter. Also include descriptions of the computer programs that are utilized at school and explain how the programs relate to the curriculum.
- Have students create computer-generated class books that they can take home to share with their families.
- Display completed computer projects in prominent locations around the school.
- If your school has software that allows you to create computerized slide shows (such as HyperStudio® or Microsoft® PowerPoint®) develop presentations that can be viewed by parents at school. For example, a slide show of a child's typical school day will be a big hit at Open House!
- Every month save each child's computer-generated assignments to an individual disk; then invite parents into the classroom to view their children's work.
- Ask parents and relatives for their e-mail addresses. Compile a list to use for communicating during the year; then send a copy of the list home with students at the end of the year to encourage summer correspondence.

Alyssa Weller—Gr. 1
South School
Glencoe, IL

Super Sites For Summer

Send your students surfing this summer—surfing the World Wide Web, that is! Packed with fun, games, educational trivia, and more, these cyberstops are sure to create miles of summer smiles!

- **Kids' Clubhouse**
  http://www.eduplace.com/kids
  This site features a variety of learning activities. Word hunts, wacky writing activities, and much more will bring your students back to this site again and again.
- **SchoolHouse Rock**
  http://genxtvland.simplenet.com/SchoolHouseRock
  This site provides the lyrics, as well as audio and video versions of popular SCHOOL HOUSE ROCK® tunes. Viewers even have the opportunity to vote for their favorite songs!
- **Aunt Annie's Craft Page™**
  http://www.auntannie.com
  This site is the perfect resource for craft-making ideas. With hundreds of projects available—difficulty ratings often included—this site will keep youngsters busy crafting all summer long!
- **Professor Bubbles' Bubblesphere**
  http://bubbles.org
  This site is bursting with information about bubbles. Brief descriptions tell about bubble tools, soap bubble history, and Professor Bubbles himself. Best of all, viewers get the recipe for the ultimate bubble solution!

LIFESAVERS

Candi Barwinski—Gr. 2
Fleetwood Elementary School
Fleetwood, PA

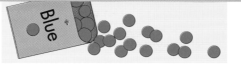

Missy Eason and Debra Wingert—Gr. 3
Moulton Branch Elementary
Valdosta, GA

LIFESAVERS

LIFESAVERS...

management tips for teachers

Collecting Class Compliments

Reinforce positive student behavior with this one-of-a-kind idea. All you need is a clean, empty container and a supply of pom-poms. Each time the class receives a compliment from you or another staff member, drop a pom-pom into the container. When the container is half-full, present each student with a sticker or another small reward; when it's completely filled, plan a class party. You can count on this incentive to keep end-of-the-year behavior in line!

Gina Marinelli—Gr. 2, B. Bernice Young Elementary School, Burlington, NJ

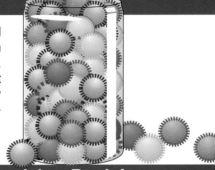

Organizing Back Issues

If you have difficulty remembering which topics are covered in your back issues of *The Mailbox®* magazine, try this! Photocopy the table of contents from each back issue and hole-punch the copies for a three-ring binder. Label one divider page for each of the six bimonthly editions. Place the divider pages in the binder and arrange the table-of-contents copies in sequential order behind the dividers. When it's time to plan for the next school year, you'll have an invaluable resource right at your fingertips!

Julie B. Pezzullo, Warwick School Department, Warwick, RI

The Motivation Station

Keep students motivated during the final month of the school year with a motivation station. Cover a large table with an inexpensive tablecloth; then place a variety of items at the table, such as markers, colored pencils, ink pens, writing paper, notepads, stickers, rubber stamps, and stamp pads. Place two or three chairs at the table and label the area "The Motivation Station." Each day before you dismiss the class, announce the names of students who have been thoughtful and responsible throughout the day. Then make arrangements for each mentioned child to spend 15 to 20 minutes of free time at The Motivation Station the following school day. Keep a record of the students who earn visits to the station so that you can personally encourage youngsters who have not yet earned the privilege.

Ann Marie Stephens—Gr. 1, George C. Round Elementary, Manassas, VA

Replenishing Prizes

Here's a nifty way to replenish your supply of inexpensive prizes for next year's class. Invite students to place any unwanted cereal-box toys, giveaways from fast-food restaurants, and other knickknacks in a designated container. Before the start of the new school year, sort through the donations and place the items that are suitable prizes in your classroom prize box.

adapted from an idea by Jill D. Hamilton—Gr. 1 Schoeneck Elementary School, Stevens, PA

Bag It!

This timesaving idea will suit any busy teacher. You need a clear, plastic suit bag labeled for each month (or season) of the school year. When you take down your end-of-the-year classroom decorations, store them in the appropriate suit bag along with any other oversized (or hard-to-store) teaching materials for that time of year. Then sort the classroom decorations and oversized teaching materials that are stored elsewhere in the classroom into the labeled bags. Suspend the bags in a classroom closet. Just think of the time you'll save next year when you have a clear view of each bag's contents!

Denise Baumann—Gr. 2, Rustic Oak Elementary, Pearland, TX

OUR READERS WRITE

Double-Sided Decorations

Double your bulletin-board border with this money-saving idea! Decorate the blank side of store-bought border using rubber stamps, markers, crayons, or stickers. Consider creating theme-related border to enhance units of study. You'll have twice the amount of border to use time and time again!

Debbie Anderson—Gr. 2, Hedding Grade School
Abingdon, IL

Seasonal Thank-You Notes

Turn die-cut seasonal shapes into cherished thank-you notes! Use your school's die-cut machine to cut several seasonal shapes from construction paper. To create a one-of-a-kind thank-you note, write a note of thanks on a cutout, and then embellish the cutout as desired. Make plans to change the shapes of your thank-you notes to match the current holiday or season. No doubt your youngsters will cherish these handmade keepsakes!

Dear Susan,
Thank you for the lovely holiday pin. It is very pretty. I'll always remember you. You are very kind. Thanks again!
Love,
Mrs. Levy

Alesia M. Richards—Grs. 1–2
Apple Pie Ridge Elementary School
Winchester, VA

Where Did It Come From?

Youngsters will give this geography activity their stamp of approval! If possible, plan to complete the activity during the holiday season when a large amount of mail is being delivered. Show your class a postmarked envelope. Explain that a postmark shows the city and state where an envelope was mailed. Next ask your students to bring empty postmarked envelopes from home. Cut the postmark from each envelope. Then, under your students' guidance, find the location of each postmark on a U.S. or world map and attach the cutout nearby. Challenge students to research the places they locate on the map. Smiles will be delivered throughout the room as students learn about geography!

Emily Goren Goodson—Gr. 3, Cary Elementary, Cary, NC

Noteworthy Notepaper

Looking for a noteworthy holiday gift to give your students? This unique idea could be just what you've been looking for! Use a rubber stamp(s) and an ink pad to create a four-sided border on a blank sheet of paper. In the left-hand corner of the paper, draw a small box about the size of a student's school photograph. Then, beginning below the box, draw writing lines on the remainder of the page. Duplicate a class set of this page. Next program one copy of the page for each student. To do this, attach a child's photo in the box and program the blank area to the right of the box with a personalized writing-related title like "A Note From Darcy" or "Wendy Writes." Make five to ten copies of each personalized page; then place each child's copies in a resealable bag along with a decorated pencil or two. (Keep the original projects for later use.) Encourage students to use their personalized stationery for writing letters and holiday thank-you notes. Students and their parents will be tickled with these unique and useful holiday gifts.

Katie's Tales

Alesia M. Richards—Grs. 1–2, Apple Pie Ridge Elementary School
Winchester, VA

Celebrating Kwanzaa

Make plans to include this festive song in your holiday sing-along. A good time will be had by all, and your youngsters will quickly learn the seven principles of Kwanzaa!

The Seven Days Of Kwanzaa
(adapt to the tune of "The Twelve Days Of Christmas")

On the first day of Kwanzaa, we will celebrate:
The spirit of unity.

On the second day of Kwanzaa, we will celebrate:
Being yourself and the spirit of unity.

On the third day of Kwanzaa, we will celebrate:
Helping one another, being yourself,
And the spirit of unity.

On the fourth day of Kwanzaa, we will celebrate:
Sharing what we have, helping one another,
Being yourself, and the spirit of unity.

On the fifth day of Kwanzaa, we will celebrate:
—Having a goal—
Sharing what we have, helping one another,
Being yourself, and the spirit of unity.

On the sixth day of Kwanzaa, we will celebrate:
Being creative,
—Having a goal—
Sharing what we have, helping one another,
Being yourself, and the spirit of unity.

On the seventh day of Kwanzaa, we will celebrate:
Belief in yourself, being creative,
—Having a goal—
Sharing what we have, helping one another,
Being yourself, and the spirit of unity.

Joyce Valentine—Gr. 1
Whitehall Elementary
Williamstown, NJ

Unique As Snowflakes

Here's a great hands-on bulletin board for the new year! If you're up to it, plan this project for the last school day before the winter holiday break. On a newspaper-covered area, position a length of dark blue paper that you have cut to fit a chosen bulletin board. In a jelly-roll pan, pour a very thin layer of white tempera paint. Add a squirt of liquid soap to the paint for easier cleanup. In turn, have each student press each of his opened palms into the pan, then press each palm on the dark blue paper to resemble a falling snowflake. When the paint is dry, mount the project, a desired border, and the title "Like Each Snowflake, We Are All Unique!"

Jennifer Balogh-Joiner—Gr. 2, Franklin Elementary, Franklin, NJ

Popcorn Reading

Pop! Pop! Pop! Try this fresh approach to oral-reading practice. Announce to a small group of readers that each time you declare, "Popcorn," the child who is reading orally is to quickly choose another group member to read aloud. Ask that every student be called on to read aloud before a student takes a second turn. Students enjoy choosing the next readers, and they are motivated to follow along closely in their books so they'll be ready to read at a moment's notice. If desired, reward students for their oral-reading efforts by serving popcorn at the end of group time.

Mary Woody—Gr. 2
Saint Ann's School
Lawrenceville, NJ

Listen To This!

Students will be all ears when it's time to read at this free-time center! Purchase two or three inexpensive handheld cassette tape players with headphones. Place each listening device in a large resealable plastic bag along with a book and tape set. Store the portable listening centers in a basket in your classroom library. A student chooses a plastic bag, settles down in a desired spot, and proceeds to listen to and read along with the book he has chosen. Reading and listening skills are sure to soar with this unique approach!

Tina McSoley—Gr. 3, Warfield Elementary, Indiantown, FL

Word Collections

Discovering new vocabulary words becomes exciting for students when their newly learned words are collectibles! Keep a supply of blank cards on hand at all times. Each time a student learns a new vocabulary word, he writes the word on a blank card and writes or illustrates its meaning on the back. Students may hole-punch their resulting vocabulary cards and collect them on large metal rings. Or they can showcase their collections in clear plastic collector sleeves. Periodically provide time for students to share their word collections with their classmates. The value of new vocabulary is sure to increase!

Pamela Walker Akin—Media Specialist
Cumberland Trace Elementary
Bowling Green, KY

A "Sun-sational" Organizer

Use this bright idea to help students organize information about a designated topic. To demonstrate the procedure, draw the outline of a large sun on the chalkboard. Write the topic inside the sun; then, on each sun ray, write a word or phrase that describes the topic. Whether students are studying for a test or writing reports or paragraphs, they are sure to agree that this activity is "sun-sational"! For added interest, change the shape of the graphic organizer to match the current theme, topic of study, or season.

Susana C. Zinser
Houston, TX

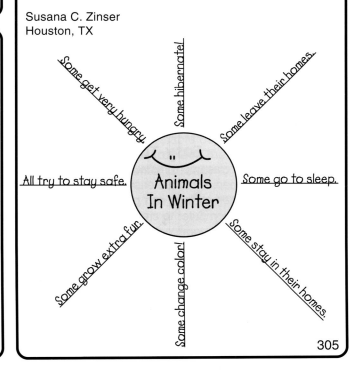

similes, self-descriptive, 72
talent, 85
writing evaluation, 309
Sentence Structure (see also Parts of Speech)
learning center, 34
subjects/predicates learning center, 25
writing center, sentences, 26
Sequence, Story
learning center, 31
Napping House, The, 68
Service Projects, 213, 242
Seuss, Dr.
Horton Hatches The Egg, 250
Oh, The Places You Will Go!, 310
Shapes
art project, 53
Sharing Time
photos from home, 300
Show-and-Tell (see Sharing Time)
Silverstein, Shel
"Hungry Mungry," 190
math poems, 164–167
Similes
self-descriptive, 72, 284
Singing Man, The, 85
Size (see Measurement)
Skeletons
unit, 170–175
Slavery
quilt bulletin board, 13
Snakes
measurement, 164
Snow
bulletin board, 305
Snowballs, 45
Snowballs, 45
Social Interaction (see Friendship)
Social Studies (see also Economics; Geography; History)
careers, 85, 288
character education, 242–253
China, 46
civil rights, 13
community, 41, 82, 126, 137, 212–215, 242, 251, 273, 276, 289, 306
government, 253
language, non-English, 258
Native Americans, 236–241
needs and wants, 72
geography, 7
Puerto Rico, 216–221
slavery, 13
Sweden, 222–229
timelines, 60, 106, 159, 214
Soentpiet, Chris K.
Around Town, 215
Songs and Chants
B-O-N-E-S, 170
coral reefs, 205
Down By The Bay, 268
hibernation, 180
Kwanzaa, 304
library, 311
Like Me And You, 215
Skeleton Song, The, 170
Twelve Days Of Christmas, 278
Winter's Coming, 179
Space
tilt, Earth, 222
Spanish, 217
Speech and Communication
book presentations, 137
consonant blends, 27
interviewing, family, 262, 306
listening, 82, 113
news report, 144
storytelling, 97, 258
vowel sounds, 25
Spelling
anagrams, 29
missing vowels game, 28
Spiders
Anansi, 76, 264
estimation, 167
life cycles, 196
Sports
baseball, 219
football, 302
Spring (see also Earth Day; Easter; Mother's Day)
basket, 50
butterflies, 198, 308
cattails, 51
chalk art, 309
lions and lambs, paper-plate, 49
rabbits, 50
weather bulletin board, 14
windsock, 48
Staff Development
National Boss Day, 302
Starring First Grade, 213
State Projects
read through your state, 138

Stone Soup, 246
Storage
art supplies, 295, 297
big books, 296
crayons, lost, 296
oversized supplies, 298
paints, 307
Stories (see Folklore; Literature)
Story Of Kwanzaa, The, 280
Strawberries
Little Mouse, The Red Ripe Strawberry, And The Big Hungry Bear, The, 70
pattern, 22
Student Teachers
gift, 310
Subjects (see Sentence Structure)
Subtraction
coins, 166
computer manipulatives, 291
Summer
baseball, 219
bulletin board, 18
camp, 100–104
classified ads, 35
Ghost In Tent 19, The, 100–104
Internet sites, 292
postcards, 285
summer memories bulletin board, 8
Swahili
number words, 231
Sweden
Santa Lucia Day, 44, 224
unit, 222–229
Swedish
vocabulary, 227
Symmetry
art project, 51
learning center, 34
Tall Tales
The Bunyans, 72
Tamar, Erika
The Garden Of Happiness, 214
Teague, Mark
Pigsty, 111
Teamwork (see Cooperation)
Technology (see Computers)
Teeth (see Health and Hygiene)
Ten Little Dinosaurs, 113
Thaler, Mike
Uses For Mooses And Other Popular Pets, 112
Thank You, Santa, 280
Thanksgiving
placemats, mosaic, 43
research, 10
turkey, construction paper, 43
turkey pattern (without feathers), 36
turkey transformation, 27
Theater (see Drama)
Thematic Units
animals in winter, 179–185
watermelons, 263–270
Thinking Skills (see Creative Thinking; Critical Thinking; Deductive Reasoning)
Tickleoctopus, The, 71
Tikvah Means Hope, 214
Time
calendar skills, 289
unit, 156–161
writing, creative, 284
Timelines
autobiographical, 106
birthdays, 60
local history, 214
telling time, 159
Titles (see Books)
Too Much Talk, 86
Tooth Fairy, 70
Tornado, 96–99
Tornados
Tornado, 96–99
Trains
reading display, 139
Trees Of The Dancing Goats, The, 276
Trickster Tales
Anansi And The Talking Melon, 264
coyote, 240
Trivas, Irene
Emma's Christmas, 278
Truman's Aunt Farm, 109
Turkeys
creative-thinking learning center, 27
construction paper, 43
pattern (without feathers), 36
Twenty-Four Robbers, 68
Uncle Vova's Tree, 277
Underwear!, 110
United States (see also Geography; State Projects)
citizenship, 253
map bulletin board, 7
Uses For Mooses And Other Popular Pets, 112
Valentine's Day
bulletin board, 13

card (arts and crafts), 47
key ring, 48
ornament, 47
placemat, 30
Values (see Character Education)
Venn Diagrams
Audrey Wood's books, 71
pen pals, 147
Verbs (see Parts of Speech; Sentence Structure)
Very Important Day, A, 253
Vikings
runestones, 225, 227
Vocabulary
anagrams, 29
bulletin boards and displays, 302, 308
character education, 243
classroom objects, 301
compound words, 33
flash cards, collectible, 305
outdoor review, 309
spelling, 28
Vowels
a, 25
game, 28
xylophone, 302
Washington, Donna L.
Story of Kwanzaa, The, 280
Watermelon Day, 268
Watermelons
bulletin board, 8
facts, 263
thematic unit, 263–270
Weather
March bulletin board, 14
tornados, 96–99
Weird Parents, 71
West Indies (see Caribbean)
What Am I? Looking Through Shapes At Apples And Grapes, 190
Where The Sidewalk Ends, 166
White Dynamite And Curly Kidd, 81
Who's Who In My Family?, 212
Wild, Margaret
Thank You, Santa, 280
Williams, Sue
I Went Walking, 126
Winter (see also Black History Month; Chinese New Year; Christmas; Hanukkah; Kwanzaa; Martin Luther King, Jr. Day; Santa Lucia Day)
animals in, 179–185, 277
helper bulletin board, 11
holiday literature, 275–280
mittens (writing project), 12
poinsettias (art project), 45
snow, 45, 305
Wizard, The, 83
Wood, Audrey
author unit, 68–73
Wood, Don
author unit, 68–73
Word Problems
bulletin board, 9
money, 166
skeleton-related, 174
Worksheets (see Reproducibles)
World Wide Web (see Internet; Internet Sites)
Writing (see also Figurative Language)
creative, 29, 31, 33, 74, 75, 84, 86, 105, 109, 115, 118, 147, 172, 219, 240, 247, 249, 264, 266, 275, 276, 278, 282, 284, 285, 291
descriptive, 7, 12, 69, 72, 115, 125, 126, 127, 144, 214, 259, 264, 279, 282, 283, 285, 301
dialogue, 70
editing, 290
evaluative, 101
informational, 35, 87, 101, 130–135, 144, 181, 189, 224, 306, 309, 310
journals, 124, 127, 303
letters, 26, 142–147, 190, 259, 280, 300
narrative, 72
paragraphs, 283
persuasive, 233, 265
poetry, 68, 189, 248, 280, 282, 284
prewriting, 115, 124
reports, 130–135
riddles, 190
sentences, 26
vocabulary-based, 26, 243
Zebra-Riding Cowboy, The, 84